Mary Purcell

The First Jesuit

ST. IGNATIUS LOYOLA
(1491-1556)

LOYOLA UNIVERSITY PRESS
Chicago   60657

ISBN 0-8294-0371-x

Preface

THE FIRST JESUIT is based on the contemporary evidence for the life of St. Ignatius Loyola, the writings of the saint himself, records left by his first Companions and the Fathers of the first generation of the Society of Jesus, the testimony of the 75 witnesses examined during the Canonization Process, and impressions of Ignatius given by various non-Jesuit acquaintances. To fill in the background of time and place, I have followed such accepted authorities as Father Leturia and Perez Arregui for the Basque scene; for the Castile period, Sandoval, the chronicler of Charles V, and Fathers Fita and Leturia. The Catalans, Fathers Creixell and Casanovas, have been the guides to Montserrat, Manresa, and Barcelona; while Father Tacchi-Venturi's works, the fruits of more than sixty years' research, have helped me to set the saint in the Rome of his time. Several visits to Spain, France, and two to Rome, following in the footsteps of St. Ignatius, have been of assistance in evoking—for myself at least—something of a bygone age in places where more than four hundred years ago the person known as Inigo de Loyola, "the pilgrim," and finally Father Ignatius, stood and walked and thought and prayed.

Three places come at once to mind. Firstly, the beautiful Basque Valley of the Iraurgi, where the old *Casa-Torre* still stands and where the early years of Ignatius were spent; where he passed the momentous months of his convalescence from the leg wound he received in the wars; where he obtained the great grace of conversion and made his first stumbling steps toward God; where he came for a few weeks in his forty-fourth year, "to give a little good example where formerly he had given so much scandal." Secondly, I remember vividly a Good Friday evening when I journeyed across the Roman Campagna, where the Judas trees waved myriads of pale, purple-tinted flags, to visit the little chapel of La Storta that stands at the fork in the great north road; there Ignatius stopped on his way to the city that was to be his home for the last eighteen years of his life; there he heard the words, "In Rome I will be favorable to you." And lastly, I like to recall the rooms where the saint lived in Rome; where he so often "celebrated Mass with many tears . . . at times losing the power of speech"; where he talked to his sons and entertained his friends and welcomed so many of Rome's saints and sinners. After hearing Mass before the same altar upon which Ignatius offered the Holy Sacrifice, I once stepped out onto the little balcony where he so often stood, heedless of the sounds coming up from the Street of the Dark Shops as he scanned the starry heavens, straining beyond created things to discern the God hidden behind creation's veil. It struck me then that the

Basque soldier-saint had more than a little in common with our Irish patriot-poet, Joseph Mary Plunkett, who wrote:

> I see His blood upon the rose
>   And in the stars the glory of His eyes;
> His body gleams amid eternal snows,
>   His tears fall from the skies.
>
> I see His face in every flower;
>   The thunder, and the singing of the birds
> Are but His voice; and, carven by His power,
>   Rocks are His written words.
>
> All pathways by His feet are worn;
>   His strong heart stirs the ever-beating sea;
> His crown of thorns is twined with every thorn;
>   His cross is every tree.

Sitting in the dark, poky room where Igantius spent most of his last years, I thought of March 12, 1622, when five saints—St. Teresa of Avila, St. Isidore the Farmer of Madrid, St. Philip Neri, the Romans' beloved *"Pippo Buono,"* St. Francis Xavier, and St. Ignatius Loyola—were canonized and the wits of Rome remarked, "His Holiness has canonized four Spaniards and a Saint." It was easy to imagine St. Philip and St. Ignatius, who had shared many a joke in that same cupboard-sized room, laughing together in heaven over the Romans' mordant sally. In this book I have tried to focus attention not so much on Ignatius the founder, the organizer, the paladin of the Counter-Reformation, as on Ignatius the man; if I have helped to highlight for readers of the twentieth century the human aspect of a man greatly loved by his intimates of the sixteenth century, I shall be happy. If he were better known, he would be better loved and oftener invoked; and in this century, which has more than a superficial resemblance to his own, his powerful assistance is something we cannot afford to do without. To know any saint it is necessary to accept the fact that he shared our common humanity; for the grace that makes saints builds on a nature not angelic but human. The key to the character of St. Ignatius Loyola lies in a simple statement of Gregory XIII, who canonized him. The pope did not mention the drive and efficiency, the genius for organization, the capacity for leadership—the only attributes later ages allowed the saint. But he declared in one sentence what all the pages of the canonization evidence said over and over in other words: "Ignatius had a heart big enough to hold the universe."

MARY PURCELL

Dublin

Contents

Part I. The Ore in the Earth

Part II. The Refining Fire

Part III. Precious Metal

PART I
The Ore in the Earth

Until his twenty-sixth year he was a man given to worldly vanities and used to take special delight in feats of arms, being filled with a great and vain desire for fame.

(Autobiography of St. Ignatius)

Inigo de Loyola, whom divine Providence deigned to choose as the first of this Company, was a native of Guipuzcoa province, belonging to one of its noblest families. . . . His education was more conformed to the spirit of the world than to that of God; as, from his boyhood, instead of proceeding to learn something more than reading and writing, he commenced to follow the court as a page.

(Chronicle of Father Polanco, the Saint's Secretary.)

. . . he profited nothing from his studies. A kind of noble ardor possessed him, his thoughts being wholly bent upon winning distinction through a glorious military career. . . .

(Father Nadal, assistant to St. Ignatius in his last years.)

S OMETIME during the year 1491, a child, last of a long family, was born in the *Casa-Torre* or Tower House of Loyola. His home was a solid, four-square structure, its peculiar, squat appearance being due to the fact that its towers and upper story had been knocked down some decades previously in obedience to a decree of the King of Castile. Though the lords of Loyola were good, reliable soldiers in time of war, they were, in times of peace, an obstreperous lot, incurring penalties for their encroachments on other men's rights. So when permission to rebuild was granted, not very long after the demolition order had been—somewhat tardily—complied with, it was stipulated that the height should be limited, and towers were banned. Nevertheless, the old stone keep was still known throughout the five valleys as the *Casa-Torre* of Loyola. It was built to last and it stands today, as it stood in 1491, in a tranquil valley of Guipuzcoa, a Basque province on the Spanish side of the Pyrenees.[1]

The name *Loyola* had associations anything but peaceful, for the men of the *Casa-Torre* came of a fighting line whose prowess in war was con-

3

siderable. Though Basques, they had frequently fought for Castile, on one occasion at least covering themselves with glory. They had, on the other hand, less praiseworthy records; the annals of the neighboring province of Navarre for the year 1309 denounce the clan as "abominable robbers, who in one of their many forays made off with 600 porkers from the Larraun Valley." And Enrique IV of Castile, thirty-four years before the birth of the child whose valor was to equal, as his glory was to surpass, that of all his kindred, made a list of the misdeeds of the Loyolas. They were, he said, responsible for violence and injuries, for robberies and assassinations, for insults and rebellions; they burned those they besieged; they sheltered and defended evildoers.

To reach Loyola, the traveler needs to turn inland from San Sebastian, the capital of Guipuzcoa; if he keeps due south for about thirty miles, at a point about twelve miles east of the picturesque fishing-port of Zumaya, he suddenly emerges through the mountain pass south of the famous mineral spas of Cestona into the Iraurgi, an enchanting three-mile reach of the Urola River. The valley is in reality only a broadening of one of the great grooves that cut northwest through the last spurs of the Pyrenees—a characteristic of the Guipuzcoan landscape being the natural corridors, magnificently walled with mountains, that run nearly all the way from the marches of Navarre to the sea. The fast-flowing Urola, its waters still bearing the icy touch of the Pyreneean springs and cataracts that nurture it, sweeps through a gap in the foothills to course through the plain known as Iraurgi. On the crest of the hill where the river enters this expanse of rich, well-cultivated land is a small town named Azcoitia; in the heart of the valley stands a sister-village, Azpeitia. Between the two, somewhat nearer Azpeitia, stands the *Casa-Torre* of Loyola.

The child who was born there in 1491, in the twenty-fifth year of his parents' marriage, was baptized in the parish church of Azpeitia.[2] The baptismal font, surmounted by an image of St. Ignatius, is still there; and parents from the surrounding districts bring their infants to be baptized in that font rather than in the other, newer font which seems to have been hardly ever used. A Basque inscription on the base of the font reads *Emenchen batiatuba naiz—Here I was baptized*. The new Christian was named for Saint Inigo of Ona, a patron much invoked against that scourge of the Peninsula, drought. Some confusion arose from the habit Inigo had in later years of signing himself one day Ignatius, the next Inigo; until 1523 or thereabouts, official documents that mentioned

4

him—and they were by no means few—gave the name Inigo. On the registers of Paris University he was inscribed as Ignacio of Loyola, Diocese of Pamplona.[3]

Little is recorded of Inigo's childhood. Hardly had his name been added to the list of Azpeitian parishioners when he was given to Maria Garin, a woman on a nearby farm, to nurse. Her husband, Errazti, worked one of the smithies owned by the Loyolas. Their farmhouse, Eguibar, on the banks of the Urola, a few minutes' walk from the *Casa-Torre,* may still be seen. A Basque farmer lives there with his wife and children. Except for a notice on one wall informing passers-by that St. Ignatius was fostered under that roof, no attempt has been made to alter the house. Built of stone, like all the older farmhouses in Iraurgi, it has weathered the centuries well; its lower floor is used as a barn, the family living in the upper storeys, as is the custom in the Basque country. Eguibar is not very different today from what it was in 1491.

When, in 1555, the Jesuit Fathers in Rome were anxious to ascertain the exact age of their Founder—Ignatius himself being seemingly unsure of the date of his birth—inquiries were made at Loyola. Azpeitia church registers having been destroyed in a fire in 1515, no record was available there. Happily, someone remembered that Maria Garin, Inigo's foster-mother, was still alive, and with mind and memory unimpaired. When interrogated, the old Basque woman was very definite: Inigo had been born in 1491—*not* in 1493 nor any other year.[4] The year 1491 had been memorable in Loyola, as in the rest of Spain; and Maria, more than others perhaps, would have had particular reason to remember it. All during the early months of that year, the lane between the *Casa-Torre* and Eguibar had been constantly echoing to the clatter of hoofs and the rattle of soldiers' accoutrements. Her good man, Errazti, had had to work night and day in the smithy, shoeing horses, forging pikes and javelins, muskets and short-swords and arquebuses, repairing visors and breast-plates, sharpening lances, tempering and burnishing swords. Many fine, strapping fellows from Iraurgi and the four valleys marched away that year with Don Beltran, lord of the *Casa-Torre,* when he rode out to join the other captains and *hidalgos* of the mountains and frontier provinces—all of whom were going south to Granada along with the armies of Aragon and Castile.[5] Maria, like the other women of Iraurgi, had spent an anxious time during that winter of 1491-1492 while the menfolk were almost a thousand miles away. Great had been the relief when they returned to Iraurgi in the springtime bringing news of the grand victory, reliving their part in the taking of Granada, the final overthrow of the invader, the last battles in the slow, long-drawn-out struggle to oust the Moors. Maria was not likely to have been mistaken when she affirmed, most emphatically, that 1491 was the year in which Inigo, thirteenth and last child of Don Beltran, had been fetched to Eguibar to be nursed and reared.

Inigo's mother, Dona Marina, was a native of Azcoitia, the village overlooking the valley; her father was patron of the church there as Don Beltran was of Azpeitia church. On her mariage in 1467 she had brought 1,600 gold Aragon crowns as a dowry to Loyola.[6] She predeceased her husband, who died in 1507. There is no record that Ignatius ever spoke of her, nor is she referred to in his letters, though occasionally others of his family are mentioned. The reasonable conclusion to be drawn from his silence regarding his mother is that he lost her before her image had had time to imprint itself upon his memory. For Ignatius of Loyola was not a man impervious to human emotion, nor was he forgetful of those to whom he was bound by blood and affection. Some forty years after Inigo's infancy and fosterage in Eguibar, he was told that a son of Errazti and Maria Garin, the "somewhat ugly-looking, squint-eyed Martin of Eguibar," wished to become a priest; he immediately interested himself in the unprepossessing candidate for Holy Orders, to such good effect that "the said Martin became an excellent priest and confessor."[7]

Being a Basque, Inigo inherited the characteristics of his race. The true Basque conceals under a courteous, even cold, exterior a somewhat inflammable nature. He likes controversy, sport—anything that involves a risk and offers a challenge. He works hard, doggedly, methodically; should misfortune overtake him, he wastes no time bewailing the damage he has suffered but sets to work at once with renewed courage to repair it. He likes to present a spruce appearance to the world; if he is wealthy, he is elegant and inclined to show off; if poor, he nevertheless contrives to turn out spick and span. Though passionately devoted to racial tradition—even today few Basque children hear Spanish spoken until they begin to attend school—he is adaptable, and being a man who delights in obliging others, the Basque who emigrates to earn a livelihood is usually most successful. Above all, Basques are intensely religious, deeply rooted in the faith.

The Basques of Guipuzcoa, Inigo's native province, are noted for their tact. More reflective than talkative, they are also exceedingly good-humored, as anyone who has spent any time among them can attest; but beneath the pleasant, easy exterior there is a steely core, some streak as unyielding as the iron ores with which their beautiful land is seamed. Through his mother, Inigo could claim descent from the Viscayan Basques, a seafaring race—hardy people, charged with the accumulated energies of generations whose lives are a ceaseless, stubborn conflict with the sullen breakers of the Cantabrian coasts. Being the last of thirteen children, Inigo Lopez of Loyola could hope for little inheritance save the qualities, neither few nor trivial, bequeathed to him by long lines of Basque forbears.

Although Inigo had at least seven brothers,[8] the family of Loyola died out in the next generation;* but the strange Basque name of the Iraurgi's *Casa-Torre*, forever linked with that of the youngest of Don Beltran's brood, has survived four hundred years and passed into almost as many languages as there are peoples. Sad news reached Loyola when Inigo was about five; the eldest brother, who had been fighting in Naples under *el Gran Capitan*, Isabella's famous general, was killed in battle. The new heir, Martin Garcia, married since 1493 to a former lady-in-waiting of Queen Isabella, Madalena de Aroaz, lived in the *Casa-Torre;* when Madalena came to Loyola as a bride, her most treasured wedding gift was a Flemish painting of the Annunciation given her by the Queen.[10] A small room, used by the family as an oratory when they assembled for prayer in common, was the repository for this memento of the great sovereign; oratory and painting are still there, after more than four and a half centuries.

Life in the *Casa-Torre* must have been trying at times for the lady accustomed to the Court of Castile. Queen Isabella was a lady with a studious mind, an astonishing breadth of vision, and a heart as brave as it was womanly. She studied rhetoric, grammar, history, philosophy, painting, Latin, and music, and liked her Maids of Honor to do the same; she encouraged and subsidized artists, scientists, and explorers, and she expected those about her to forward these and similar interests and enter-

* Recent researches have discovered that a son, Francisco, went to Granada with his father in 1491. He contracted an illness on the way and was taken into the home of a wealthy family of Murcia province and cared for until he recovered. As a result of his illness—and also, possibly, from the effects of the glare of the southern sun—he lost his sight and remained blind all his life. Francisco however found compensations; he married a rich lady, daughter or neice of his kind hosts, and settled down in Murcia. A direct descendant of this brother of Inigo, the Conde de Velle, died in Madrid in 1926.

prises. At Loyola there was little learning and the talk was mostly of war and conquest. None of Inigo's five sisters ever learned to read or write, except one, who could sign her name.[11] Soon after Martin Garcia's marriage, Inigo would have been old enough to run to the *Casa-Torre* alone; when Madalena went to visit a nun cousin in the Azpeitia convent, the small boy would have been brought along occasionally. Nuns were a seven days' wonder in the Iraurgi area, the Isabelita foundation in Azpeitia being the first and only convent for miles around. Like their patroness, St Elizabeth, the Queen-Saint of Hungary—from whom they got the name Isabelitas—the nuns followed the Franciscan rule.[12] One can imagine the fuss the Sisters made of Inigo, stuffing him with gingerbreads, almond cakes, and apples, while he listened uncomprehendingly to the conversation between the elegantly dressed Madalena and the brown-robed cousin. As yet Castilian was a foreign language to him.

Another brother sailed to the Indies in 1510, returning a few years later only to die, like his eldest brother, in the Italian wars. There was a Beltran, named after his father, and a boy named Ochoa. Of the five sisters, three were married during the childhood of Inigo, one to the notary of Azpeitia, the others to landowners in neighboring valleys. Then there was Pero Lopez, who was ordained priest in Pamplona and given the parish of Azpeitia by his father.[13] As patron of the church, Don Beltran not only had a say in the appointing of its clergy, but, like patrons of other churches in that century and particularly in the Basque area of Spain, took three-quarters of tithes and offerings, made regulations for both clerics and laity, and yielded precedence only to the Alcalde at all church ceremonies and processions. The Bishops of Burgos and Pamplona protested more than once, both to royalty and to Rome, about this abuse, but to no avail.[14]

Don Beltran, like his father and grandfather, could produce documents signed *I, the King*, and others bearing the Fisherman's Seal to prove the privileges the Loyolas had been given and which he and his meant to maintain in the teeth of all opposition, both lay and clerical. When Pero Lopez was appointed priest of Azpeitia, his father, the lord of the *Casa-Torre*, probably flourished several imposing parchments to bolster up his authority. The appointment was the source of much trouble and scandal; it provoked a feud with the Anchieta family, one of whom had to resign the benefice in favor of young Loyola. The latter brought little honor either to his family or his cloth. He was a bad influence on Inigo, as will be seen. In the will of this priest of the Loyola family, provision was made for children he openly acknowledged as his. Don Beltran also left three natural children, one of whom died on a Hungarian battlefield fighting the Turks.[15]

> Into these hidden valleys, the lax morals, common to all Europe had penetrated. Not even the reforms initiated by Isabel *a Catolica* succeeded in extirpating them. One need only glance at the list of illegitimate children, legatees in wills made by the Loyolas, at the concubinage, the quarrels, and the sloth of the very priests of Azpeitia to realize the need for prayer and atonement in the Iraurgi and its surroundings.[16]

Thus one of the greatest writers on Ignatius in modern times describes the milieu in which Inigo's boyhood was spent. But although wills and other documents in the archives of Loyola and Azpeitia reveal something of the sins of the successive owners of the *Casa-Torre*, they also attest to their faith and piety. One commends his soul to God, humbly acknowledging and imploring pardon for his transgressions; another arranges to have thirty Gregorian Masses offered for his soul's repose; all leave strict instructions regarding the discharge of unpaid debts and the righting of injustices that troubled consciences suddenly roused to action by the realization of approaching judgment. Money was left to send pilgrims west to Compostella, or south to Our Lady of Guadalupe, there to pray for the souls of the dead Loyolas. Relying on the gracious and unfailing advocacy of our Blessed Lady, the Refuge of Sinners, they died invoking her aid and calling upon the powerful name of her Son; the many Marian shrines that sentinelled the mountain passes and all the roads of Iraurgi were provided for through legacies left by various heads of the family. Neither were the poor forgotten when a Master of the *Casa-Torre* dictated his last testament to the notary; whether the times were bad or good, alms were to be given to the beggars, God's ambassadors, for their prayers were powerful in heaven.[17]

The bequests of wills made in Loyola during the lifetime of Inigo are interesting, for they reflect something of the life in the valley. Apart from a few costly heirlooms which included silver and gold plate, some for use in the oratory, some for the table, the things that made the warp and woof of daily life are itemized: "... Two mules and a mare; three casks of my own cider standing in the wine-press ... and the other casks as well. ... My jewels, my furniture, my clothes, my beds, and all my valuables what-

9

soever. . . . All the livestock on each and every one of the farms. . . . The rent of Agaunza farm. . . . The ash-trees surrounding the House of Loyola, those that I myself planted as well as the marked ones. . . . " And other documents mention mills, foundries, villages, farms; cultivated land and pasture; meadows and sheep-runs; mountains and water-sheds; woods of oak and chestnut; fresh-water and mineral springs; apple orchards, rents running to thousands of *maravedis* yearly. A letter from one who visited Loyola in the sixteenth century describes the Iraurgi:

> I doubt if there be a fairer sight than this valley. In the midst stands Loyola, surrounded by flowers and a great variety of fruit trees; so dense are the trees all about it that one hardly sees the *Casa* until at the door. . . . One very ancient evergreen oak, so high that it quite overshadows the roof, stands at the northern corner of the building.[18]

A witness for the canonization of St. Ignatius recalled the hounds kept for hunting, dogs so good that the neighbors often borrowed a brace for a day's sport.

Thus, in the first formative period of his life, Inigo was influenced on the one hand by the rather feudal life of the *Casa-Torre*, on the other by the life of the farm-cum-smithy at Eguibar. The latter forged unbreakable bonds between Inigo and ordinary men; it helped to make him "a good mixer"—which partly explains his extraordinary attraction in later life for so many different types of people. His family, with its pride of lineage and the sense of loyalty so evident among its closely-knit members, gave him an appreciation of the value to any society of obedience to its acknowledged head. Because he had heard what was said in the *Casa-Torre*, the forge, and the farm, he saw life from the viewpoint of both the rulers and the ruled. Order and discipline were taught—unintentionally, perhaps—through the Loyola writ that ran undisputed in Iraurgi and its confines. For extreme examples of regular and irregular living, he had Azpeitia, with its Isabelitas, a zealous community careful in the observance of the rule, and with its unworthy pastor, his own brother, Pero Lopez. In his father, Don Beltran, he saw authority centralized, efficient, strong. Its efficiency derived not only from its strength but from the fact that it was well reinforced; for the Loyolas, however dissentient on other matters, were always united in upholding the authority of their clan's accepted head.

The sensations first imprinted on his infant mind need not be altogether a matter for conjecture. In a smithy, the light and heat and roar of the fire are inescapable; the child, beginning to notice, could gaze from over his foster-mother's shoulder at the shower of sparks that flew each time Errazti's hammer rang off the anvil; he could blink, solemn-eyed, at the flames that leaped to obey the hoarse orders of the great leathern bellows. The customers waiting in the shadowy forge meant no more to the baby than the tools, weapons, field implements, kitchen pots, and pans Errazti turned out. For as yet, men, iron, work, conversation conveyed nothing to Inigo; the fire was the great object of attraction; it was pleasant to stare at; its ruddy glow was warm; and, in Maria's cradling arms, all was peace. In Eguibar he heard only Basque; until old age he remembered the prayers and turns of speech learned in Iraurgi valley; an aquaintance remarked upon his Basque knack of "driving in nails that could not be drawn out." The proverbs that flew to and fro above the head of young Inigo had a topical flavor: *More go to the Indies than ever return. A shut mouth is the best mouth when in company with Kings and Inquisitors. The ocean once crossed, God is forgotten.* His delight in old age when presented "with a few roasted chestnuts on feastdays" evokes pictures of a small boy waiting, teeth watering, while the smith obliges—turning the spoils of an autumn evening's nut-picking clumsily, carefully with his heavy tongs. Directions given more than fifty years later to those who would teach the young hint at a childhood that afforded opportunities for watching kittens at play—the observer having a ground-level view! In the shadows of the past, little Inigo, shouldering the responsibility entrusted to him by Maria Garin, can be heard urging and arguing with rebellious and unruly hens that refuse to enter the low, narrow door of the hen-house.[19]

Childhood over, his days were spent mostly at the *Casa-Torre.* There the conversation was sometimes in Basque, sometimes in Spanish; very poor Spanish, spiced with soldiers' lingo. Occasionally there was mention of exciting events, wars and voyages and adventures in faraway places over the edge of the world. Usually the talk was of Iraurgi matters: the yield of orchards, fields, mills, quarries; the opening of a new lode by the miners; the quality and quantity of the year's wool and timber and wine and cider. There was full and plenty; refinements might be few, but scarcity was unknown. For entertainment there were the *fiestas,* with songs and dances commemorating epics of other days. There were pelota games, and contests of speed, strength, and endurance.

A time came when Don Beltran engaged a priest from the village as teacher and gave orders that Inigo was to present himself for daily lessons.[20] The preliminaries to reading and writing—"the hard apprenticeship of the primer and the practice of the down-strokes"—began. There had been a long-standing offer from a relative, Juan Velazquez, a high official of the Court of Castile, to take a son of Don Beltran's as a page into his own household; Velazquez, related by marriage to the family of Loyola, and a life-long friend of the master of the *Casa-Torre*, had promised to see to the education of whichever one of his sons Don Beltran might decide to send; later on, he would have the lad well placed at court. As the youngest Loyola was on the small side, "not tall or well-built like his brothers,"[21] his father must have had some misgivings as to his ability to make his way in the world. Smallness of stature might well be an asset to a page at court, but after a few years Inigo would be too old for page duties; a small courtier was another matter. Sixteenth century Spain was no place for small men; everything was on an exaggerated, larger-than-life scale.

During the last years of his life—he died in 1507—Don Beltran had more to worry about than Inigo and his future. The priests in Azpeitia were trying to turn the Isabelitas out of town; the Franciscans had come to direct the nuns, and, in consequence, stipends that should have gone to the parish went to the friars; disgraceful quarrels were the order of the day; the altars in the convent had been overturned and the Isabelitas denounced in Azpeitia parish church.[22] Don Beltran knew all this; he also had to face the fact that—even allowing for his two sons lost in the wars—he still had boys to settle in life. So Pero Lopez, having been ordained, was given Azpeitia. Sometime between 1504 and 1507, just in case of accidents—for anyone could get the plague, and all the Loyolas had their enemies—the father thought that Inigo should receive the tonsure. It is not certain whether the boy was tonsured then or not.[23] As will be seen, there is evidence for and against. At that time Inigo was in his early teens; too young for the Indies; too small for the wars. And, worse still, "he was not attracted to study, which cost him a tremendous effort of the will."[24]

Then Juan Velazquez de Cuellar, the Treasurer of Castile and royal Major-Domo, renewed his offer. Besides setting the seal on an old friendship, it was, for the Loyolas, no small honor. Up to the three or four generations preceding that of Don Beltran's, the importance of the family and their renown in battles was purely local and provincial. The wars of the reconquest had hardly touched them except on one notable occasion a century before. They had seemed, somehow, to miss the opportunities the Moorish wars offered to enhance their fame and forward their fortunes. The offer of Velazquez held the promise of a footing at court provided Inigo made the best of his chances; it was an offer gladly accepted. Inigo was then sixteen; it is not known whether he left the *Casa-Torre* before or after his father's death; no Polonius-like farewells are recorded.

Except for Dona Madalena, few in Iraurgi could have given the prospective page and courtier any Maxims-for-Correct-Deportment-in-High-Places. And Madalena, if asked, could reply with truth that the court would be a changed place since the time when she had been Maid-in-Waiting to Isabella. For the Queen's death in 1504 had been quickly followed by Ferdinand's marriage to young Germaine de Foix, a niece of the King of France. Germaine was saucy-tongued and fat and not always sober—anyone less like the great Queen whose place she now most inadequately filled could hardly be imagined. The Spaniards, outraged, persisted in calling her not *Queen*, but *Dona Germana*. The court was filled with her frivolous friends, mostly French and Neapolitan nobles. It was different from what it was when Madalena Araoz had been there.

Inigo was not altogether lacking in courtly accomplishments; he could sing and dance and play music. Like everyone in Azpeitia he was familiar with Anchieta's hymns and ballads. He knew, too, the songs of his people, those primitive chants of a race whose origins are lost in antiquity: the hymn to the sun; the lament for a lost love; crooning songs, shearing songs, milking songs; songs of the plough and the scythe, of battle and victory, of adventure and achievement; echoing choruses where the anvil answered the hammer, the stream the millwheel, the valley the mountains. His last days at home could have been worse spent than in practicing the Basque dances. In later years he was to perform those same dances in circumstances vastly different from those of his boyhood in Loyola or of his life in the courts of Castile. It is on record that he was always very fond of music and also that he "refrained from playing music on Fridays and Saturdays," but the instrument or instruments on which he performed got no mention.

There were farewell visits to make. To the Isabelita cousin, to the rakish brother, Father Pero Lopez. To Maria and Errazti, with their family at Eguibar, squint-eyed Martin and young Catalina and Juan and the rest. And to all the neighbors, many of whom, several years later, were to attest that Inigo had been regular in his assistance at Mass and

Vespers—and a frequent visitor to the Marian shrines in the valleys and mountains—during the few years he had spent among them.[25] As he left Eguibar, Maria's lamentations and parting blessings following him along the river bank, the shrine of Our Lady of Olaz, on the slope of the nearest mountain, would have caught his eye. As a member of the leading family of the district, one which had made generous gifts to Olaz, it is not likely that Inigo left Loyola without visiting this shrine so close to his home.

It was eighty leagues from the Iraurgi to Arevalo, the principal residence of Juan Velazquez, and the journey into Old Castile would take young Loyola some thirty miles south of Valladolid. Riding over the tawny, grassless plains, Inigo, his "bright blond hair flowing to his shoulders,"[26] was probably as excited and delighted as any boy his age going away from home to a new life. Everything was so strange that he hardly noticed how he had left the mountains behind. He was galloping south to become a great man in the king's service. Already he saw himself famous.

... in the household of the Catholic King. ... He was much given to reading certain worldly and fictitious books known as caballerias: "Amadis of Gaul" and similar romances. ... And his mind became so filled with the adventures these books related that he used to imagine himself facing hazards and performing great deeds, like knights he read of. ...

(Autobiography of St. Ignatius.)

... He was valiant and loyal, spirited and enterprising. ...Although attached to his faith, his life was not in keeping with his beliefs, and his mind was far from spiritual things; he did not avoid sin, being particularly without restraint in gaming, affairs with women, duelling, and armed affrays. ... Once he composed a poem in honor of St. Peter. ... In affliction and trials he never blasphemed against God. ...

(Chronicle of Father Polanco, the Saint's Secretary.)

... he was spirited and hot-blooded, fond of fighting and other excesses. ... He was tempted and overcome by carnal vices ... he was ingenious and prudent in settling disputes. ...

(Lainez, one of the first Jesuits; Ignatius' successor as General.)

... When challenged (to a duel) he would go before Our Lady to fortify himself. ... He never played music on Fridays or Saturdays. ...

(Father Araoz, relative of St. Ignatius.)

A T AREVALO, Inigo found himself in a different world. For the next ten years he lived the life of a courtier, his *pied-a-terre*—that of Velazquez and his household—sometimes at Arevalo, as often as not elsewhere. The Treasurer's official duties involved so constant an attendance at Court that his entire entourage was continually moving about in the Royal orbit. In July, 1507, for example, the court was at Valencia, welcoming the sovereigns home from a tour of their Neapolitan dominions, the celebrations there being followed by a royal progress through the dozen cities that lay between Valencia and Burgos. In the course of his ten years with Juan Velazquez, Inigo would have visited all the towns of Castile. He knew something of Seville, so it is probable that, at some time, he was with his lord in the beautiful cities of the south. Sometimes the officials and their retinues were lodged in royal residences or in castles of noblemen; occasionally, when the accommodation proved inadequate for the numbers, the pages and gentlemen-in-waiting got lodgings nearby.

Juan Velazquez de Cuellar, Treasurer of Castile, was Alcalde of Arevalo and other fortified towns in Castile. The lands surrounding these walled towns, all Crown property, were his by virtue of his office; he governed these estates as though they were really his own, treating the inhabitants so extraordinarily well that historians recorded the phenomenon:

> He was careful for their well-being, and would not allow them to be evicted or loaned or conscripted for war, or to be exploited or suffer any of the other impositions to which peoples were then often subjected. He maintained many out of his own pocket ... in all of Old Castile there was not a kinder lord.[1]

He was prudent and upright; somewhat conscientious; perhaps a trifle stubborn. He had a fine appearance and was exceedingly generous, giving munificent donations to churches and charities. A convent of the Poor Clares had been founded by him; and when Inigo arrived at Arevalo, the finest and newest building in the town was a hospital for women, also built by the Treasurer. Velazquez was well connected, as was his wife—daughter of an old Basque lady related to Inigo through the latter's mother. This old gentlewoman lived in a small house adjoining the San Miguel hospital built and endowed by her son-in-law; if Inigo went to pay his respects to her, he would have found her in the hospital, for she spent her time and her means in the service of the sick and poor.[2] But apart from this aged relative and her daughter, Dona Maria, the Treasurer's wife, Inigo did not lack for Basque friends. Twenty years before, the chronicler of Castile wrote to a friend, a Basque nobleman:

> The homes of our merchants and lawyers are simply crowded with Guipuzcoans; some of them are content to serve as lackeys, but

most of them endeavor to become lawyers and secretaries, while still others are adopted by nobles and learn to joust. I have four of them in my own house and forty others—whom I trained and set on their feet—are now honorably married in this district. You will find more from that province (Guipuzcoa) in the homes of Castilian grandees than in your own or in the Lord High Constable's, though both you and the Constable hail from Basque country.[3]

Behind him, in Azpeitia, Inigo had left Franciscan friars and Isabelita nuns, the former having fallen foul of the local clergy—including Pero Lopez of Loyola—the nuns resisting determined attempts to drive them out of their convent. In Arevalo he found Franciscans being held in high honor, while everyone, from the Treasurer and his lady down to the street beggars, respected the Poor Clare nuns and saw to it that they had sufficient both for their own meager needs and for the hospital and the charities they administered. The Poor Clares, the Isabelitas— sometimes called Concepcionistas—and the Friars following the Franciscan rule formed the spearhead of the ecclesiastical reform movement begun by Queen Isabella and continued by her confessor and friend Cardinal Ximenes. Himself a Franciscan, Ximenes was a man of the highest integrity. He led a most austere life; a hairshirt was concealed beneath the Franciscan habit he always wore under the Cardinal's purple or that armor he so often donned—the command of troops being no unusual thing for churchmen in the time of Julius II, a Pope who was constantly in the saddle riding with his army.

The only clue Inigo himself gave to his life at that time was the statement that he "wrote a fairly good hand"[4] and that his reading followed certain trends, then the fashion in Spain and elsewhere. It is safe to assume that, as a page and later a Gentleman of the Household of the royal Major-Domo, he had a very thorough training in formal manners; the ceremonial that surrounded court life everywhere at the time of the Renaissance being nowhere more rigidly observed than in Spain. The King often stayed at Madrigal, one of the towns of Velazquez, and Dona Maria was one of the few ladies of Isabella's court who found herself welcome at the court of Dona Germana. In fact, she became first favorite of the new Queen, who "could not bear to be a single day without her Maria attending on her and entertaining her—even more than was proper." The allusion to impropriety refers to the young, French-born Queen's drinking habits. A contemporary chronicler described Ferdinand's fifteen-year-old second wife as "a heavy drinker and fat."[5]

The lady of Arevalo being in such constant attendance on her Queen, it is reasonable to suppose that Inigo also was often in the royal presence. The intelligent young Basque would have soon noted that, between 1507 and 1516, one had to walk warily in the court of Castile. The King, Ferdinand of Aragon, accepted for Isabella's sake, after her death was regarded as a foreigner. His harsh, suspicious, niggardly, and sulky nature did not help to make him popular. His marriage to young, flighty Germaine de Foix within a year of his wife's death gave grave offense to his subjects. From an international viewpoint the alliance was a masterstroke of diplomacy, as it broke down the three-sided opposition to Ferdinand on the part of the latter's son-in-law, Philip, the King of France, and Emperor Maximilian. But in view of the internal situation in Spain the marriage was most impolitic.

Before his first marriage Ferdinand had had limited prospects as heir to Aragon; the Castilian nobles conceded him the title of King only by courtesy—as Isabella's husband. By Isabella's will he was only Regent of Spain until such a time as Charles, grandson of Ferdinand and Isabella, should attain his majority. The only nobleman he could rely on was his uncle, the Duke of Alba, yet he did not seem to realize the hostility and indignation his marriage caused in Castile. Though the French were unpopular in Spain at the time, Ferdinand's bride brought not only French lords but also several Neapolitan noblemen—dispossessed when Spain annexed the Kingdom of Naples—to the court. Even in her own country, people raised eybrows at "the marvellous audacity" of Dona Germana. At an international banquet during the royal tour of Naples, "she made little of all the French, including her brother, the noble Duke of Nemours." In Spain she saw no reason to curb her wit; she chided the Constable of Castile on his second marriage, implying that his second choice was decidedly inferior to his first. The Constable retorted that he was "but following the precedent set by His Highness, Don Fernando." The reply scored such a direct hit that "the Queen, much upset, made a lady in the Constable's household do him the favor of sitting on his knee and giving him a doughnut to eat, of which he died."[6]

Dona Germana was the center of that court in which Inigo of Loyola served. When he had mastered Castilian he found that to be in the fashion one had to have read the romances then enjoying a tremendous vogue. So Inigo read them until "his head was filled with them." To later, more sophisticated ages these books seem incredibly ridiculous. Dragons, ladies in distress, wizards, spells, heroes whose lives were one succession of preposterous and impossible adventures and fantastic amours, were the ingredients of these *caballerias*. Written at a time when chivalry was, if not dead, in a state of decadence, they persisted until Cervantes with his immortal parody on them laughed these extravagant romances out of existence. The Spanish writer, Menendez Pelayo, describes *Amadis* thus:

> A book in which the "eternal feminine" predominates, the lady of Amadis being the equal of her knight if not more important than he. The lover's passion, constant and noble, is not absolutely pure, nor could such be expected of the society that engendered such books. . . . Their gravest fault is the false idealizing of woman. In *Amadis* and similar books she is made into an idol, receiving a worship both sacrilegious and absurd, being served in an extravagantly amorous fashion. . . . A certain effeminacy, . . . a sensual idealism pervades the book.[7]

Against this court background of intrigue, effeminacy, dalliance, and corruption Inigo stands. In these surroundings he falls. The strong passions of his Loyola blood, the insidious solicitations of his new environment are too much for him. Two pictures of him at this period give, one the young courtier's appearance, the other his character:

> Although alledgedly tonsured, he never had his hair cut at the crown as the statutes required; his blond hair fell curling to his shoulders. He wore a suit of gaudy colors, again contravening the ecclesiastical statutes for the tonsured; his suit was slashed with another bright colour; he had a small scarlet cap with the insignia of his ancestors and a gay, waving feather. He strode about with his cape slinging open to reveal his tight-fitting hose and boots; a sword and dagger were at his waist. He had been seen to come and go (on visits to his native Azpeitia) with breastplate, coat-of-mail, sword, dagger, a crossbow with darts, and every kind of weapon.[8]

Azpeitia, no doubt; indulged in some hearty laughs at the sight of the undersized knight swaggering about with intent to impress all and sundry.

But there were days when such exhibitionist behavior was out of the question—days on which Inigo wished to be anywhere but in the courtiers' company.

In the flower of his youth and his glory, he contracted a nasal ailment which was accompanied by an odor so insupportable that when an attack came on him no one could bear to be near him. At such times, his shame and affliction were so great that he used to wish himself in some inaccessible solitude, not from any desire or will to serve God, but that he might be spared the spectacle of the tightly-held nostrils and averted faces of his fellow-courtiers. He consulted all the doctors, tried all the remedies, but to no avail. In the end he cured himself by frequent cold-water douches.[9]

This incident brings into high relief both the sensibility of the young courtier and the dogged streak that would not admit defeat in spite of the failure of all the doctors and their prescriptions.

During these years he seems to have visited home occasionally. He certainly was there during the carnival days preceding the Lent of 1515, for charges of law-breaking were made against him and his brother the Azpeitian priest. Documents relevant to the case still exist in the Azpeitia archives. The first document is from the Corregidor, or magistrate of Azpeitia, to the Bishop of Pamplona demanding the person of Inigo de Loyola, then safe from the civil powers in the episcopal jails at Pamplona. Anyone accused of a crime who could claim that he had been tonsured was tried by an ecclesiastical tribunal, and civil courts had no jurisdiction over such. Inigo, who evidently had been warned of the warrant out for his arrest in Azpeitia, decided to claim ecclesiastical exemption and rode to Pamplona where he got himself lodged in the Bishop's prison—a very astute move, for the bishops and corregidors all over Spain were constantly at loggerheads on the fine boundary-line dividing the civil and ecclesiastical jurisdictions.

The Corregidor, balked, listed the rules laid down in various papal bulls regarding tonsured persons; he tells the Bishop that he is gravely mistaken in his prisoner—

... who is no tonsured youth but a layman, who should be in my jurisdiction, not having been tonsured nor having kept the rules for the tonsured and therefore not entitled to claim clerical privilege.

The second document, dated March 6, states that Pero Lopez de Loyola, chaplain, and his brother, Inigo, both of Azpeitia, have had informations lodged against them because of certain excesses commited by them at carnival time. The Corregidor had by this time sent his notaries and officials to the ecclesiastical authorities in Pamplona, reiterating the demands previously made. The third document is in Latin, and is a brief, terse note asking that Inigo Loyola, "self-styled cleric," be handed over to stand his trial. Document number four again appeals to the diocesan authorities to obey the papal bulls; in case the Bishop is not familiar with them, the Corregidor reminds him that he has sent him copies, and asks him to note certain points, to wit:

> ... that the churchmen should not admit and receive *laymen*, married or single, who claimed tonsure. Neither should threats be uttered against the Corregidor or other civil judges until the cleric in question had first proved that for four months before the crime he had worn the habit and haircut laid down by Canon Law, in proof of being ton-sured. And, whereas the said Senor Corregidor, on asking for Inigo de Loyola, has received nothing but threats, though the said Inigo has not fulfilled the four-month law as to dress or haircut—on the contrary it being public property and notorious that he has always carried arms, gone about with cloak open, long hair and not a sign of a tonsure—the Corregidor asks that the law be not impeded but that Inigo de Loyola, without whom the case cannot proceed, be handed over at once . . . the crimes commited coming into the category of crimes of enormity, both because they were commited by him and his brother, Pero Lopez, by night, with malice aforethought, and because he had advised as to the strategems to be adopted. . . . And the Corregidor finally asks that the competent authorities arrest Pero Lopez de Loyola, cleric, and give him the penalty due him, and send Inigo to the Corregidor that he may get the punishment he deserves, but is evading, by remaining in Pamplona.[10]

In no document was Inigo called a cleric, though he was referred to as "the criminal." No difficulty was made about the Bishop's right to try Pero Lopez; the guilt of both brothers seems to be taken as certain and proved. In the final long document in Latin, the Corregidor patiently goes over the same ground, holding the trump card till the end:

21

The name Inigo de Loyola does not appear in the lists of Pamplona Diocese as having been matriculated; he has not done so; nor is ever likely to bother himself to do so.

It was a ruling in Pamplona Diocese that the tonsured wishing to enjoy ecclesiastical privilege should have matriculated and signed a register as proof of the same.

But despite the persistence of the Corregidor, Inigo was not handed over. In no document are the crimes specifically named; one states that it was not only at carnival time but on previous occasions; Inigo is mentioned as having been "disgraceful in his dress and worse in his conduct."[11] Is it only coincidence that the priest Anchieta returned from the court to Azpeitia where Pero Lopez had supplanted him, in 1515; that 1515 was the date of the burning of the Azpeitia Registers; and 1515 the year when Inigo was arraigned on charges that were evidently serious? Four years later, relatives and supporters of the Loyolas stabbed a nephew of Anchieta to death in Azpeitia.[12] Whatever his crime, Inigo himself, when he visited Azpeitia in 1535 after a long absence, said that "he wished to give some edification there, where he had been a *cause of scandal* to so many."[13]

On his release from the Bishop's prison in Pamplona he returned to Arevalo. Early in December, *el Gran Capitan* died in his home in Andalusia; of all Spaniards he had done most to drive out the Moors and to make Spain the first power in Europe; in all Spain no subject had deserved more and been treated more despicably in his latter days. A modern historian has summarized his life thus:

> An admirable man, the bravest and most adventurous captain of all those who, during these many years past, have set forth from Spain. The ingraditude with which he was treated only increased his glory and even preserved him from becoming his own stumbling-block in the end of his days; for it is a difficult and rare thing to make many voyages without suffering shipwreck. . . . Time cut short his life; his fame time cannot tarnish. . . .[14]

The news of the great Gonsalvo de Cordoba's death revived his memory throughout Spain. Inigo would have heard older courtiers and soldiers tell of his nobility of character, his greatness of soul, his unequalled military career. Many lords of Castile rode to Granada to salute for the last time the beloved commander. Two hundred standards and pennants, his insignïa, all the trophies won from the enemies in wars at home and abroad, told above his tomb the tale of glory. The visitor to Granada today will find the tomb, but the banners were torn to shreds and all the souvenirs of *el Gran Capitan* thrown into the streets when the Reds sacked San Jeronimo friary during the Spanish civil war. In death, as in life, the hatred and jealousy of lesser men followed him. Ferdinand, always inimical to Cordoba, had added insult to the ingratitude and suspicion that were the lot of Isabella's greatest soldier at the end. Inigo of Loyola could not but have heard comments on the ingratitude of the great to those who serve them best. Very soon he was to witness for himself, at closer quarters, poor reward for faithful service.

King Ferdinand died early in 1516, at Madrigalejo, one of the fortresses of Juan Velazquez. The Treasurer was with him to the end. Dona Germana, by her husband's will, was to receive an ample annuity, which was to be levied on the kingdom of Naples. Spain was in a state of great unrest; Cardinal Ximenes, Regent until Charles V came of age, had no easy task to keep rebellion in check. During the summer, Charles wrote saying that Naples was not to be asked to pay such a large yearly income to the Queen, but that certain Crown estates, including Arevalo, Madrigalejo, and others, were to become Dona Germana's property, Velazquez to retain his office and to continue governing the estates now to become the Queen's. The Treasurer did not stand to lose anything by this arrangement, but he considered that the rights of his towns had been violated, and that Crown estates were Crown estates and should not go to Dona Germana. The Cardinal agreed with Velazquez and wrote to Charles in Flanders advising against the dismembering of Crown lands. But Charles was immovable.

When a decree came from Flanders ordering him to hand over his estates, Velazquez determined to resist. All his people rallied to their "kind Lord's" assistance; he prepared for a long siege, gathered his supporters into Arevalo and closed the gates. After a two-month siege, during which most of the fighting was done by the scriveners of the legal documents passing between the besiegers and the besieged, Velazquez gave in. He was a ruined man; he owed sixteen million *maravedis*. Dona Germana, now become the sworn enemy of his wife—formerly her favorite—and himself, ordered them to be banished, their goods destroyed, and deprived them of all honors. The erstwhile Treasurer was a "disloyal" man in the new King's eyes; the previous spring he had lost his eldest son; now his friends forsook him. Sadly he moved to Madrid, where Cardinal Ximenes received and provided for him; he died some months later. Among the few who remained with him to the end was Inigo de Loyola; instead of leaving the latter "well-placed at court," as he had promised Don Beltran so many years before, Juan Velazquez died "leaving Inigo unprovided for."[15] But the Treasurer's wife gave him 500 *escudos* and two horses and advised him to go visit the Duke of Najera, to whom he was related; so he left for Pamplona, capital of the Kingdom of Navarre.[16]

The man of twenty-six who rode back north in 1517 to enlist in the army of the Viceroy of Navarre had a good deal for which to thank Velazquez and the courts of Castile. He had had a training in formal manners, in courteous speech and deportment, that Loyola could not have given him. To the end of his life he retained a liking for the self-control and serenity that he had been taught to associate with good breeding and correct behavior. When distinguished visitors came to dine with Ignatius and the first Companions, the Jesuits deputed to serve at table aquitted themselves "with a decorum and elegance such as could not have been surpassed in any prince's court; and an air of court ceremony prevailed," though the bill of fare was simple and often poor.[17]

At Arevalo the ideals of loyalty and obedience to acknowledged authority, already implanted in him because of his Loyola blood, were strengthened. He had been in the service of royalty; if his post had not been of great importance, if he had not—as yet—succeeded in appeasing that "great and vain longing for fame," he had served the greatest king of the greatest country on earth. Spanish diplomats were the most astute in Europe; the Spanish infantry, an instrument of war brought to perfection by *el Gran Capitan*, had shown the possibilities of lightly armed forces that could be moved rapidly. In 1512 Ferdinand conquered nearly all of Navarre. Except for Portugal, all the Peninsula was Spain's. Now the heir to Spain, Prince Charles the Hapsburg, was spoken of as likely successor to the Emperor Maximilian. What a king Inigo would then serve—King of Spain, and of that New Spain beyond the seas; King of the Netherlands and Sardinia, and Emperor of "that huge slice of Europe called the Holy Roman Empire." The Spaniards, like the Irish, gave their loyalties more to persons than to ideals. Men had died for Isabella, for *el Gran Capitan*; men were to die for Cortes, for Don Juan of Austria; allegiance was to the person of the king or leader. Inigo of Loyola was imbued—because of his service under the Treasurer of Castile as much as by that reading which "filled his mind"—with ideals of devotion and service. During his time in Arevalo he lived under the roof of an upright and conscientious servitor of the Crown; he would have heard something of the regard and honor and loyalty accorded to Queen Isabella by those in her service; of the disinterestedness and enthusiasm with which el Gran Capitan had served his sovereigns. As he rode towards Najera—a town about sixty miles south of the Casa-Torre of Loyola—Inigo, knowing that he was now commited to soldiering and finished with the court, probably felt a thrill of exhilaration. The life of a soldier promised more hope of achieving fame and glory than that of a courtier.

But he was under no illusions. The five hundred escudos, the parting gift of Dona Maria Velazquez, would not last very long; a night's gaming could see him penniless; Loyola estates could not be relied upon to afford much—too many brothers had to draw incomes, too many sisters had had to be dowered from the patrimony—and he was the last; a last, moreover, whose future was supposed to have been assured when he left for Arevalo. Now he had to succeed alone; his deeds would have to supply what fortune denied him.

Perhaps the most lasting lesson learned in Castile was the bitter one of disillusionment; in the fall of Velazquez from honor, power, wealth, and high station, Inigo de Loyola realized the dangers and vanities besetting the courtier; his decision to take up the profession of arms was an instinctively Loyolan reaction. His fellow page attested: "The Contador dead, Inigo wished much to follow soldiering."[18]

Don Antonio Manrique de Lara, Duke of Najera, had been named Viceroy of Navarre and Alcalde of the fortress San Juan de Pie del Puerto—St. John-Standing-in-the-Gate—one of the most important fortresses in Spain, as it barred the main pass between France and her old ally Navarre. Already there was skirmishing in that area, the Duke having to hold off the dethroned Juan d'Albret who was only waiting his chance to recapture Navarre. It was a likely place for a young soldier to win his spurs.

III

When he was in a fortress which was besieged by the French . . . a cannon ball, passing between his legs, shattered one and wounded the other. . . . The French treated the wounded man very well, being courteous and kind to him. . . . They sent him on a stretcher to his native place. . . .

(Autobiography of St. Ignatius.)

. . . He was a soldier, disorderly and vain. . . .

(Life of St. Ignatius, by Ribadeneira.)

. . . He used to spend three or four hours on end imagining how he would serve a certain lady: the means he would take to get to the country where she was, the witty remarks and fine speeches he would make to her, the feats of arms he would do in her service. And, so puffed up was he with these conceits, that it never dawned on him how impossible of achievement were his dreams; because the lady was of no ordinary rank, being no mere countess or duchess, but someone of far higher estate than either. . . .

(Autobiography of St. Ignatius.)

B ECAUSE St. Ignatius, in his memoirs dictated to Father da Camara, said that "up to his twenty-sixth year he was worldly," some biographers consider that he experienced a conversion of life, partial at least, when he set out for Najera. If 1491 be accepted as the year of his birth, he was then twenty-six; but there is little evidence of any conversion of life or manners. One of the Duke of Najera's family, who later became Bishop of Salamanca, related the following incident:

"With my own eyes I saw Inigo one day in Pamplona, when a file of men who were going along the street collided with him, flinging him against the wall. He drew sword and chased them the length of the street where, if it were not for those who held him back, he would either have killed some of them or they him."[1]

From 1514 until 1521, Inigo of Loyola was in Navarre—a captain fighting under the Duke of Najera. They were stirring times for

Spain. At faraway Cempoal, Cortes was running his caravels aground, cutting off the possibilities of retreat and revolt, and leaving his handfuls of Spaniards faced with two alternatives—to march on unknown Mexico and conquer a foe that outnumbered them by heaven knew how many to one, or die. Posterity was to transform this bold, heroic decision from fact to flaming legend until the expression "to burn one's boats" passed into the speech of every people in western Europe. His fellow conquistadors were swooping like hawks over other regions of that New World just then beginning to unfold its wonders before the amazed eyes of the Old. The Pizarro brothers were preparing to scale the passes of the Andes, enter the innermost Inca strongholds, and take Peru; de Leon was in Florida, Valdivia in Chile, de Soto on the Mississippi plains. Balboa, "silent upon a peak in Darien," was to be cheated of his acheivement in discovering the Pacific by no less a man than Keats, who attributed that Cortes-like feat to the man who conquered Mexico. Magellan was on his voyage around the world. All these enterprises were being carried through in 1519 and 1520, while Inigo de Loyola was sentinelling the marches of Navarre.

It was a time when greatness was in the very air of Spain. Within the walled city of Avila, in that Castile Inigo had left behind, an infant Teresa was lisping over and over, "For ever, and ever, and ever..." Though she would never leave Spain, she was to travel far over the vast spaces of the spirit and into the realms of prayer, leaving a name unequalled by any of the conquistadors, her contemporaries. A century ahead, Teresa of Avila and Ignatius of Loyola were to be raised to the altars on the same day—March 12, 1622.

Towards the end of 1520, Inigo distinguished himself in the taking of the town of Najera which had rebelled against its lord. This rebellion was but an extension of the *Comunero* revolt which had broken out in Castile earlier that year, arising mainly from the preferment the Flemings—who had followed Charles to Spain—were getting in the matter of Crown appointments. A revolt in Najera was a horse of a different color, as Najera was a fortified frontier town guarding ever-seething Navarre. The Duke sent a trumpeter ahead into his town, telling his subjects that if they submitted at once and quietly they could hope for equitable treatment. They replied "with salvos of artillery directed at the very spot where the Duke waited." Whereupon Najera sent other nobler envoys demanding surrender on promise of pardon; these were seized and were about to be executed when the Duke rode in, storming the city and sacking the fortresses, imprisoning the leaders and hanging the four principals as a warning to all. It is on record that Inigo de Loyola fought with great valor and "displayed a great and generous spirit when Najera was taken and sacked; though he might have taken much booty, he deemed such an action unworthy and would have none of the plunder."

Early in 1521, Inigo is again in the news. The people in his native Guipuzcoa refused to obey their new Corregidor. If Najera was important because it stood on the borders of Navarre, Guipuzcoa was infinitely more so, being the key province between France, Spain, and Navarre. So the Duke sent "persons of my household" to negotiate. Inigo, a member of one of Guipuzcoa's leading families and a soldier who had proved his worth and loyalty at the seige of Najera, was the leader of the embassy. On the 21st day of January, the Duke could write to the Constable of Castile that "all was well and the province was all in peace."

In the meantime, Navarre was causing much anxiety. The Constable of Navarre wrote to the Emperor complaining that it was unwise to leave his territory so unprotected. Henri d'Albret, son of the last King of Navarre, was reported to be massing troops just across the Pyrenees at convenient mountain passes; the French were preparing to send him large-scale support. It was madness, argued the Constable, while enemies were at the very gate of Spain, Navarre, to leave that province so inadequately guarded.[2]

In the spring of 1521, the Viceroy himself, back in Pamplona, writes in similar vein. Henri d'Albret is at Bearn, he says; only a mountain lies between the Pretender and his waiting Navarre. But Castile, instead of sending reinforcements, demands that Najera's son and artillery—sorely needed in Pamplona—be sent to the forces fighting the Comuneros. The Duke's own men are mutinous "because of ten months' arrears in pay." Of his fine retinue of royal guards "dressed in the fashion of the soldiers who crucified our Lord . . . I can only rely on two hundred veterans, a few auxiliaries, and the mounted retinue of my own household." A message was sent to Guipuzcoa for help, but the Guipuzcoans replied that their own province was on the frontier and that they had all they could do to defend themselves. One family did not fail. The messenger sent to Guipuzcoa was Inigo de Loyola and he brought back his brother, Martin Garcia, with a sizable army from the Iraurgi area; forced marches took them through the mountains to Pamplona in less than two days.[3]

Meanwhile, news of Spain's troubles—civil war in Castile, armed revolts in Valencia—seeped through to the north, convincing the free-

walls—a long argument with the city fathers and commander Beaumont. The upshot was that, when the Council and Beaumont did not agree with him, the lord of Loyola, in a huff, rode back to Iraurgi with all his troops.[5]

Inigo remained, with a handful of brave volunteers from his native valley. "He left his brother and entered the city, spurring his horse to full gallop."[6] If his brother's behavior was bad, that of the commander to whom their master, Najera, had entrusted the defense of Pamplona was no better. Beaumont told his fellow captain that he wished to abandon the city; it was useless to oppose an army the size of that which the French had brought and the populace could not be trusted. He was going to move out to the southwest; Inigo would be well-advised to accompany him. But such an action was the farthest from Captain de Loyola's mind; not for nothing had he lived through those years in Arevalo, where knights were weaned on el Gran Capitan's motto: Por la honra pon la vida; y pon los dos, honra y vida, por tu Dios. For your honor give your life; for your God give both your honor and your life. To leave would be admission of defeat; Inigo would be ashamed to ride away; it would look as though he were running from danger. So he saw his commander ride away on the heels of his brother.

The enemy were bivouacked in strength little more than a mile outside the city walls. They had a decided advantage in that the high winds blowing all ten days between Ascension and Pentecost enabled them to enjoy the fresh breezes blowing along the Arga, while the beseiged had to suffer the whiff of the corpses brought them on the East wind.[7] Inigo, having put himself at the head of those willing to defend Pamplona, had the satisfaction of seeing "a former rival" join him, with a few other knights. There was little else for satisfaction. On the eve of Pentecost the mobs finished looting the Viceroy's house, and citizens, suddenly turning soldiers and showing a surprising acquaintance with the defenses, began to man high places and armed positions. They had no intention of helping the defenders, for they killed and robbed any of Najera's men found alone and unaccompanied. Deputations of prominent Pamplonians were preparing to go out after sundown to swear fealty to Don Henri d'Albret. And in deep conclave in the cellars beneath the fortress sat Herrera, Governor of the city, with his captains. Herrera was from Aragon, and Cardinal Ximenes—a good judge of men—had advised against his appointment as Governor in Pamplona. The general opinion of the Herrera group was that they should surrender. Out of courtesy for the missing Viceroy, they sent for Najera's representative; but the garrison Comdom-loving Navarrese that the time was opportune for striking off the Spanish yoke they had so unwillingly borne for five bitter years. Each night contingents could be seen moving through upper Navarre, slipping into France by the Pass of Roncesvalles to join d'Albret's army. Among the Navarrese leaders were Miguel and Juan, captains from Xavier Castle near Sanguesa and brothers of the boy Francis of Xavier, in the shaping of whose future destiny Inigo of Loyola was to play so noble a part.

A letter from Sanguesa in that spring of 1521 told of:

> . . . multitudes of men advancing through the mountains; one town after another declaring for Henri d'Albret. The Duke of Najera has fled Pamplona, which city is now its own master. The French should be that far by tomorrow, and indeed they will not need to take their feet out of their stirrups to capture it. All Navarre and all the mountains are for Don Henri, and if the Duke of Najera succeeds in reaching Castile, he may thank God. . . .[4]

The invasion was no rumor but a fact; the French were in Navarre. It was not fair to the Duke to say that he had fled the Navarrese capital. Having sent ten couriers to Castile and eliciting no better response than the Constable's jibe: "Navarre isn't worth a chestnut; the King can regain *that* any day he likes," he decided, even at the eleventh hour, to go for help himself. Najera felt desperately anxious; the Constable of Castile was his life-long enemy, while the Constable of Navarre, his own son-in-law, was of very doubtful loyalty. Worst of all, the Royal Council seemed inclined to think that the Navarrese affair was but a faction fight compared to the rebellions in Valencia and Castile. *They* had not seen the French armies sent by Francis I, the rival of Charles V, pouring in through the mountains by Maya and Roncesvalles and San Juan.

Before his departure the Viceroy set up the defense cannon, issued the defenders with corselets and crossbows, and laid in food and ammunition. He left Francis de Beaumont in command, having sent Inigo de Loyola the previous day to bring what reinforcments he could from Guipuzcoa. Hardly had the Viceroy and the Bishop of Avila gone posting for Segovia, where the Royal Council was sitting, than the Loyolas and their forces arrived. The gates were closed. Inigo, being one of the garrison, was already known to the townspeople and had a permit to enter. Martin Garcia, insisting that he and his brother should have command and could be counted upon to save the city, conducted—from outside the

mander was well on his way to Logrono by then, so Inigo was called. When asked his opinion as to what should be done, he replied, "Defend the citadel or die." In 1553 he was to recall that meeting in the cellars of the fortress . . . "he gave so many reasons that at last he persuaded the Governor to defend the citadel, though against the better judgment of all the knights."[8]

The city fathers, ready to go out to meet Don Henri, were prudent men who believed in keeping in with both sides. They called upon the Governor and pointed out that if the garrison in the fortress resisted, the French, already in outlying parts of the city, might fire, and the citizens would be the worst sufferers in a bombardment at such close quarters. They extracted a pledge from Herrera that he would only fire outwards, beyond the city walls; in return, they promised to obtain from the French a pledge to attack only the portion of the fortress that jutted out from the walls. Then they sallied forth, met the French, and offered the town to Don Henri. The French general was ready to agree to all the conditions mentioned, save that of not attacking the fortress from within the city. In Pamplona, on the evening of Pentecost Sunday, the defenders were left in no doubt as to where the citizens' loyalties lay; when the first three hundred French troops entered the town they were cheered to the echo.

On Whit Monday the French cannon, the best in Europe, were brought up and set in position. The French general made the customary demand for the surrender of the citadel before beginning the bombardment; he made a special appeal to Inigo not to remain in the fortress; possibly they had met in Arevalo. Herrera and the other captains must have been wavering, for Father Polanco records that "Inigo persuaded them not to accept the terms promised by the French if they surrendered, terms which seemed disgraceful to him. He induced them to arm and defend the fortress."[9]

The French captains went away. The defenders prepared for a defense they must have known was hopeless. They were vastly outnumbered. They had enemies within the city gates. There was no hope that help could arrive from Castile—even if the Duke had arrived there and had got help—for several days. They had no priest among them and death was imminent; so Captain de Loyola took one of his comrades aside and asked him to listen to his confession.[10] This custom of confessing to a layman in the absence of a priest was very prevalent in earlier times, and devotional manuals in vogue in Inigo's youth sanctioned the practice. The Loyolas might be lacking in morals, but they were strong in faith.

There was a little chapel of the Virgen del Pilar in the fortress. It is more than likely that the man who, as a courtier in Arevalo, always prepared himself before fighting a duel by going to pray before our Lady's altar, now visited the Lady-chapel in the fortress. After that he might be noted bobbing up and down behind the breastworks, for he fought like a demon in the vain attempt to hold a city the citizens of which were all for the enemy and all against their defenders.

The siege lasted six hours, by which time one wall of the fortress had crumbled and the gates had been breached; the attackers began to storm the place, so Inigo, with the other captains, dashed to man the gap in the walls, ready with drawn sword for the first rush of the French. It was there, while fighting bravely, that "a cannon ball, passing between both his legs, shattered one and wounded the other." And, "as soon as Inigo fell, the garrison surrendered to the French." With a broken right leg and his left limb badly gashed—from flying fragments of the wall when the ball ricocheted rather than from the missle itself—Captain de Loyola lay bleeding and groaning on the ground. Around him there was nothing but noise and confusion; the shouts of the French, the cheers of the citizens, the smoke and dust of the cannonade; the rushing of soldiers hither and thither. Herrera and his men, having surrendered, were intent only on saving themselves from instant execution at the hands of the enraged infantry; they had no time to spare for the wounded Inigo. It was left to the French to search for him. Though seemingly infuriated with the other defenders, the enemy had nothing but admiration for the little Basque captain.[11]

> Finding him streched upon the ground, they carried him down into the city, for he was very well known. There they, his enemies, attended to him, fetching doctors.... Among all his afflictions and during his labors (at the siege) he harbored no hatred against anyone; neither did he blaspheme against God.[12]

While the French surgeons were looking after Inigo de Loyola, the Governor, Herrera, anxious lest the fall of Pamplona imperil his future, hastened to get his version of the surrender to the right quarters.

No mention of Inigo de Loyola appeared in his account. Herrera demanded the Governorship of his native province of Aragon as a reward for his bravery. But there was no talk of the man who had been most grievously wounded in the action at Pamplona, and no mention of a reward. Inigo was still in enemy hands; speaking of his capture in later years, he told of the courtesy and friendliness with which he had been treated. He, in turn, gave the doctors what he could: "to one his shield, to another his dagger, to another his corselet." There was almost a year's pay owing to the Duke of Najera's men, it will be remembered; so the poor captain was probably penniless. Sometime in the first week of June, ten or fourteen days after his misfortune, the French sent Inigo of Loyola home in a litter to the *Casa-Torre,* taking a roundabout route to keep in French territory.

The rough mountain roads and the unknit fracture rendered the travel a torture, and at one point the wounded man had to rest for eight days. They finally reached Loyola, coming down the hill from Azcoitia. Martin Garcia was away; Guipuzcoa, thoroughly alarmed since the news of the fall of Pamplona had come, was mobilizing a militia. But Dona Madalena was at the *Casa-Torre* with her three grown-up children and her three little ones. It was after mid-June when Inigo was carried into his home, up the wide stairs—where today the pilgrims throng—to a large, bright, low-ceilinged room at the very top of the house. It had two windows, one looking north, the other east; the giant oak tree blocked most of the view. They laid him on the canopied bed in the center of the room, the spot now the site of the main altar; and the family retainers, hanging about on the staircase and in corners, told one another that here was a true Loyola, a warrior if there ever was one.

Inigo himself, towards the end of his life, described the sufferings he endured in that room:

> As he felt poorly, doctors and surgeons from many places were called in. They were of the opinion that the leg should be broken again and reset, saying that, having been ineptly set the first time, the bones were out of place and could not heal. So the butchery was done again; during which, as in all which he had gone through up to then and afterwards, he spoke never a word, nor showed any sign of pain beyond the constant clenching of his fists.
>
> His condition getting still worse, he was unable to eat and the signs of approaching death became apparent; and, come St. John's Day, as the physicians had little hope of his recovery, he was advised to make his confession; so he received the Sacraments on the Vigil of Saints Peter and Paul, the doctors saying that if he did not improve by midnight he could count himself a dead man. The sick man had been

devout to St. Peter, and God so willed that that same night, at midnight, he took a turn for the better, the improvement continuing so that,within a few days, he was judged to be out of danger.

And now, the bones beginning to knit together, one, just below the knee, was found to be overlapping another, thus shortening the leg; and there it remained, protruding in such a way that it was an ugly sight—the which he could not abide, because, being determined to remain in the world, he considered that this would be a disfigurement. On inquiring from the surgeons if it could be cut, he was told that it could indeed, but the pains would be greater than all he had undergone before, for it had already healed, and it would be a tedious task to cut it again. Nevertheless, his self-conceit determined him to face this martyrdom, although his eldest brother, scared, said that he would not dare to put himself in such agony; the wounded man, however, endured it with his customary patience.

The flesh and the protruding bone cut away, remedies were applied so that the leg might not remain shorter than the other; many ointments were used and instruments which kept the leg extended, for many days, during which he suffered excruciating pain. But Our Lord was restoring him to health and he soon found himself getting better in every way except for his leg, on which he was not able to support himself; so he had to lie on his bed. And because he used to be so fond of reading those worldly works of fiction known as *caballerias*, and feeling in good health, he asked for some of these to pass the time; but in that house no reading of the type in which he formerly indulged could be found. So he was given a Life of Christ and a book of the Lives of Saints written in the style of the *caballerias*. Reading and rereading these books many times, he began to relish what they contained. During his reading he paused occasionally to think on the things he had read. At other times, he thought of the worldly things which hitherto had so much engaged him. And of all the vanities that presented themselves to his mind, one in particular had a strong hold on his heart: that he remained lost to all, never feeling three or four hours slipping by, so engrossed was he imagining what he would do to serve a certain lady—the means he would take to get to the country where she was, the witty remarks, the fine speeches he would make to her, the feats of arms he would do in her service. And so puffed up was he with these conceits that it never dawned on him how impossible of achievement were his dreams; because the lady was of no ordinary rank, being no mere countess or duchess but someone of far higher estate than either.[13]

This account covers the three months from mid-summer to early September in 1521. The dates mentioned, June 24 and June 29, were two special feasts in the Loyola area. The former, St. John's Day—still kept as a Basque *fiesta* at Tolosa, not very far from the *Casa-Torre*—celebrated a famous victory of the Loyolas in battle when the head of the house and his seven sons gave a good account of themselves, routing an enemy force which greatly outnumbered them. It was also the feast of a nearby hermitage. The sufferer, lying between life and death, would have been dimly aware of the bells ringing through the valley. And, on the evening of the 28, when the doctors pronounced him in grave danger and he received the last sacraments, the bells were ringing again in the dying man's ears, for the shrine nearest to the *Casa-Torre* was that of St. Peter.[14] Many neighbors, good Maria Garin and Errazti among them no doubt, were at the shrine for the Vespers of the valley's titular feast, and probably praying for the poor captain, on the threshold of eternity. Father Leturia, one of Spain's leading authorities on St. Ignatius, wrote concerning his devotion to Saint Peter:

> This devotion to St. Peter had taken root in him in his infancy in Loyola; in Arevalo, living in the parish of St. Peter, and with the family of the Duke of Najera—where the very air breathed devotion to the Prince of the Apostles—it had its period of growth; now it flowered forth in ardent supplication. . . . There was nothing in this incident denoting a change in the worldly tenor of his life; nor did it impel him to make a vow to go on a pilgrimage or do penance. . . . It was only the agonized supplication of one who hoped in that moment of crisis for the protection of the Saint to whom he had consecrated his ventures of knighthood and poetry. . . .[15]

During the Arevalo period, he had at one time composed a poem to St. Peter.[16] As the writings left by St. Ignatius are in a labored sparse prose, this poetic flight has aroused considerable speculation. The German, Heinrich Boehmer, remarks that such a poem could have been "no jewel of Parnassus"; the Spaniard, Father Astrain, says, "one is curious to know how a man, who always found such difficulty in writing ordinary prose, would express himself in verse."

36

When, some days afterwards, he was pronounced out of danger, there were other reasons for rejoicing. The bells of all the valleys were ringing peals of joy—the Duke of Najera's army of Basques and Castilians had routed the French, capturing their commanders. Once again the flag of Castile flew over Pamplona. The first back to the Iraurgi with the news was a man from Azpeitia, leader of the local militia recruited some weeks previously by the lord of the *Casa-Torre*. Azpeitia, which had supplied "one hundred and two men, a drummer-boy, two priests, a flag of silk from the church chest, and silk ribbon to sew a cross on the flag"—the ribbon a gift of the town's leading business-woman—rewarded, with 100 *maravedis*, the leader who came home bringing the good news that the war was won. Other fighters soon returned, and two visited Inigo giving him an account of what had happened; lastly, the lord of Loyola, Don Martin Garcia himself, reached home with full details for his convalescent brother, who was eagerly awaiting news.[18]

There was an item of rather galling news for Inigo. His fellow captain, that de Beaumont who had ridden away before the siege, had captured de Foix, the French Commander, and was to get ten thousand ducats ransom-money. Herrera was still Governor of Pamplona and had been commended to Charles V, then back in Flanders; it was fairly certain that he would be made Governor of Aragon.

De Beaumont was rich; Herrera was to be powerful. But Inigo de Loyola was poor—unpaid for over a year; he had gained no honors; he had been knocked out just before the fortunes of war began to turn. He had, it was true, come back from the door of death, but his leg was not yet healed. It was poor consolation to know that he was not as badly off as Andre de Foix, the brilliant young French Marechal, several years Inigo's junior, who was not only crippled, but blinded and imprisoned, his huge ransom price payable to his captor, lucky de Beaumont. Don Martin, a Loyola to the core, would have cheered Inigo with the thought of opportunities awaiting him on recovery. His share in the conflict should be told to King Charles; as a leading Guipuzcoan captain and a member of one of its best families, any honors coming to the province might reasonably be expected to come his way; the Duke of Najera knew his worth and loyalty and valor, and would speak to the King for him.

But Inigo had not yet recovered. There was the discovery of a horrid deformity below the kneecap, resulting in the decision to face a second crude operation with its ensuing torture. He does not tell us in his own account of how "Dona Madalena and her daughters wept and begged him not to undergo the butchery."[19] The surgeon of Azpeitia got ten ducats for fee.

The pain, both of the operation itself—in those days when anesthetics were unknown—and of the stretching device he was placed in to pull the shrunken sinews to their original length, must have been appalling. But he would have consoled himself by looking forward to the days when he could again dress up in his riding boots, his tight-fitting hose, his slashed doublet and sleeves, his belted, bright-colored tunic and swinging cape. There is no sign of melancholy or discouragment; failure is the Basque's best spur. Thirty years afterwards Inigo could say, commenting on himself at this stage:

> In general, he proved himself a man of worth in his undertakings and acheivements. And, although—because of his ignorance of the things of God and the bad habits he had acquired—he sometimes put his natural gifts and ability to bad use, yet one can see in him a man whom God had made for great things.[20]

Before taking leave of Inigo of Loyola, Captain of Castile, some mention must be made of his last salute to romance. There was no library in Loyola. The only book owned by Martin Garcia was an account book bound in red leather. His will refers to it more than once; . . . . "in which is written by my own hand what such a one owes to me and what I owe to such a one."[21]

When Inigo asked for books of the *Amadis* type, to pass the time, Don Martin could not oblige. Dona Madalena, trained in the school of Isabella, had been used to reading books of a more spiritual tone; the two she now produced had been published eight to ten years after her time at the court of Castile. The *Life of Christ* was a finely-bound volume, the first work published by the Alcala printing press founded by Cardinal Ximenes at the time of the founding of Alcala University. It was a handsome production, the Gothic lettering being in black and red; the preface would have induced the convalescent to read on, for it was by the famous Court poet, whom he had known in Arevalo, Fray Montesino. The same Franciscan was also responsible for the translation of the book; Montesino's foreward was a panegyric to Isabella and Ferdinand, at whose command the translation had been made.

The other book, *Flos Sanctorum*, or *Lives of the Saints*, had a special attraction in its resemblance to the books of chivalry he had been so fond of; it was, in fact, what today would be described as fictionalized hagiography. This illustrated volume contained a translation of the Golden Legend—rather extravagantly embroidered tales of Saints; the title of one narrative gives the general tone of the remainder: *St. Amarus' adventures in quest of the earthly Paradise and his meeting with Leonatis and the duenna St. Baralides.* "Although," says Father Leturia, "this book lacked style and had certain bizarre and grotesque features, it was tremendously popular just then throughout western Europe, and by 1500 there were 74 Latin, 13 Italian, 8 English, 6 French, 3 Dutch, 2 Bohemian, 1 German, and some Spanish editions; its historical basis was remarkably correct; its pages exhaled a simple, profound piety."[22]

It is interesting to note Inigo's first reactions. He read and reread the books; several times, his own account says. There was nothing else to read and, the wars over, there were few visitors. Martin Garcia and others who had been away earlier in the year fighting, were now busy making up for lost time and had to see to their various affairs. The room at the top of the *Casa-Torre* was sometimes stiflingly warm during the July and August days, and, by degrees, his periods of reading became shorter and the meditative intervals between, longer. It came as a surprise to him to find himself attracted by what he read; Christ the fountainhead of all sanctity, the saints, who had drunk deep of those living waters, drew Inigo towards holiness. But, some days, for hours on end—like Augustine centuries before—old, seductive memories plucked at his heartstrings; he gave himself up to romantic daydreams of "a certain lady."

Endless speculation on the part of Ignatian biographers, and no little research in Spain, have failed, so far, to establish the identity of this fair unknown. Inigo's words, "he pondered the means he would take to get to the country where she was,"[23] indicate that the lady of his affection was, in 1521, living outside Spain.

It is more than likely that his infatuation for his high and unattainable star never went beyond wishing and planning. If morals were lacking in castle and court in his time, etiquette was ever so strict and few survived any breach of its rules. In any case, Inigo would have been slow to transgress against the social code, which, during his stay at Arevalo, had become as second nature to him. And if any lady had at any time received a letter or gift or poem from the little Basque captain, in later times when Ignatius Loyola became a European name, is it likely that she would have kept silent about the tokens of love and esteem she had had from so great a man? What woman—a saint excepted—would, or could, have kept secret

39

the earlier indiscretions of the officer who, before the end of his days, became the *Gran Capitan* of a new army recruited for the service of God and the Church? To Inigo's list of natural virtues may be added the ability to keep certain things to himself—no small attribute in a time when it was the fashion to love, ride away, and then tell.

As he lies musing in the summer evenings, looking out from that upper room of the *Casa-Torre*, Captain Inigo Lopez de Loyola can look back on his four years of soldiering with pride. At the siege of Najera he had distinguished himself, by his bravery in the attack as by his magnanimity in refusing to take his share of the booty. He had led an embassy to Guipuzcoa, bringing about peace by his prudence and tact in negotiation. He had fought with honor at Pamplona. Though misfortune had befallen him, though fame and victory had evaded him at Navarre as in Castile, his life as a soldier had taught him much. In Arevalo he had become acquainted with the theories of the new military tactics planned and perfected by *el Gran Capitan;* in the wars of Navarre he had learned how to employ such strategy. On one basic principle—troops equipped lightly enough to be capable of shifting positions quickly as need arose, yet without any lessening of their effectivness as a fighting force—*el Gran Capitan* made the Spanish armies the finest and most victorious on the continent, transforming the strategy of European warfare within a few decades. The Duke of Najera, whose aunt had been married to *el Gran Capitan,* was a soldier of the latter's school, a brave and competent commander. From him, more than from any other, Inigo learned the science of war in all its practical aspects.

Meanwhile, in the Iraurgi valley, life went on much as usual. Errazti, in his forge, worked iron into the familiar utilitarian shapes, sometimes bending the hard metal into intricate, beautiful designs, as he fashioned wrought-iron balconies or archways with hanging lanterns or other occasional orders for special patrons. The ring of his hammer was a sound that would have often carried up-river to the convalescent in the *Casa-Torre*. Maria Garin, no doubt, sometimes paid a visit to her foster son, telling him the gossip of the valley, the happenings in Azpeitia—happenings in which Inigo's brothers did not play a very creditable part.

Since the murder of his nephew by a Loyola faction in 1519, the priest Anchieta had become the champion of the nuns whom he previously tried to drive away from Azpeitia. Pero Lopez of Loyola, having traveled to Rome to get his own pastoral rights recognized, was now in complete charge of the parish and shortly before Inigo's injury obtained a papal bull ordering the nuns to pull down the belfrey and "other public signs" that proclaimed their little convent for what it was.[24] The summer dragged on. In his attic Inigo waited, probably with some impatience, for the bones of his leg to knit. Now and again, looking down at the injured limb, he must have known moments of anxiety, wondering if ever his tight-fitting hose, his boots of soft Cordoba leather, would pull on again. Tradition has it that, when at last his leg would bear his weight, he began to take little walks,[25] first in the meadows about the *Casa-Torre*, then to Eguibar, that home of his infancy. Still standing a little way from the farm is a stone which marks the spot where in those days Inigo used to stand, steadying himself on his crutches, as he saluted Our Lady of Olaz.

> . . . And his great consolation was in gazing at the heavens and the stars, in which occupation he often spent a long time. . . .[26]

"When the night was in the midst of her course" and cool winds sprang up in the river valley, he gazed at the starry expanses above and beyond the giant oak—where the heavens hid God. The night skies in the Iraurgi are a peculiarly entrancing sight, the great bulk of the mountains on either side seeming to lend the stars an extraordinary brilliance. Though the night falls swiftly, the dawn comes slowly, the skies passing through many grades and shades of ink-black, ink-blue, and all the greys—leaden, steely, pearl. It is easy to imagine the watcher at his window as the heavens pale and torches of night are extinguished until none remains but one—the morning star.

PART II

The Refining Fire

IV

. . . When reading the Lives of the Saints he used to stop and think, reasoning with himself thus: "How would it be if I did this, as did St. Francis? And this, which St. Dominic did?" . . . Afterwards, being interrupted, vain and worldly thoughts displaced these, engrossing him for long periods. . . . This see-sawing of his mind detained and hindered him considerably. . . .

(Autobiography of St. Ignatius)

. . . One thing above all others he desired—to set out for Jerusalem as soon as he was well enough, and to do such fasting and penance as a generous soul, enkindled by God, would wish to do. . . . And so, mounted on a mule, he set off for Montserrat. . . .

(Ibid.)

S T. FRANCIS and St. Dominic, the two saints who stand as that point in the life of Inigo de Loyola when he first turned towards God, seem to have attracted him more by their external actions than by the intense inner life of the spirit that underlies, as it explains, the activity of every saint. Both saints had been mentioned at great length in the Golden Legend or *Flos Sanctorum*, which Inigo had been reading. In the life story of St. Francis he must have noted a certain similarity to his own. And St. Dominic's complete disdain for money would have appealed to the soldier who had scorned to take his share of booty at Najera.

In his reading Inigo also came across the account of a vision vouchsafed to Dominic in which Our Lady, kneeling at the feet of her divine Son, interceding for the souls redeemed by Him, pointed to St. Francis in heaven and to St. Dominic still on earth, one of whom had finished as the other was then accomplishing great work for the establishment of Christ's kingdom in the hearts of men. The Blessed Mother referred to these two faithful servants of God as "men of fiery zeal and courage." Captain de Loyola, who had undergone without a murmur the most excruciating pains just to have his leg set straight, fclt that he, too, was capable of undertaking penance similar to that of Dominic—

> ... who each night scourged himself three times with an iron chain; the first discipline he took for his own sins; the next for the sins of all the sinners in the world; and the third for the sins of the souls detained in Purgatory.

Although, in the memoirs he dictated at the end of his life, Ignatius mentioned only Sts. Francis and Dominic, other saints about whom he read in the Golden Legend included several of the Desert Fathers, St.Patrick of Ireland, St. Augustine of Carthage, and the great monastic founders, St. Benedict, St. Bruno, and St. Bernard.

The convalescent's active mind began eventually—perhaps inevitably—to study its own workings. Noticing how his mental process kept vacillating between worldly and spiritual thoughts, he set himself to examine the aftereffects of each. A new element, hitherto absent, now manifests itself in the pattern of his thought; he begins to be introspective, to psychoanalyze himself, to note the manner in which these periods of reflection affected him.

> ... He noticed that while worldly thoughts delighted him at the time when he gave himself up to them, afterwards—when through weariness he desisted from them—he found himself discontented and dry. But when he thought of such things as going barefoot on pilgrimage to Jerusalem, or living on nothing but herbs, or practicing the austerities of the saints, not only was he consoled while thinking on these things but afterwards he remained joyful and contented.
> ... And so, he learned from experience how after some kinds of thought one is left sad, and after others joyful. And, little by little, he came to know by what different thoughts a man may be agitated. And this was the first reasoning he did on the things of God; afterwards, when making the Spiritual Exercises, it was this experience of his own which enlightened him as to the diverse inspirations by which men are swayed. ...[1]

This probing for the general principle underlying seperate facts or occurrences was a characteristic of Inigo throughout his life. Having now, in the words of Pere Dudon, "lighted a beacon on the horizon of his past life," he began to feel the need of doing penance for the sins of former years. The saints he read of provided examples of mortification: a pilgrimage to the Holy Land, severe fasts, bodily austerities. Rather sensibly, he deferred his penitence until his health was restored. Concerning the grace received one night when he "beheld clearly a likeness of Our Lady with the Holy Infant Jesus," he adds:

> By the effects of this experience, it may be taken as having been from God, yet he (Inigo) would not dare to determine it as such, nor to say anything further about it, save to affirm what has been related.[2]

This vision, which he himself dares not proclaim as a supernatural manifestation, is generally accepted as having taken place in August, 1521. It is not without significance that before that month ended the long-standing differences between the Loyolas and the Isabelitas, between Pero Lopez and his sons—also priests in their father's parish—and Father Anchieta, were settled. A servant was sent from the *Casa-Torre* all the way to Burgos to fetch the Franciscan Provincial; conferences took place in Martin Garcia's home at Loyola and an amicable agreement was reached. In token of the genuineness of the reconciliation, Pero Lopez and Father Anchieta arranged that, after their deaths, they would share the same grave in the plot of ground Martin Garcia presented to the nuns as a peace offering. But despite all Inigo's efforts in this matter, the year after he left Loyola the old feud flared up worse than ever, Martin Garcia and Pero Lopez going so far as to threaten to burn down the convent if their niece, a novice with the Isabelitas, did not leave at once; they also refused to allow the corpse of Father Anchieta to be interred in the convent cemetery.[3] In the autumn of 1521, however, the reconciliation pact seemingly sealed for evermore, Inigo continued his reading and meditations; the decisive phase in the mental tug-of-war between worldly and other-worldly thoughts having been resolved, he now gave most of his days to God.

> His anxieties vanished; when those of the household came to speak with him, the conversation was about the things of God and the good of their souls. And the thought occurred to him that he ought to make extracts from the books that afforded him such delight—the Life of Christ and the Lives of the Saints; so he commenced with great care to write this anthology. Now that he was able to move about a little, he got 300 leaves, quarto size, wherein he wrote the words of Christ in red and those of Our Lady in blue; the paper was shiny and

lined, and the lettering finely formed, for he wrote a very good hand....

> And his greatest consolation was in gazing at the heavens and the stars, in which occupation he often spent a long time; for it inspired in him an immense courage to serve Christ our Lord....[4]

The varied reactions with which Inigo's change of heart was received in Loyola may be imagined. Dona Madalena and her daughters, sitting with their mending or embroidery, would have made good listeners while Uncle Inigo, already an enthusiast for the perfect life, told and retold some of the stories from the Golden Legend. It was probably for Madalena de Araoz a reliving of the old days in the courts of Castile, when Queen Isabella read similar books with the Maids of Honor, or invited holy men to speak on such subjects. The heir, young Beltran, a great favorite of Inigo, was no doubt nonplussed at the changed demeanor of his uncle; after Pamplona, all the Captain's talk had been of the wars and the court, of gaiety and adventure; now he spoke of nothing but piety and pilgrimages, fasts and vigils and disciplines, death, judgment, hell and heaven. As for Martin Garcia and the priest-brother Pero Lopez—both with their irregular attachments—after a session or two with the zealous convert in the attic of the *Casa-Torre* it is more than likely that they made themselves exceedingly scarce!

Until his leg healed, Inigo had to curb his desire to rush headlong after that kingdom which only the violent bear away. He had, at first, no definite ideas as to what he should do when he returned from the pilgrimage to Jerusalem, but was resolved that his life should be one of unceasing penance. Despite his admiration for St. Francis and St. Dominic he did not contemplate becoming either a Franciscan or a Dominican, though for a time he flirted with the idea of becoming a Carthusian. At Arevalo he had heard of the famous Carthusian monestary of Las Cuevas in Seville. In a century when many Orders had relaxed their rule, the Carthusians preserved the strictest observance, and the Priors and Fathers of the Chartreuse of Seville were held in the highest esteem not only in Spain but throughout a great part of Europe. A German traveller, describing his visit to Spain and Portugal in 1494 and 1495, writes: "Outside the walls of Seville, to the west, beyond Betis, there lies a celebrated Chartreuse called Our Lady of the Cuevas (Caves), the architecture of which is truly admirable... there are forty Fathers, thirty lay Brothers, and a venerable Prior who is a profound scholar." Cristobal Colon frequently visited Las Cuevas to speak with his friend, Fray

Gaspar, both before leaving for the Indies and after his return from his various voyages.

Inigo, to carry out his resolve of leading a life of unceasing penance, thought of offering himself as a postulant in the Carthusian monastery at Seville, but without telling who he was, so that he might be held in disesteem; there, he told himself, he could live on herbs. But, on second thoughts, remembering the penances he yearned to undertake during his passage through life, the desire to become a Carthusian cooled, for he feared that in Las Cuevas he might not be able to give his self-hatred full rein. Nevertheless, he sent a servant of the *Casa-Torre*, who was riding to Burgos, to the Chartreuse of that city (Miraflores) to enquire regarding the Carthusian Rule; he was pleased with the information brought back, but because of the aforesaid reason and also because he was engrossed in the thought of his coming departure, he did not pay further attention to the matter, which could be left until his return.[5]

A story was told at the canonization process of St. Ignatius which illustrates the complete change that had come over Inigo at this time. One day a relative from Cestona, some six or seven miles away, sent a messenger to borrow a brace of Martin Garcia hounds to go for a day's hunting. As the master of the *Casa-Torre* was away from home, Dona Madalena was asked for the dogs. She said that they were not about the house, though she knew the hounds *were* there. "Inigo," says the narrator—a witness on oath—"greatly abhorred lying; and when he knew that Dona Madalena had told an untruth, he took her to task, saying that he would not sit down to table with her and, for some days afterwards, he would not even speak to her."[6] This rather harsh treatment of a lady to whom he was always extremely devoted and to whom he was, since Pamplona, particularly indebted,* is only understandable as a flare-up of untempered zeal—the typical reaction of the newly reformed, who have

---

* St. Ignatius always retained a great affection for Dona Madalena, whom the early biographers called "his second mother." Once, when consoling a Jesuit novice who was pining for his relatives, the saint, after telling of his own family and his conversion, confessed to the novice that the face of Our Lady in a picture reminded him so much of a certain lady, a near relative, that during prayer he found his heart going out to this lady, "in such manner that his devotion was disturbed. To curb his imagination and to preserve reverence he pasted a piece of paper over the picture; so he told me the day he came to my cell and sat down for a friendly chat." The relative mentioned is generally taken to be Dona Madalena.

little patience with anyone unable to keep up the fast spiritual pace at which they themselves progress.

It is noteworthy that, at this stage, Inigo does not seem to have had the undertaking of any special apostolate in mind. He had to see to his own soul first. He was filled with shame before God:

> ... like a knight who finds himself before his king and the whole court, ashamed and covered with confusion, his manifold offences against one from whom he has received so many gifts and honors having been discovered and disclosed.[7]

Realization of his sins led to the desire of atoning for them. Whether the atonement should take place in a Carthusian monastery or in some hermit's cave was a question as yet undecided. The first item on his program was the pilgrimage to the Holy Land. To get there he would have to go to Barcelona; as he needed to prepare his soul before visiting Jerusalem—the city sanctified above all others since the Savior had walked its streets—he decided to visit Montserrat, the great shrine of Our Lady near Barcelona.

It was nothing unusual in the west at that time to do the Jerusalem pilgrimage. Although the Crusades were long over, pilgrims continued to set out, year by year, from all over Christendom, converging on Venice where the pilgrim galleys waited, the ships' masters haggling with the prospective passengers and fighting with one another as to who should bring whom. Von Harff, the German noble, Canon Casola of Milan, an English lord's chaplain, and others who went to Palistine shortly before or after Inigo did, kept journals of their pilgrimages which have been preserved. In the Basque provinces, there had always been a great devotion to the Holy Places, for the upkeep of which annual collections were made; noblemen of Guipuzcoa and Castile, men with whom Inigo was acquainted, had made the pilgrimage. There were ballads about Jerusalem pilgrims which Inigo would have heard; and the Golden Legend not only told of saints' pilgrimages to the Holy Land but had illustrations of places there. One of these latter—a picture showing the footprints which, according to tradition, were left by Our Lord on the stony summit of Mount Olivet at the Ascension—particularly impressed Inigo, and he resolved to see those footprints for himself when in Palestine.

Eight long months had passed since the wounded warrior had been brought home from Pamplona, every stride of his bearers being agony to the man borne in the rough litter that swung from their shoulders. During these eight months there had been fresh alarms and excursions. The French had marshalled another army, this time on the Guipuzcoan frontier. In August 1521 they attacked Fuenterrabia, near Irun. The tocsins sounded again in the Iraurgi, summoning all to arms; Maria Garin's son, Juan, a foster brother of Inigo, proudly captained the eighty-three Azpeitians who rallied at Martin Garcia's call. Pero Lopez went as chaplain, and even the shoemaker left his last and marched away to hold the mountain pass. The French might be sure of a welcome in Navarre but they would never enter Guipuzcoa, swore the lords of Loyola, Zarauz, and Lizaur, as they joined forces and hastened north. In Fuenterrabia Martin Garcia and his men were besieged; they were short of bread and water, "so much so that they had to cook their meat in cider," but they decided to hold out or die, for Martin Garcia of Loyola declared that they "had not come there to lose their honor but to win more."[8] For all his fine words, the master of the *Casa-Torre* had to surrender Fuenterrabia and come home; thus the war fizzled out in that area for the time being.

His brothers and those who lived in the house realized from the demeanor of Inigo that some great change had taken place in his soul.[9] Martin Garcia's accounts of the Fuenterrabia campaign did not evoke the expected response from the most seasoned soldier of them all, and the Loyolas began to wonder. Early in 1522, when the days began to lengthen, Inigo, though his leg was not yet completely healed, knew that the time had come to speak, so he said to his eldest brother: "Senor, as you know, the Duke of Najera is well aware of the fact that I am now almost well. I ought to go to him at Navarrete."[10]

The Duke, like Juan Velazquez in 1517, had now lost the royal favor; there was another Viceroy in Navarre and the brave Najera was living in straitened circumstances at the small village of Navarrete, ten miles to the Loyola side of what had formerly been his Ducal town and estates. Knowing that the Duke's household was now considerably reduced both in size and prestige, Martin Garcia felt sure that Inigo was not going to take up his old post. Why, then, was he so bent on going to Navarrete?

His (Inigo's) brother and others of the household had been suspecting that he wished to make some great change. Now his brother brought him, first into one room, then to another, and with admiring words began to beg of him not to waste his life, entreating him to consider the great hopes people had of him, the honors in store

51

for him; and with similar arguments he tried to turn him from his good resolutions. . . . His answer was such that, without departing from truth, concerning which he was already most scrupulous, he managed to put his brother off the scent. . . .[11]

Inigo wasted no time saying farewells. He left, "mounted on a mule," and accompanied by two servants and one of his brothers, who was going on a visit to a married sister at Onate.[12] Father Larranaga says that this brother was none other than the sorry priest of Azpeitia. They had hardly started out when Inigo, all afire for conversions, persuaded Pero Lopez—his codefendant in the summons served by the Corregidor seven years previously—to accompany him to the shrine of Our Lady of Aranzazu, there to keep a night's vigil. The other agreed; though neither knew it, that night at the shrine was the last time they were to be together in this life.

Aranzazu—a Basque word signifying you-are-in-the-bush—was a popular shrine in Guipuzcoa; only fifty years before some shepherds had found an ancient statue of Our Lady concealed in a shrub; it had probably been hidden there by someone flying north before the Moors several decades or perhaps centuries previously. It was customary for the pilgrims to enact scenes from the Passion during these nocturnal vigils; some would carry crosses and walk about the church while others stretched their arms for three hours against the thwart-beam of a cross; some pilgrims—come there to do penance for sin—scourged themselves to blood.[13] A note in the margin of the memoirs Ignatius dictated to Father da Camara states:

> From the very day he left his home, Inigo was accustomed to discipline himself severely every night. . . . At Aranzazu he prayed for renewed strength for his journey.[14]

It is more than likely that he was among those who "scourged themselves to blood" that night at Aranzazu; one wonders what were the reactions of Pero Lopez to this spectacle; his behavior the following year when he threatened to burn the convent in Azpeitia and dragged his niece out of the novitiate there does not give a picture of a changed man; but Inigo, though yet only a layman, could not part with this poor priest-brother without doing something for him. Hence the night of prayer and penance at the shrine of Our Lady of Aranzazu—Our Lady in the Bush.

Towards the end of his life Ignatius was asked what he meant by saying that he prayed at Aranzazu for renewed strength for his journey; he replied that he feared that he might be again overcome by the temptations of the flesh to which he had formerly yielded and which, *more than any others*, had conquered him.[15] Now that he was riding back to the scenes of former vanities, the captain of Castile felt the need of our Blessed Lady's special protection, his virtue being as yet of a brittle, untried quality. On this account, and also "because God filled him with ardent desires of doing things pleasing to Him," he made a vow of chastity to Our Lady, beseeching her to take him under her protection. Some think that he made this vow further along on the road to Montserrat, perhaps at the shrine of El Pilar in Saragossa, or at Montserrat itself, but the general opinion is that the vow was made at Aranzazu. In later years he was to tell Father Lainez that "although this vow was acceptable and pleasing to God, it was not quite theologically correct"; Lainez remarks that "God Our Lord, who had inspired him to make the vow, used His Mother as His intermediary to help this creature (Inigo). He showed that He accepted the sacrifice and took him under His protection."[16]

The vigil ended with Mass at dawn. The brothers rode on to Onate near the home of one of their married sisters. Then Inigo, accompanied by the two men of Martin Garcia's household, rode on to Navarrete.[17]

> Having remembered that the Duke owed him some ducats, he thought it would be a good idea to claim them, so he wrote a note to the Treasurer; the latter told the Duke that there were no funds, whereupon he (the Duke) said that whoever else went short, Loyola should not go unpaid, and for sake of his past deeds, the Duke would be pleased if he would accept a lieutenancy also. But, the money paid over, Inigo divided it, giving part of it to some persons to whom he considered himself obliged, and spending the rest on the restoration of a certain dilapidated statue of Our Lady. Then bidding farewell to the two servants who had come with him, he set off alone on his mule from Navarrete for Montserrat.[18]

The servants rode home to Loyola, bringing the message that Captain Inigo "had dismissed them because he was going to Montserrat on a pilgrimage of poverty and penance."[19] Meanwhile the solitary pilgrim was riding his mule through country he knew well since the days of his brief but brilliant military carrer, "pondering, as was his habit, the great deeds he would perform for the love of God." Externally there was not much change in the little captain riding northeast through Navarre and Aragon on his way to Montserrat in Catalonia. He had a good mount, was well dressed, wore a dagger and sword in his belt; his well-kept hair was "sweeping his shoulders"; his complexion "usually of high color" was somewhat paler since his long illness; his "lively, penetrating eyes," under the broad forehead," did not, perhaps , glance about as much as hitherto. His demeanor is little altered; but riding along, he thinks of his first goal—Montserrat; there he will try to prepare his soul before setting out on the journey to that Holy City he so longs to see—Jerusalem.

The winter, which in the south of Spain is but a matter of weeks and never very cold, is long and extremely rigorous in the north, particularly along the Ebro, which river route Inigo followed until past Saragossa. Having traversed the Navarre-Castile border he entered Aragon where he would have soon encountered the cierzo, a depressing wind that ceaselessly drives across the plateau from the northeast, scorching like a furnace blast in summer and in winter piercing the traveller through and through. Aragon might well be called the roof of Spain; to Inigo, as to all Spaniards of his time, it was the spearhead of the reconquest—the cradle of the nation.

While riding through Aragon, Inigo was soon presented with an opportunity for putting some of those virtues he had been reading of into practice:

On the way a Moor, riding a mule, overtook him. And in the course of conversation, the talk turned on Our Lady. The Moor said he could well grant that the Virgin had conceived by supernatural means; but that she should remain a virgin after child-birth, that he could not believe; and despite many reasons given him by the pilgrim, from this opinion he could not be budged. As the Moor then rode on very fast and was soon out of sight, he (Inigo) was left pondering on the incident; and many thoughts disquieted his soul, for it seemed to him that he had not done as he ought; besides, he was filled with anger against the Moor, and felt that he himself had acted badly in allowing a Moor to say such things of Our Lady; things he was in honor bound to make the fellow a return for. So a desire to go after the Moor and stab him hard for what he had said seized him. After weighing these thoughts for a good while, he was still in doubt and unable to decide what to do. The Moor, who had gone on, had told him that he was bound for a destination not very far ahead, on Inigo's road, close to the royal highway, though the road did not exactly pass through the place. Wearied from debating with himself where his duty lay, and unable to come to any definite decision, he finally decided to give the mule the bridle at the spot where the road to the Moor's destination turned off from the high road, and let his mount take one road or the other. If the mule took the road to the town, Inigo would follow the Moor and let him feel the dagger-point; if the animal kept to the royal highway he would let things be. Inigo did as he had planned, but our Lord willed that—although the town was a little more than thirty or forty paces from the high road, and the road approaching it very wide and good—the mule took the highway and did not turn down the side road.[20]

This was the first time, during the dictation of his memoirs to Father da Camara, that Ignatius referred to himself as "the pilgrim." He gives himself this title for the remainder of his "autobiography."

If the character of the countryside through which the pair were riding be considered, the odds against the poor Moor and the unsuspecting fellow's good fortune in escaping with his life may be appreciated. The side road, with food, water, and a promise of rest—only thirty or forty paces away—must have presented the mule with attractions far beyond any the royal highway could offer! For interminable stretches that road runs through country resembling nothing so much as an ocean of rock, thrusting endless, stony waves against a pitiless sky. The former soldier, accustomed to fighting on the grassy plains and rolling hills of southern Navarre, familiar too with the strategy favored by war captains in his native Guipuzcoa—a terrain peculiarly suited to guerilla tactics—would have marvelled as, riding over these arid wastes, he recalled the military feats accomplished by the Aragonese in times not long past. There the Arab invaders had been pushed back, mile by mile, to the south. Across these selfsame plains Ferdinand of Aragon had come west to Castile, traveling as a muleteer with—ostensibly—a merchant caravan, the "merchants" being in reality the escort of the Prince of Aragon, riding to wed Isabella of Castile, to unite the two kingdoms first freed from Mohammedan rule.

The cold was intense. Inigo's leg was giving him some trouble; he still kept it bandaged. At last he sighted Saragossa, not on a great height, as the *Song of Roland* describes it, but on a hardly noticeable rise on the right or south bank of the rolling murky Ebro. Special celebrations were then being held in the capital of Aragon, noblemen and churchmen from all central and northern Spain were pouring into Saragossa; as he did not wish to be recognized or to let anyone know of his secret resolves, it is quite possible that he bypassed a city where there would be every danger of running into some old acquaintance.

And reaching a large village before he came to Montserrat he wished to buy pilgrim garb, which he would need for his Jerusalem journey; so he bought some coarse sacking, loosely woven and with no selvedges; and he gave orders to have a garment made at once, loose and reaching to his feet; he also bought a pilgrim's staff and a gourd which he tied to his saddle, and some rope-soled sandals, of which he wore only one, and this not for appearance's sake, but because one leg was still in bandages and in a rather bad state; so much so that, although he went mounted all the way, each night he found this leg swollen; therefore he thought it necessary to wear a sandal on that foot.[21]

At last he left Aragon behind and rode through Catalonia, one of Spain's Mediterranean provinces; it was the third week of March, always the most beautiful time of the year in northeastern Spain. Now that the saw-toothed peaks of the Holy Mountain, the Monte Serrata, were already visible on the distant horizon, Inigo fell awondering what he was to do when he got there.

He began thinking, as was his wont, of the great things he meant to do for the love of God. And as his mind had been always full of the deeds described in *Amadis of Gaul* and similar books, he now found himself thinking in terms of chivalry; so he determined to keep a knightly vigil watching by his arms (as knights were accustomed to do) without sitting or lying down, but sometimes standing, sometimes kneeling, before the altar of Our Lady of Montserrat. He determined to leave there the clothes he wore and to don the uniform and insignia of Christ.[22]

When he arrived at Montserrat . . . he made a general confession . . . And at Vespers of Our Lady's Annunciation, March 24, 1522, he went as secretly as he could and, divesting himself of his fine clothes, gave them away to a beggarman; then clad in the longed-for garb (the pilgrim gown of sackcloth) he kept vigil all that night before the altar of Our Lady.

(Autobiography of St. Ignatius.)

. . . As there were many there who knew him, for fear of recognition he turned aside to a village named Manresa . . . where he lived on the alms he begged daily. He ate no meat; neither did he drink wine . . . and he allowed his hair, which he formerly tended so carefully, to go uncombed and uncut; his head now went uncovered. And, as he had always been very particular about his fingernails and toenails, he now began to neglect them, leaving them to grow unpared. *(Ibid.)*

It was while at Manresa that he first read the "Imitation of Christ" and ever afterwards he preferred it to any other book of devotion.

(Ibid.)

T HE SHRINE of the Black Virgin, Our Lady of Montserrat, towards which Inigo and his mount were climbing in the early morning of March 21, 1522, is perched upon a shelf of rock less than a thousand feet from the summit of a mountain some thirty miles north of Barcelona. The fantastic outline of the Montserrat range, formed by centuries of erosion, is in keeping with the mountains' weird coloring—forever changing as the light and its reflections strikes from different angles. High above the buildings, hunched on the shoulder of that mountain which is the goal of so many pilgrims, tower the conical shapes of further heights; and on clear days, away on the eastern horizon the Mediterranean can be glimpsed, a tranquil mirror for the blue of the skies and the gold of the sun. Since the ninth century the Benedictines of the great monastery surrounding the shrine have kept open house for all who ascend from the plains, two thousand feet below, to pay homage to the Dark Lady of the Sierra, Our Lady of Montserrat. A village, complete with hotels and hostels, restaurants, shops and post office, caters to the needs of modern pilgrims; the monastery has accommodation for those who wish to stay there. In Inigo's time there was a large pilgrim-hostel and booths at which food, votive candles, disciplines, manuals, and objects of devotion were sold.

The arrival of the elegantly dressed captain with the bandaged leg did not go unnoticed. Several decades later, the servant of a priest who was on a prolonged visit to Montserrat in 1522 testified:

> When I was at Montserrat in 1522, there arrived at the monastery a knight, well-mounted, wearing very fine clothes and bearing arms as soldiers do. . . . I saw him with my own eyes. . . . People took him to be Castilian for he spoke the language of Castile.[1]

Inigo could hardly have planned a better day for his arrival than March 21st, St. Benedict's Day. The feast of the father of the monks of the west, then held on that day, was a great *fiesta* at the Monastery. He possibly got to the shrine in time for High Mass, celebrated that day with full liturgical splendor. Montserrat was the Benedictine equivalent of the famous Carthusian monastery in Seville, Las Cuevas. On ordinary days the shrine drew hundreds of pilgrims, on festivals several thousands. Each pilgrim got free lodging for three days besides being supplied with a platter of soup, bread, wine, oil, salt, and vinegar; he also received sufficient fuel to make a fire—for the nights were cold at that altitude. In the crypts, pilgrims might stable their mounts; Inigo's mule was tethered there among the other animals while his master hastened to the church to be in time for Mass and to witness the other ceremonies peculiar to the feast.

The captain could have had some trouble in obtaining an unobstructed view of the altar, for the congregation on that date would have filled the church and Inigo was not very tall—barely five feet. But his love for music would have been gratified by the chant, for the singing in Montserrat was worth going a long way to hear. The abbey housed fifty monks and forty brothers and thirty schoolboys; these latter were known as Our Lady's Pages and assisted in the choir, their clear trebles alternating with the robust voices of the ninety Benedictines in the singing of the antiphons and hymns and litanies. On Saturdays, Sundays, and major festivals the choirboys accompanied their singing with instrumental music, "and one might have thought that they were a choir of angels descending from the sky, so entrancing was the melody they made with their youthful voices and various instruments, filling the hearts of the pilgrims present with most sweet and heavenly devotion." It was a Saturday and a major festival combined, that March 21, 1522, so Inigo could have heard all this entrancing music and beheld the choirboys in their livery of white and sapphire and silver, Our Lady's colors.[2]

On that day, too, the number of Benedictines was augmented, for thirteen monks who had become solitaries and lived, each in his hermitage further up the mountain, descended from the heights to join in the community celebrations. During the Mass they stood in the big circle with the other monks; like these they received Holy Communion from the hands of the Abbot, enacting the liturgy of the day which speaks of the great Patriarch—Benedict—"surrounded by the ring of his brethren." Later they would partake of the midday meal at the monastery before climbing up again to their eyries poised between earth and heaven, those cells where their days were lived out in silence, austerity, labor, and ceaseless prayer.

Inigo lost no time in seeking the hermitage of one of these Benedictine solitaries; the monk he sought was a man with a considerable reputation as a confessor. Dom Juan Chanones was a saintly, kindhearted man, as noted for his spirit of mortification and strict fidelity to the rule as for his kindness and zealous care for such pilgrims as ventured up to his high cranny. His hermitage was dedicated to Saint Dismas—the Good Thief.

After interviewing the penitent who came on St. Benedict's Day, Dom Chanones was obliged to make a second descent from his cell. The limping gallant had been refused admission in the hostel, for Inigo would not tell his name—a formality with which all pilgrims had to comply. When the confessor intervened, the Captain from Castile was given a cell in the monastery without further ado. There he could have the privacy which the church porches, the hostel, and other lodgings lacked, for his prayers and meditations and for the scourgings in store for the flesh that had sinned. A boy who noticed Inigo at Montserrat, when questioned sixty years later, had a vivid memory of him.

> He did not undress during his three days at the shrine, nor ever remove his shoes; and he did not take his soup but fasted on bread and water. . . . He made a general confession with many tears, and was constantly to be seen before the altar of Our Lady, weeping. . . .[4]

Penitents who came to the shrine asking to make a general confession were given a manual which the Montserrat Benedictines printed on their own presses. It posed Benedict's question to those who came seeking admission to the order —"What seek you here?"— and was designed to sift the postulant, to prove his intentions, to see if he could honestly give the one answer Benedict wished to hear: "I come seeking God." Sinners wishing to set their souls right at Montserrat were expected to be somewhat similarly disposed. The manual contained reflections on the severe punishments with which God visited Lucifer's single sin; on the penalties imposed on humanity through the first sin of Adam; on the enormity of sin, which necessitated an atonement infinitely great—the passion and death of the Son of God.

Father Nadal states that:

> Inigo prepared for his general confession by meditating, noting down (in the book of three-hundred pages which he had carefully carried all the way from Loyola) whatever struck him, and conferring with his confessor, a man pious and learned.[5]

The penitent records nothing of his reflections and sentiments during the three days preceeding March 25, save to state that he wrote out lists of his sins. His catalogues could have contained little that was new. Sin is the most hackneyed thing in the world. The dispositions he brought to the holy tribunal may best be judged by the remaining thirty-four years of his life.

His confession over, he told the Benedictine of his resolution to become a knight of God. The mind that "had been filled with the doings of Amadis and the knights of the legends," the man who had spent the most formative years of his life in the rather romantic atmosphere of the courts of Castile, could find expression only in the idiom of chivalry. In his *caballerias* he had read rsuch about the investiture of knights. He had, no doubt, witnessed the ceremony more than once during his service at Arevalo and Najera and was well acquainted with the rules prescribed: confession, a bath, the donning of knightly insignia, a night-long vigil beside the arms that were to be used honorably and nobly in defense of the weak and the oppressed, in battle for God and for good, for all that was right and true and honorable; and after the vigil, Mass and Holy Communion. It is almost impossible for the modern mind to understand Inigo's ambition to become a knight of God, for concepts of kingship, knighthood, service—common to all Europe in his day—are lost to our time. The very word "service" has lost its former sacred meaning—joyful service rendered freely to God, or to one's fellowman for love of God—and has come to mean time-serving tasks performed without love, without any reference to God; to modern men the word "service" is but another expression for hateful thralldom and galling servility.

> This man (Dom Chanones) was the first to whom he confided his secret resolve . . . and the confessor arranged that his sword and dagger should be placed on Our Lady's altar in the church. His mule he presented to the monastery; this he also arranged through the confessor.[6]

Already Inigo had met with a refusal when he offered his fine clothes to the monk-custodians of the shrine. The brothers had every reason to be chary about accepting such a gift. Montserrat drew sinners from the four corners of Europe. Malefactors came there to confess their crimes, or on a pilrimage of penance and expiation for evil deeds already confessed. The livery this lame fellow was so anxious to get rid of—who knew how he came by it? Perhaps the clothes of this Castilian captain had been taken from a murdered body, flung to rot in some ditch. The monks would not have anything to do with the garments; the pilgrim who proferred such a gift had done little to warrant his good intentions. His behavior had been peculiar from the very day of his arrival at Montserrat, when he refused to disclose his identity to the brother-porter and put good Dom Chanones to no end of trouble dragging him down from his hermitage to ensure that his anonymity might be preserved. Was it not significant that the limping pilgrim had gone to the Saint Dismas confessor—that he had chosen a thief—albeit the Good Thief—for his patron?

Repulsed when he offered his clothing, that last link with the gay days of old, Inigo reasoned—rightly—that the offer of his damascened sword and jeweled dagger would also be looked at askance. But Dom Chanones was both understanding and cooperative: he agreed to dipose of the sword and dagger as his penitent wished; during the night they would rest on Our Lady's altar; afterwards they would be hung in the grill seperating the Lady chapel from the main portion of the church, with the other ex voto offerings. The insignia of the knight of God—a sackcloth gown and pilgrim staff—were in readiness, but it would never do to invite notice by going about in sacking while carrying costly looking garments.

So when darkness fell, Inigo went out in search of a beggar to give him the clothes. He would not have had far to go, as there were many beggars at the shrine for the big feast days of the 21st and 25th, such times being their harvest. The lucky fellow who had a complete and magnificent outfit pressed upon him must have got the surprise of his life and thanked Our Lady loudly for each and every item of this heaven-sent wardrobe—the bright cloak lined with contrasting satin; the doublet with velvet facings; the slashed sleeves and finely worked girdle; the soft, cuffed, dressed-leather riding boots, the hat with its gay feather, the linen with fine stitching done by some fair hand —"he gave the beggar even his shirt," writes Ribadeneira.

Inigo, without waiting to be thanked, went at once to the Lady chapel, peering through the grille to see if his sword and dagger were on the altar. Dom Chanones was a man of his word; they were there. His hands, always beautifully manicured, must have looked incongruous against the sackcloth. Since his long illness they were unusually white and soft—not the hands of a beggar or a poor pilgrim—so he tucked them well into the ample folds of his robe. Then he began his vigil. That night saw him, no longer the son of Loyola, the courtier, the soldier, but a man standing girt and ready, like the Israelites of old, about to set forth in the night in quest of the promised land.

At midnight the monastery bell rang out, calling all to rejoice with the monks of Montserrat who were in their places in choir waiting to celebrate the day of the Annunciation, to commemorate the great mystery of the Incarnation. Our Lady's pages made melody, accompanying the antiphons with their music. The pilgrim in sackcloth "knelt and stood by turns, his staff in hand."[7] Possibly his bad leg was troubling him; it was often swollen and sometimes throbbed or suppurated within its bandages. Inigo renewed the vow made at Aranzazu. It was an ideal night for a dedication such as his—the night when the Word so humbled Himself as to assume the sackcloth of human nature, the dawn on which the Eternal became a pilgrim in time. But Inigo tells not a word of how he prayed that night or of the emotions that welled up within him. Stating laconically that he made the vigil, he goes on at once to tell what happened next morning:

> At dawn he left, so as not to be recognized, and went not the direct road to Barcelona, because on that highway there would be many who might know him and show him honor. Instead he turned

aside to a village named Manresa, intending to stay in a hospital there for a few days and also to note a few things in his book which he brought everywhere with him—well guarded—and which afforded him much consolation.[8]

Father Nadal states that before leaving the holy mountain that morning Inigo received Holy Communion; this would have been at the first Mass celebrated at dawn. At the entrance to the chapel where Inigo kept his vigil a tablet was placed in 1602. The inscription, which is in Latin, translates thus:

> Here Blessed Ignatius of Loyola, with many prayers
> and tears, consecrated himself to God
> by the hands of the Virgin.
>
> Here he donned sackcloth, as though it were spiritual armor,
> and kept vigil all the night through.
>
> Hence he went forth to found the Society of Jesus
> in the year MDXXII.

His hurried departure he himself explains. A great shrine like Montserrat, with its concourse of pilgrims from all parts of Spain, was no place for a man wishing to avoid acquaintances. The Duchess of Najera was a native of the Catalan province and Inigo may have seen some of that lady's relatives at the shrine. Perhaps his limp had already betrayed him, and glances were being cast in his direction, his sackcloth disguise easily penetrated. If the news of the beggarman's windfall had got about—and, as will be seen, it was the talk of Montserrat that morning—the pilgrim could have overheard whispered comments on the strange metamorphosis of the Senor Captain, who only yesterday was so splendidly accoutred and who was now going about in sackcloth. More likely, he heard someone express the opinion that he was a holy man. He told later on that after Montserrat he found himself so beset with temptations to spiritual pride that he went to extraordinary lengths to conceal his identity. His amanuensis, Father da Camara, having told him that he was troubled with temptations to vainglory, Ignatius replied:

> For two years this same vice plagued me so much that, when I embarked at Barcelona for Jerusalem, I did not dare to reveal to anyone

that I was bound for the Holy Land, and similarly in other matters. As a remedy for these temptations, you should frequently refer all that is yours to God, striving to offer Him any good of which you may find yourself capable, recognizing that it is God's and thanking Him for it.[9]

Already a great change was apparent in the man who, but a year before, had chased passers-by with drawn sword simply because they jostled him in a narrow and crowded street. For a man of independent and strong character—evidenced not only in his career at court and in the army, but in the months of his illness and the earlier phases of his conversion—Inigo had won notable victories over nature, even in a short time.

About an hour after Inigo left the shrine he was overtaken by the Constable of Montserrat, a rather important official responsible for the maintainance of law and order at the shrine.

... This man came at a great pace in pursuit of Inigo. He asked if it were a fact that he had given some fine clothes to a beggar, which beggar had declared the same, when accused of having come by the garments unlawfully. The pilgrim replied that he had given clothes to a beggarman, and tears of compassion welled up in his eyes, for he was given to understand that they had ill-treated the poor fellow— thinking that he had stolen the suit. "Alas!" he reproached himself interiorly, "sinner that you are! You don't even know how to go about doing good to your neighbor, but must needs bring him danger and insult."

But although the Constable asked who he was and whence he had come to Montserrat, and the name of his family, he did not reply to any of these questions, as such queries did not seem to him to have any connection with the freeing of the innocent beggar.[10]

Satisfied that the beggar was no thief, the Constable hastened back to release the man unjustly detained. Inigo plodded along, taking a side road that led down a steep hill, and continuing until he came to a hermitage dedicated to the Holy Apostles where he entered and remained some time praying. On the same day a group of pilgrims, also returning from Montserrat, came by the hermitage about noon. One of these, a boy, Juan Pasqual, later testified to their meeting with Inigo. He and his widowed mother had shut up their Barcelona home some time previously and had come to a house in Manresa to see after some property Juan's father had left in that town. Ines Pasqual, with "three honorable widows of Manresa," her son Juan, and two other lads, had gone on pilgrimage to Montserrat, nine miles from Manresa. Juan, a rather loquacious witness, described their encounter with the strange pilgrim in detail:

> We were walking along on the homeward journey, all together,and chatting a little, when, just as we neared the little chapel of the Apostles, a poor beggar dressed all in sacking just as pilgrims wear came towards us. He was not very tall; his skin was white and his hair blond; he was good-looking, if somewhat serious, and kept his eyes fixed on the ground. . . . He walked very wearily and with a limp in the right foot. . . . (Here follows a long digression about how Inigo came by the limp and the sackcloth.) . . . He asked my mother if she knew of any hospital nearby where he could find lodging. She noted that he looked a good and honorable person whose glance moved one to devotion and piety; she also noticed that he was beginning to go bald. She told him that the nearest hospital was three leagues away in Manresa, from which town she had come and towards which she was now returning; she added that if he wished to accompany or follow our group, she would endeavor to secure accomodation for him. Thanking her in Christian and honorable words, he decided to follow us, we all going slowly because of his lameness, so that he could come along in our company. . . .[11]

Before they entered Manresa, Ines Pasqual thought that it would be wiser if their pilgrim companion did not enter the town with them, "so as not to give the low-minded and malicious cause for whispering, she being a widow and he a good-looking man and young. So she sent him on ahead to the hospital of Santa Lucia, with a message that would ensure his admittance and accommodation; there he would get a bed and a small room, while she herself would see to his other needs, and send him in food from her own house."

The Roman bridge across the river Cardoner and the Tower of Breny proclaimed the antiquity of Manresa. It was old even in the days of Hadrian. Pompey refers to it as "*Munorisa,* a municipality with good shops." When Inigo first saw it in 1522, it was a dilapidated town which had been reduced—by recurring wars and their aftermaths of plague and famine—to three hundred households. Outside the walls stood three hospitals, one of which, Santa Lucia's, was for the poor; it stood about forty paces from one of the town's eight gates and an inventory of 1465, a time when Manresa was still prosperous, lists Santa Lucia's as having only eight plank beds.

To this poverty-stricken institution Inigo limped. A little room was assigned to him. He meant to spend just a few days there "writing in his book." His first moments of privacy were interrupted by a messenger from Ines Pasqual; the widow's family had prepared "a pullet and good hot broth" for Ines and her son on their return from Montserrat; she sent the pullet and a bowl of broth at once to the pilgrim who had so impressed her on the return journey. But Inigo gave it away—probably to the sick poor in the hospital.[12]

His stay in Manresa was to be of far longer duration than he thought when going there. He remained almost a year, not leaving for Barcelona and the Holy Land until February, 1523. The plague had appeared in Barcelona, causing a panic and the complete close-down of the port.

Inigo does not seem to have been much ruffled by this setback to his plans. After staying some days at Santa Lucia, he went to the convent of the Dominican Fathers who gave him food and lodging. On April 12, he changed to lodgings which Ines Pasqual found for him but he does not appear to have stayed there for long, for he was back with the Dominicans again during the early summer. It is difficult to ascertain the times of his stay with the Dominicans, at the hospital, in the cave about two hundred paces outside town, in the houses of the Amigants and Canyelles (families who took him in and looked after him during his three illnesses while in Manresa), for in his recollections dictated to Father da Camara, Ignatius does not observe chronological sequence, but puts important spiritual events first, last and in between; all else he just records as afterthoughts. But from what he has told, it is possible to reconstruct in part his ten months in Manresa.

Before long he became the most stared-after man in the town; people spoke of the life that he led; the staff of the hospital and the Dominicans could tell that he rose at midnight to pray, that he prayed for seven hours daily and assisted at the Missa Cantata and the divine office. Everyone saw that he went to confession and Communion weekly, and his spare figure was often noticed kneeling at the various shrines in Manresa and the vicinity, or in one of the lesser churches and chapels of the town. He helped the sick in the hospitals, and though his own scholastic record hardly entitled him to set up as a teacher, "he taught doctrine to children and poor beggars." "The teaching of catechism began in Manresa with Father Igantius," said a priest who gave evidence for his canonization.[13]

The Manresans were of two minds concerning their pilgrim. Some called him "the sackcloth fellow," others the "holy man." No one knew his name, his origin, nor his past history. Inigo had succeeded in submerging his identity in the sea of humanity. After some weeks in Manresa, he no longer had need to fear that any former aquaintance would recognize him. The unkempt hair, matted with the dust and sweat of the hot summer days, the unsightly nails, the shapeless robe of sacking, the girdle of cords, with its knots to denote so many victories or so many defeats in the day's spiritual combats, the fasting on bread and water, the frequent scourgings, the constant curtailment of food, sleep and rest, all had their effect on his appearance. "His face and figure," says Lainez, "underwent a complete change—he who had been so robust, and of such a fine constitution. But in his first four months at Manresa he understood little of divine things, although God helped him, particularly in giving him the virtues of constancy and fortitude."[14]

Sometime during the summer, searching for a spot where he could be alone, Inigo found a secluded cave about nine feet long and four feet wide some two hundred yards from the town on the same side of the river as the Santa Lucia hospital. The entrance was overgrown and there was little danger of anyone coming to the spot to interrupt him at his prayers. In the cave he had full scope for his penances; one of his first actions on taking up his abode there was to scratch a rough cross on the ledge of rock on which he rested his book when writing. He had a particular devotion to the Holy Cross and, up to 1936, the Dominican nuns of Santa Clara convent preserved as a treasured relic a heavy penitential cross which Inigo had frequently carried up and down the corridors in 1522, when the house was a Priory. During this time at Manresa, Inigo read for the first time the *Imitation of Christ*. There were several Spanish editions of the *Imitation*, the one he had being known as the *Gerconzito*, a version the translation of which was attributed to Gerson, a famous Chancellor of Paris University in the early fifteenth century. Regarding this book, Inigo said:

> I first came across el *Gerconzito* while at Manresa and since then I prefer it to any other devotional book.[15]

Father da Camara adds that the Jesuit founder recommended the *Imitation* to all with whom he had talks; he used to read a chapter a day, beginning at Book I, Chapter I, and going right on to the end of Book IV—which meant that he covered the book three times a year, or about one hundred times from then to the end of his life. After meals and at other times he had a habit of opening his *Imitation* at random "and he always chanced upon something which just then he had at heart, and something which he needed."[16]

The first months at Manresa were, generally speaking, a time of great spiritual peace; but temptations were not lacking.

> The very day he came there from Montserrat, dressed as a beggar, being alone in a room in a hospital (Santa Lucia's) the thought came to him: "If you had your clothes now, how much better you could dispose of them." And as this thought depressed him somewhat, he went and sought the company of the other beggars, when the thought immediately left him.
>
> On various occasions, while in this same hospital, a strange thing befell him, each time in clear daylight. He used to see something in the air beside him, some object which filled him with intense delight, its splendor being on a magnificent scale. But when the object vanished, he found that the recollection of it filled him with disgust.[17]

This caused him to apply the rules he had taught himself at Loyola for discerning the origin of the inspirations that moved him. The same diligent introspection he applied to another difficulty he had. He had carefully divided his day—so many hours for praying, for visiting shrines, for helping in the hospital, for reading and writing, for "speaking with certain souls who came asking him to help them." Little time was left for sleep but, when he lay down—on bare boards or on the earth of the cave—his "mind became so filled with great ideas and torrents of spiritual consolations that much of the time allotted to sleep went to loss. When he looked into the matter and considered it . . . he began to doubt the source of these thoughts and consolations and ended by deciding to have no more to do with them, but to sleep for the time he allowed himself." And so he did.[18]

When he had persevered for some months in this stupendous program of prayer and penance, a new temptation beset him. At Mass and at Vespers and Compline, when he found great consolation in the chant, a recollection of the rigorous life he was leading used to obtrude itself between him and his prayers; the contrast between the delight the music afforded his ear and the misery to which he subjected his other senses was too great. His soul asked itself, "How can you bear this dreadful existence for the seventy years ahead?" However, once he recognized "the enemy" by the disquiet this thought caused him, he braced himself interiorly, replying with all the force he could summon. "Miserable one! Can you promise me one hour of life?" The temptation vanished never to return.[19]

Again, he found himself one day with no relish for prayer or spiritual things, the next quite elevated in spirit. Polanco tells of further trials:

> God, like a good surgeon, had to cut deeper. He [Inigo] began to develop an intimate understanding of the nature of sin, and to weep with great bitterness for his own past sins. [Then followed temptations and intense anguish and afflictions of the spirit and various scruples which caused him particular torment] in all of which God our Lord gave him the strength and humility to seek the remedies, tempering betimes his many and grave afflictions with consolations by no means small.[20]

Possibly the unrelenting and severe austerities he practiced had so worn him out that these sufferings of mind were but a back-kick of the body—that poor, ill-used Brother Ass. The general confession he had made with such care at Montserrat now seemed to be wanting in integrity. The ghosts of first one, then another, again whole battalions of past sins, rose up from the sepulchre of the past to taunt him with "You did not confess this" or "You did not fully confess that." He sought a confessor and put right everything that troubled him. But like many another soul before and since, he was hardly out of the confessional before his mind became more agitated than ever. He made confession after confession, and wrote out another general confession, but still had no peace of mind.

The climax of this period of depression and scruples came when he was violently tempted to commit suicide by throwing himself out of an opening in a room put at his disposal by his friends, the Dominican Fathers. So terrible was this temptation that, in desperate plight, Inigo threw himself upon his knees, shouting over and over again "Lord, I will not do anything that offends You."[21] The Dominicans knew of his struggles with his scruples, just as they knew of "the long hours he spent praying in their church, the rivers of tears he shed when visiting the various altars, the constancy with which he frequented the sacraments, the delicacy of conscience so obvious." They prayed for him, but his battles of spirit he had to face alone. One day he prayed, begging God to show him a remedy for the state in which he found himself: "Since I find no helper among men or created things, do Thou Thyself help me. And even though I should be sent to follow a puppy-dog to get help, I would do so."[22]

If he did not throw himself from the opening in the wall of the Dominican Convent, he all but ended his life through an indiscretion:

> He recalled the incident from the story of a certain saint, who, to obtain a greatly desired favor from God, refrained from eating for many days until he got that which he asked. After thinking about this for a good while, he determined to do thus, saying to himself that he would neither eat nor drink until God gave him ease (of his scruples), or until he felt that death was near; in that case he would ask for bread and eat it.[23]

One Sunday after communion he began his fast, eating nothing all week, but not omitting any of his usual prayers and penances. When he went to confession the following Saturday, he told his confessor of his fast, and was at once ordered to break it. He did so, and that weekend he was free from scruples; but on Tuesday the phantoms of past sins began their interminable patrol up and down the paths of memory. Suddenly he was delivered from these agonies of conscience, "like one who has been awakened from sleep; and he determined, being quite clear in mind, that never again would he confess any of his past life; and from that day on, he remained freed from those scruples, and he regarded it as certain that it was our Lord who in His mercy delivered him."

These months of prayer and penance, of severe spiritual trials, took—as might be expected—a heavy toll of Inigo's health and strength. The wonder is that he did not lose either his life or his sanity. He had various bouts of grave illness. Once some Manresans found him unconscious near the shrine of Our Lady of Villadordis and carried him to the Santa Lucia hospital. Andres Amigant, head of a noble family in the town, hearing of his illness, had "the sackcloth fellow" brought to his home, where he nursed him back to health. A month later he again fell ill and the same family took him in a second time. During one of these illnesses the wife of Senor Amigant thought that the sick man was going to die in her home.

So she opened a chest which she thought contained whatever belongings he had, hoping to find some garments which she meant to keep as relics, which all in Manresa were clamoring for. Inside she saw various instruments of mortification and penance, a hairshirt big enough to cover his whole body, some chains—the very sight of which struck terror in her heart—some pointed spikes nailed into the shape of a cross, and a tunic studded with iron points, made not only to cover torso and shoulders but even the arms.[24]

The annals of the Amigant family relate wonders seen by those who attended to the pilgrim "seemingly at the point of death." Once they saw him enraptured, lifted into the air, where he knelt without visible support, repeating, "O, my God, how can I love You as You deserve. If men but knew You, they would never offend You; for they would love You too much to do so." In one of these illnesses the temptations to vainglory tormented him, suggesting to him that he was holy and pleasing to God. When he rejected the thought as presumptuous, it only annoyed him the more; finally his struggle to resist the temptation exhausted him more than the fever. But as his spiritual temperature rose, that of the fever fell. Death moved away and Inigo asked those about him to oblige him, if ever again they found him in danger of death, by shouting into his ears: "Sinner! remember all your offenses against God."

Not all Manresa had the same high opinion of him as the Pasquals and the Amigants, and those who despised him made things miserable for Inigo's friends. Senor Amigant was nicknamed Simon the Leper, and his wife Martha. Ines Pasqual, his first friend in the town, was derided and ridiculed. But Inigo was probably in blissful ingnorance of what his friends had to endure because of their championship of the "sackcloth fellow." During the later months of 1522 he was too taken up with the things of heaven to notice mundane matters.

At this time God treated him as a schoolmaster a boy whom he teaches ... whether this was because of his stupidity and ignorance of mind or because he lacked a teacher or because of the gift God Himself had bestowed on him—that intense will he had to serve Him— he does not know. But he thought and has always thought since that God was his teacher at this time.[25]

There were occasions when his mind received illuminations regarding the Blessed Trinity, the Creation, the humanity of Christ, and the Real

Presence of our Lord in the Blessed Eucharist. It is noteworthy that during this period "at the school of God," he began to cut his nails again and trimmed his hair and beard; "seeing how he was enabled to help other souls by means of the consolations God had given him, he ceased from this time forth, to practice such extremes of penance, and he now kept his hair and nails cut."

The last and greatest of these visions or "illuminations of spirit" took place on the banks of the Cardoner near the chapel of St. Paul:

> He sat facing the river, which at that spot runs deep. And while seated there, his understanding was enlightened. It was not a vision, but understanding and knowledge of many things, some concerning spiritual things, others concerning faith and human learning. . . . All the helps God gave him during his whole life, together with everything he himself learned in his sixty-two years on earth, was less than the graces he received that day sitting by the river. Moreover this enlightenment remained with him so that he seemed to himself afterwards a different man, possessed of a new intellect.[26]

Various references made by Saint Ignatius in the closing years of his life indicate that it was during this final and greatest "enlightening of the understanding" vouchsafed to him at Manresa that he first had the idea of forming a company not for the defense of Castile or Spain but of all Christendom. It was then he first envisaged that spiritual militia he was later to recruit and train for the greater glory of God and the service of the Church of Christ. When Fathers of the first generation of Jesuits asked him why they did not have a distinctive habit, or assemble for office in choir, or enquired the reason for various divergences in the Jesuit rule from rules of older or contemporary orders, Ignatius invariably replied with one word—"Manresa."[27]

Once he told Father Nadal about his unforgettable experience sitting by the swiftly flowing waters of the Cardoner: "I saw, felt within me, and penetrated with my mind all the mysteries of the Christian faith," he said. This comprehensive grasp of divinely revealed truths, interlinked to form one chain of unbreakable strength, this extensive, sweeping view of the relation of all created things to the Creator, the Redeemer, the Sanctifier, the Three who are One and the same God, this light that enabled him to glimpse how these immensities had been translated, taught and explained by Christ and transmitted to succeeding generations by His Church—

all this and more was comprised in that single illuminating grace which Ignatius Loyola ever afterwards regarded as the greatest of his life. In its beam he saw clearly how good and evil struggled not only for possession of his soul, but for the soul of every human being. From his clear realization of all these things came his masterpiece, the book of the Spiritual Exercises, upon which so many missions, retreats, sermons, and exhortations have since been based and to which so many souls have owed first their conversion and finally their salvation. At Manresa the Exercises were forged. "At Manresa," says Father Orlandini, "Ignatius envisaged the *fabrica Societatis*, the blueprints of the Society of Jesus."

... Saint Ignatius has left nothing more precious, nor more useful, nor of more lasting worth, as a heritage to his sons, than that golden book which has constantly received the highest praise from sovereign pontiffs since Paul III, and from very many saints in the Church. If it is true that the book of the Spiritual Exercises was the first-born of St. Ignatius, it can equally be affirmed that the saintly author was himself the first child of the Exercises. For it was those Exercises that enlivened his spirit, directed his first steps in the way of perfection, and gave him strength to choose a divine King who was worn out with labor, who was loaded with insults, and who suffered torments and death in the service of His Father. They enabled him to follow this King to the greatest heights of charity, so that burning with the flame of divine Love, he wished to bring not only himself, but the whole world to the feet of Christ our Savior. Ignatius, having experienced the tremendous force of the Exercises, once testified that they contain "all the best means that I can think of, and feel, and understand, whereby a man may make progress himself, and bear fruit so that he may be a help to the progress of others."... From the Exercises he himself had drawn new life. From them he wished his sons to imbibe the spirit that gave birth to the Society. That wonderful and holy fire of spirit, aroused by God's grace working in the Exercises, would render them not only desirous, but eager and prompt to serve the divine glory and to undertake strenuous labors to that end....
    (Letter of Pope Pius XII to the Father General of the Society of Jesus on the occasion of the 1956 fourth centenary celebrations in honor of St. Ignatius.)

... The time was approaching for the intended departure for Jerusalem, so in the beginning of 1523 he left for Barcelona, to embark from that port.
    (Autobiography of St. Ignatius.)

A S REFERENCES to the Spiritual Exercises of St. Ignatius will occur from time to time in the course of the present book, some mention of them must be made at this juncture, though adequate assesment of them is hardly possible in a biography of this kind.

The *Book of the Exercises* was begun at Manresa; there Inigo planned the Exercises; there he himself did them; there he drafted the main outlines. From time to time during his life he made various additions or changes as experience showed him what was likely to be useful; for instance, his "method for examination of conscience" was added at a much later date, while the "method for making a choice" was based on his own earlier experiences at Loyola when, in the first gropings towards conversion, he noted how good and evil strove within his soul, impelling his will in directions forever opposite.

The title given to this slim book by its author—*Exercises*—is the key to the contents. The casual reader, perusing it, curious to see what makes it so famous, is apt to be disappointed or bored—probably both. Exercises are meant to be practiced, not read; and this manual is rather for those who give the Exercise to others than for the exercitants themselves. The only European country where the Spiritual Exercises seem to be popular reading is, fittingly enough, Spain, the land of their origin; there they circulate freely in pamphlet and booklet form and run into several editions. They were intended by St. Ignatius for use in times of retreat and their subtitle defines their aim:

> Spiritual Exercises for the conquest of oneself and the ordering of one's life so that one's decisions are not influenced by any inordinate affections.

The purpose of the Exercises is further developed in another note:

> A method in which the soul may prepare and dispose itself to free itself of its disordered affections and, this achieved, set itself to seek and find the will of God concerning the ordering of life, for that soul's salvation.

The preliminary exercises are framed with the intention of reforming what deformities a man may find in his soul; the reformed soul is then taken through graded efforts to ascertain God's will in his regard; he is shown the further disciplined exertions he must undertake to ensure that his life conforms to the divine plan for him; then follow exercises calculated to ground and confirm the soul in its good resolutions; the final exercises aim at the transformation of the soul to the ideal expressed by St. Paul: *I live now, not I, but Christ liveth in me.* Besides the Exercises so called—the meditations, contemplations, methods for examining the conscience, various methods of prayer—there are several directions and a good deal of advice for directors, explaining how the various exercises are to be made, how they are to be adapted to various types of exercitants, how the retreatant is to be helped and encouraged. The meditations are based on the truths of the Gospel, but in this book St. Ignatius did not develop them; he just indicated the subjects for meditation. Even in the few chapters where he develops the theme slightly, he gives only the barest outline, leaving the development to the retreatant under the guidance of the director.

The author of the Exercises is at pains to point out that their success will always depend on the measure of generosity, good will, and docility brought to their performance by the individual who elects to make them. Beneath and sustaining the whole framework of this program for spiritual development is the experience of Inigo himself, who struggled and searched and suffered and prayed, and finally emerged a transformed man from his Manresan retreat. His book, based on the Gospel and on works of ascetical writers of an earlier age than his, is, says one of his modern biographers, "an inexorably logical unfolding of Our Lord's own words: *If any man will come after Me and be my disciple, let him deny himself, take up his cross daily and follow Me.*"[1]

To make the Exercises in their complete form would require a period of about thirty days. They may be prolonged or shortened, according to the circumstances of those making them. Members of the Society of Jesus do them in their entirety, first after admission to the novitiate, and again after ordination to review the past and rekindle zeal for the sanctification of the Jesuit himself and of the souls to whom he will minister in the years ahead.

☆ ☆ ☆ ☆ ☆

As 1522 drew to a close, Inigo began to think of the future. But on December 13, the feast of Santa Lucia, patroness of the hospital, a strange occurence took place in a room adjoining the hospital chapel. He was kneeling there on that Saturday of Santa Lucia, assisting at Compline, when he suddenly fell unconscious. People ran to his aid, "all the devout of Manresa," among them the Amigants and a godson of Ines Pasqual, a lad named Juan Torres. Juan ran as fast as he could to tell his godmother the news, and charged into that good woman's house yelling, "The Santo has dropped dead! The Santo has fallen dead in the hospital." Thinking—and probably praying—that it was only another weakness brought on by lack of food, Ines waited only to snatch a pot containing the inevitable Pasqual hen from the fire, "and rushed off with it at top speed, hoping to revive him with the hot broth," or to persuade him to break his abstinence and try some of the chicken.

But Ines Pasqual had her race out of town for nothing. This time nothing revived the sackcloth man, and Manresa mourned him as dead. Some days later they began to make arrangements for his burial when, fortunately for Inigo, Senor Amigant, coming to pay his last respects to his friend, bent to kiss the hands folded by the devout across the dead man's breast; to his amazement he discovered the heart beating steadily. The doctors being called, they affirmed that Inigo was alive; he remained in this extraordinary swoon for eight days; on Saturday, December 20th, at the hour of Compline, he sat up, "opened his eyes like one awakening from a peaceful and refreshing sleep, and devoutly called upon the name of Jesus." This wonder was known to all Manresa and is very well attested in the process for the Saint's canonization.[2]

In his memoirs Ignatius himself says nothing of this. He mentions that he had a grave illness during the final months at Manresa, in midwinter, when "he was taken to the house of people named Ferrara, so that he might be properly looked after." There he got every attention. When he recovered, he was still very weak and subject to recurring gastric attacks; it was an exceptionally cold winter, so the Ferraras and some noble ladies of Manresa insisted that he should wear "two robes of homespun—very thick cloth and dun colored, with a sort of bonnet or hood of the same material which they made for him."[3] When he was up and about again in January, he resumed his former life, but not the severe penances; he tended the sick in the hospitals, attended many Masses and the divine office in the various churches, looking a bit more respectable in his new clothes.

At this time, however, the fame his eight days' swoon had won him in the minds of Manresans previously opposed to him underwent a sudden eclipse, brought about by Inigo's enthusiasm for the Exercises. He was so eager to induce others to make a trial of them, so that they might reap benefits similar to those he himself had gathered, that he began to get some of his friends to do the Exercises—probably the full thirty days. He himself was a wiser man when, over thirty years later, he told Father de Camara:

He was avid to speak of spiritual things of which he himself was so enamoured and to find others who had the capacity to discuss them . . . but neither in Manresa nor Barcelona, despite the time he spent in both places, could he find persons to aid him as he desired. He found, after all his searching, only one little old woman in Manresa who could converse on the things of God. And so, when he left these places, he ceased altogether this anxious seeking for spiritually-minded persons.[4]

The loquacious Juan Pasqual tells in greater detail something of Inigo's first retreatants—who evidently had not the slightest idea of solitude or silence—and the not altogether unreasonable and angry reactions of their families:

Honorable ladies, some married, some widows, used to chatter about him for hours on end, with their mouths open, dying to hear or to retail the little lectures and spiritual parables of which he always had such a store; and they talked about his good works in the hospital where he waited hand and foot on the sick, and his charity towards the poor and the orphans on whose behalf he went begging from door to door. . . . But there was no lack of envious and malicious toungues that publicly contradicted and murmured about the holy Exercises, and their author, and those who practiced them. . . . And my mother, Ines Pasqual, got the worst backbiting of all; for they said she was the inventor and fomentor of all this fuss and novelty—she being the one who fetched him to our town and who had supported and shielded him all along.

Finally things came to such a pass, and these murmurings were so general and so detrimental to the honor of holy Ignacio and several good women—my own mother more than any—that she was forced to send for my uncle Antonio, an assistant of the Bishop of Tarragona. He came, and she told her story . . . also how and where she had first met this man (Inigo) and how she had helped him and how good he was. But because idiotic rumors had been scattered everywhere in Manresa by both men and women concerning her conversations with this holy man about her soul's salvation and the road to heaven—our town being so small and it's citizens so malicious and coarse—she thought it best my uncle should escort him to her house in Barcelona.[5]

The uncle, a Canon Pujol, went to visit Inigo and came away completely won. When he told Inigo of Ines Pasqual's suggestion, the pilgrim seemed pleased and agreed to go whenever the Canon wished. Before leaving he paid a last visit to Montserrat. The priest who with his servant had been staying in the monastery in 1522, was still there and told Inigo that he was going to Rome. They agreed to travel together, so Canon Pujol and the other priest and his servant set out with Inigo for Barcelona in February. Before leaving Manresa, the pilgrim left his hair shirt and spiked girdle on the altar of Our Lady of Villadordis. Pieces of the former later went as relics all over the world, a scrap of it going as far as Japan, where a Jesuit, Charles Spinola, three days before his martyrdom in 1622, sent it to his Provincial, another martyr, Francis Pacheco. The spiked girdle was a precious heirloom in a Manresan family who had befriended the saint during his sojourn in their town; when the wave of vandalism that overran the place in 1936 subsided, this relic of Ignatius, with many other holy things, was no more.

So, passing through the gate nearest the shrine of Our Lady of Villadordis, and taking the royal highway, Inigo left Manresa, that little town he so often spoke of afterwards as his "novitiate," his "primitive church," his kindergarten where he was the sole scholar—"stupid and ignorant"—but with God, infinitely patient and kind, for his teacher. When he eventually founded the Company of Jesus, it bore the marks of its forging place. His six tests for novices were: the making of the Spiritual Exercises in their complete form; the serving of the sick in the hospitals; pilgrimages which had to be made on foot, the novice-pilgrims begging alms on their way; employment in humble tasks; the teaching of the catechism; and for those who were priests, preaching and hearing confessions.

The group of four arrived in Barcelona about the third week of February. The Canon lodged himself and his new-found friend in the house which Ines Pasqual had closed up the previous year after her husband's death. The street was narrow and tortuous and the house small and unpretentious. Inigo had a little room on the second floor, except for a time while he was ill when he occupied an alcove on the first floor. Some days after their arrival, Juan Pasqual and his mother came to Barcelona to see how things were going; they found Inigo very content and occupied with his prayers and good works, visiting hospitals and prisons, and "outside one of our window lattices, a queue of beggars was always waiting to waylay him; you would think our house was a church or hospital," adds

Juan.[6] Among the friends Inigo made in Barcelona were the Rosers, a wealthy nobleman and his wife. Dona Isabel Roser noticed Inigo one day when she was in church listening to a sermon; she wondered who the poor man could be who sat among the children on the altar steps, his gaze riveted on the preacher, his own face "glowing." She felt impelled to call him afterwards but waited until her husband had heard of this holy looking man. They had their servants search for him and, when Inigo was located, they invited him to dine with them. At table, they asked him to speak about spiritual things, "to say something about Christ our Lord." Inigo needed no spur, he said, to do so; he only longed for the occasion when he might speak on that theme nearest his heart. His hearers listened, enthralled, and became his devoted friends.[7]

Two sailings were due to leave Barcelona for Italy about this time, an armed brig and a ship which was at the repair docks having her seams caulked. The brig was to go first and Inigo thought he had better make arrangements to go by that sailing, as it was less costly and only a few passengers were being taken. "He was anxious to travel, if possible, alone." When the Rosers heard that he meant to embark on the brigantine, they remonstrated with him. It was too small a vessel for that time of year, they pointed out, a season when storms frequently swept the Mediterranean. Their cousin, a bishop, was sailing on the other vessel, and they knew it would not be too long delayed. Inigo allowed himself to be persuaded to wait; he took his few books and provisions, which he had already placed in the brig, ashore. He was probably among the crowds who watched, helpless, when the vessel sank, a few hours' distance from the land; all aboard perished.[8]

The master of the other ship agreed to allow this poverty-stricken pilgrim to travel free, but he made the condition that Inigo must put aboard sufficient rations to last him for the voyage. During the remainder of his time in Barcelona, therefore, Inigo went about begging food. The nuns in the Hieronymite convent were particularly good to him, and he did not forget them for it later. But not all thought so well of him. One day a lady stopped him in the street and, concluding from the nobility of his features and the whiteness of his hands that he was the prodigal son of some noble house, took it upon herself to bring him to his senses. "For shame!" she said. "A man of your sort begging. Go back to your parents from whose home I suppose you ran away to find adventure. Going about begging like a stray child! Shame!" Inigo listened to her harangue and then thanked her quietly: "I am indeed a stray—a great sinner," he said,

81

which answer so mollified the lady that she filled his knapsack with provisions for the journey.[9]

During all this time he never divulged his name or his place of origin. Once when some friends were warning him against venturing to Rome alone, "seeing that he knew neither Latin nor Italian," he replied that "though he had the son or the brother of the Duke of Cardona himself for a companion, still he would rather go unaccompanied except by faith, hope, and charity."[10] This probably raised a laugh, the family of Cardona being the leading grandees of the province; his hearers little guessed that the pilgrim knew most of the family; he certainly knew the Duke's sister—the Duchess of Najera!

Neither did he tell anyone that his real goal was not Rome, but Jerusalem. Pilgrims to Jerusalem were usually praised and honored, and the temptations to vainglory were always lying in ambush for him. So when he asked for alms, he did not cry as most intending pilgrims did: "Alms for the Palestine pilgrim! Help the poor palmer who will requite your alms with prayers when he visits the Holy Places." He just stood there in his homespun coats, a man in the prime of life, who, for all his mean-looking clothes, had a courteous demeanor and the stance and appearance of one used to standing in the presence of the great, and begged, "Alms for a pilgrim." He seems to have attracted particular attention from the ladies. One, passing him by and hearing him ask for alms to enable him to go on a pilgrimage, stopped and asked sharply, "Pilgrimage—to where?" He hesitated a moment, wondering if such a forthright question had to be answered; then he stammered out, "To Italy—and Rome"—not daring to add the rest. But his hesitation and his halting reply were his undoing. The lady had heard enough to convince her that here was either an imposter or a simpleton. She rounded upon him. "To Rome!" she repeated. "You ought to know what they say of those who go on pilgrimage to Rome:

> Take the pilgrim road to Rome
> You'll be worse when you come home."

Everyone knew that pilgrimages had deteriorated; in the sixteenth century they were not the journeys of devotion and penance they had been in ages past; former pilgrim faith and fervor had given place to frivolity and show; few palmers came home as holy as when they set forth. Ignatius himself told this story, adding that he did not dare tell the lady he was going to Jerusalem—"for fear of vainglory; the which fear so much afflicted him that he never dared to tell anyone who his people were or from which province he came."[11]

There was greater reason for fear, though Inigo does not advert to it at this stage of his memoirs. Possibly, having lived so aloof from the affairs of men for the previous year and more, he did not know or failed to appreciate the nature of the catastrophe that had befallen Christendom in the loss of its strongest southeastern bastion, Rhodes. A generation before, the West had vanquished Mohammedanism at Granada. But though beaten at one end of the Mediterranean, Islam was steadily increasing its territory and power at the other. The Turks, with their magnificent armies, were lords of the Balkans; their Sultan's rule extended right around the eastern rim of the Mediterranean. Suleiman the Magnificent, the latest and greatest of the Osman dynasty, in taking Rhodes, the island stronghold of the Knights of St. John of Jerusalem, had won as great a victory in the eyes of the Moslem world as the taking of Granada by the Catholic sovereigns had seemed to Christian Europe in the days of Inigo's father.

If Inigo knew nothing of the taking of Rhodes at this time, he certainly learned all about it soon, for on his passage to Italy he was to dine with a Knight of St. John. Besides, he sighted Rhodes from the ship that took him to Palestine and the topic was one being discussed all over Europe at the time. The soldier in Inigo could not but have been interested; the Christian in him could not but lament the loss of Rhodes. With the collapse of Rhodes died all hope of ever again reviving the spirit of the Crusades. It was a body blow to the West; the menace from the southeast became immeasurably stronger and more threatening; Suleiman could pray in his mosque in Belgrade; he held the line of the middle Danube; with Rhodes as base, he could sail up the Adriatic any day and attack Venice. All this Inigo heard, if not before he left for Italy at least on the journey.

They set sail from Barcelona on March 21 or thereabouts, a year after his arrival at Montserrat. It was probably the pilgrim's first sea trip of any appreciable length. A strong west wind was blowing, which drove them to Gaeta within five days "though not without fear, because of the storms." One passenger, the fifteen-year-old page of a Knight Commander of St. John of Jerusalem—probably one of the survivors of Rhodes, an anachronistic figure unhappily strayed into the sixteenth century—gave evidence regarding the voyage:

I saw Inigo continually praying in the ship, sometimes under cover, sometimes in the lowest and most solitary corners below decks. He never took supper and ate but once a day. That was with my master; for when the Commander saw him so poorly clad and so given to prayer, he invited him, for the love of God, to dine with him during the voyage.[12]

When they landed at Gaeta, the Rome-bound pilgrims set off in groups. Inigo walked with some of the poorer of his fellow passengers. The journey to Rome was not without adventure. The plague was rampant and already people were beginning to look askance at the gaunt, pale pilgrim with a slight limp as a person to be avoided. At first he journeyed with a mother and daughter and another young man; the mother had dressed her daughter in male attire, a common enough practice then for young women venturing long journeys. They were begging, too, all three; Inigo made a fourth mendicant. Coming to a farmhouse, they found a big fire, with soldiers all about—one wonders did Inigo's blood race a bit at the sight of this campfire with soldiers sitting around! The travelers were given food and much wine, in such a way that it seemed as though the soldiers only wished to be kind and let them get warm. Neither party knew the language of the other; it was evening and the pilgrims decided to stay with the kind strangers, the mother and girl going to an upstairs loft, Inigo and the young man bunking down in the stable beneath. At midnight, Inigo heard screams and yells from overhead. He does not say that he was awakened—as it was either March 25 or a day or so later, however, he may have been praying in commemoration of his vigil at Montserrat just a year before—but he was in bed, for he gives the following account of the incident:

He arose to see what was happening; he found the mother and daughter both down in the patio, in floods of tears, complaining that attempts had been made to violate them, whereupon he (Inigo) flew into such a rage that he began to shout, yelling, "This is insufferable" and similar remonstrances. So effective was this anger of his that all in the house got a good fright, so that no evil was done by anyone to anyone. The boy having already fled, all three pilgrims set off walking through the night.[13]

Following Father Genelli, one of St. Ignatius' early biographers, many

84

later writers have taken the boy's flight as proof that he was the guilty one. Such could not have been the case, as the women, complaining of the attempted outrage, spoke of attackers, not an attacker. Besides, the boy's identity has been established, since he testified at the canonization processes; he was none other than Gabriel, the page of the Knight-Commander who befriended Inigo on the voyage from Barcelona to Gaeta. In his account of the incident he identifies the ladies as his own mother and sister, and says that he fled, "being panic-stricken"; when the other three overtook him next day, Inigo consoled him and allayed his fears. Gabriel adds that "on the following day, the Knight Commander came with armed men and, unsheathing his sword, put those malefactors to flight."[14]

Inigo goes on to relate that the group then came to a town, the gates of which were closed. It was a pouring wet night so they took shelter in a church outside the town. Next day, being refused alms in the castle nearby, his companions decided to move on towards Rome.

> He was overcome with weakness, partly from the seacrossing, partly from all they had gone through, and was unable to go a step farther. So, when they went off to Rome, he remained outside the castle. That same day a great concourse of people came out of the town escorting the lady of the castle to her home and, when he heard this, Inigo went before her and told her how he had fallen ill through sheer weakness and asked if she would allow him to enter her town to seek some remedy. She readily agreed, so he went into the town and begged in the streets and before long was richer by a good many farthings (*quatrini*); rebuildiing his strength with some food, he stayed there two days and then resumed his journey, arriving in Rome on Palm Sunday.[15]

In 1523, Palm Sunday fell on March 29, so he probably saw Rome at its best—in the glorious Italian spring, and when the days of Holy Week, Easter Sunday, and the octave were being celebrated with solemn and magnificent ritual. As usual, in his memoirs he gives no hint of his first impression of Rome. He simply says: "After having obtained the benediction of Adrian VI, he left for Venice eight or nine days after Easter Day."

He was only three days north of Rome when his conscience began to reproach him for having so lacked confidence in God as to accept six or

seven ducats from some people who had told him that without money he
need not hope to obtain a passage to Palestine. He first decided to leave
the money by the wayside; on second thought, he reflected that "on this
journey, as on former ones, he was bound to fall in with some beggars in
which case he could do no better than to spend his ducats liberally on any
poor travellers he might encounter." God did not fail to send him some
poor companions; having treated them royally, Inigo arrived in Venice
with a few farthings, "just enough for that night."

Although it was his first experience of travel abroad, he is tantalizing-
ly silent on sixteenth century Italy, its citizens and their customs, its
towns and its countryside. Nor does he mention the itinerary, which
would have taken him by Tivoli, Spoleto, Tolentino, and Loreto. One can
hardly imagine such a devout client of Our Blessed Lady passing by her
great shrine in Loreto without stopping to salute her or keep a vigil there.
But it must be remembered that he did not know a word of Italian, so he
could have passed that and other famous places without having an ink-
ling of their significance; he was unable to inquire and unable to understand anyone who might undertake to enlighten him. Besides, the plague
was then raging throughout Italy and sanitary cordons were patrolling
the roads leading to every town; travellers from Rome and other plague-
stricken cities were not allowed to enter walled towns; at nightfall the
gates were shut, while watchmen stood guard to make sure that no
itinerant gained admission. Inigo relates that he had to sleep in door-
ways, and once when he arose in the morning, his extreme pallor
frightened a man whom he met, causing him to fly in terror.[16]

Somewhere near Chioggia or Chusi, he fell in with other travellers
who spoke Spanish; these told him that he would need a passport to enter
Venice, and for that he would have to make a detour to Padua. They were
making for that town, but Inigo, because of his lameness, was unable to
keep up with them. They strode along quickly, leaving him at nightfall all
alone in a great plain:

> And as he stood there, Christ appeared to him, as He used to at
> Manresa, and comforted him exceedingly. And, with this consola-
> tion, he came next morning to the gates of Padua and entered, the
> guards letting him through without any questions. And when leaving
> Padua, he was allowed to pass by in the same manner. His compa-
> nions wondered greatly at this, they having procured passports for
> Venice with some trouble, whereas he had not been bothered. And

when they arrived at Venice, they got into a boat and the guards came to inspect all the travelers' papers; they searched the travellers, one by one, until they came to him; and he was the only one they did not examine.[17]

It was the middle of May when he arrived in Venice. There he was to have a two months' delay before sailing for Palestine. Being a veteran of the wars of Navarre, and a member of a leading Guipuzcoan family, he could have approached the Spanish Ambassador and obtained help. But he preferred to beg his bread in the squares and along the waterways of the city. He slept in the porticoes on the famous Piazza San Marco; there he could enjoy the sight of the selfsame stars he had so often admired from his attic-room in the *Casa-Torre* of Loyola.

One night a rich Spaniard, Trevisano, who had become not only a citizen but a Senator of Venice, woke from his sleep with a voice ringing in his ears: "So you go delicately and richly clad, well-sheltered in your fine house, while My servant goes half-naked in the Piazza; and you sleep soft in your richly adorned bed while he must needs take his repose stretched on the hard ground." Trembling and afraid, the Senator arose and went out to the Piazza San Marco and found a poor Spanish pilgrim, poorly-clad, sleeping there. Understanding that this was the man whom he had been sent forth to find, he brought him to his home and kept him there.[18]

And while with that household, the pilgrim resumed a custom he had at Manresa, which was that, when anyone brought him in for a meal, he never spoke at the table, but listened very carefully, noting what interested his hosts; and then afterwards, by means of these interests, he brought the conversation round to the things of God. This habit of his resulted in this good man and his household becoming very fond of the pilgrim, so much so that they were so desirous of having him with them that they forced him to remain. And the host fetched him to the Doge of Venice, and got him an audience. When the Doge heard the pilgrim, he ordered that he be given free passage on the boat of the Governor who was about to sail for Cyprus.[19]

It is interesting to note how many people in so many different walks of life "became fond of Inigo." He seems to have had an easy spontaneous manner, a nature that led him to make friends quickly. In the places where he lived, people soon got to know of him; he was hardly a convert himself, says Father de Iriarte, before he became a catechist. He had an extraordinary flair for knowing exactly which approach would win the heart of the particular individual or group he was contacting at any given time; "with one man he played a game of cards, for another he danced a Basque dance, he threw his arms around the shoulders of another." And "When he gazed at one," writes a contemporary, "while his conversation was benign, his eyes seemed to pierce the heart, to see all; conversing with him only once, you felt that he knew you through and through."[20]

Inigo at this time, if not earlier, heard all about the capture of Rhodes. Many intending pilgrims to the Holy Land, having arrived in Venice and hearing of the disaster to the Knights' stronghold, refused to proceed any further and returned to their own countries. Because of these defections the departure was delayed as the master of the pilgrim ship did not think the number travelling sufficient to justify a sailing. Two whole months went by before the twenty-one pilgrims who decided to travel—Turks or no Turks, Suleiman or no Suleiman—could set sail. These two months were not without some grand events in Venice. The new Doge of the Republic celebrated the traditional pageant of the marriage of Venice with the Adriatic; that was on Trinity Sunday, May 31. On the following Thursday, June 4, the Feast of Corpus Christi was held with magnificent ceremonial. A fellow pilgrim of Inigo's has left an account of these *fiestas*. After describing that of June 4, he says:

> All the pilgrims (waiting to leave for Palestine) were called out and each was given a lighted candle. This procession went out from the Cathedral to the Palace, around the courtyard and back into the Cathedral, then back again to the Palace where the Doge sat on the throne to receive each pilgrim; he shook the hand of every one of us and said he would do whatever he could to help us.[21]

On the Friday all the pilgrims were summoned to meet the owners of the two ships, the usual pilgrim ship and a smaller vessel, at the White Lion Inn. The haggling between the parties went on far into the night, the ships' masters raising their prices because of the fewness of the passengers, the pilgrims refusing to budge if the fares were raised. The dispute did not directly concern Inigo, who had been guaranteed a free passage by the Doge; but he was at the meeting.

> Two Spaniards were there who did not wish to go in the small
> boat; they told us of a boat sailing, the owner a man named Ragaz-
> zoni. We met him on June 11 and arranged to sail with him to Beirut,
> he to wait thirty to forty days there for us and fetch us home again. His
> price was thirty-six ducats a man for food, drink, and other fare; he of-
> fered two meals a day and soup every morning.[22]

This ship was the one carrying the new Govorner to Cyprus; the master,
Ragazzoni, although he made his bargain with the pilgrims on June 11,
did not leave Venice until July 14. Meanwhile one careful and far-seeing
Swiss, Peter Fussli, availed himself of the extra week's delay to make his
purchases and preparations. He went to the Greek church in Venice to
become acquainted with the Mass of the Greek Rite. He bought biscuits,
cheese, ham, onions, sausage, cow's tongues, three casks of wine, 150
eggs, suet, candles, lanterns, dishes, plates, jugs, chickens, plums and
prunes, sugar, salt, and various drugs, and some gunpowder. He, with
two other Swiss, and a Tyrolean baker who lived in Rome, and four
Spaniards—Inigo, the Knight Commander already mentioned, his servant, and an unknown priest, probably the one who had come from Montserrat—made up the eight pilgrims embarking on the Governor's vessel.
When Fussli and his friends had put their huge stock of provisions on
board, they went ashore to make further purchases:

> Each bought a bed case on which he lay, and a straw mat, two
> linen sheets, and a coverlet and pillow. I myself also bought paper,
> writing materials, ink, and balsam, licorice and other sweet smelling
> things to ward off bad odors when in the ship.[23]

Inigo, travelling free, hardly bothered to buy anything. God had provided for him thus far, so he would trust Him for the remainder of the
journey. He had no intention of returning; "he was firmly resolved to remain in Jerusalem and to spend the rest of his days visiting the holy
places; and, as well as this devotional work, he meant to assist others to
save their souls." Besides the eight pilgrims, the Negrona carried many
passengers; there were 150 in all, about a hundred silk merchants and
some forty persons—high officials and the household and suite of the
Governor of Cyprus. Their vessel was a fine, solid one, with nineteen
canon and a crew of thirty-two.

When the morning for departure came, Inigo was laid low with a fever; the doctor—called in by the family with whom he stayed—when asked if the sick man could travel said, "Certainly, if he fancies a grave at sea." But Inigo relates that, notwithstanding this cheerful forecast, he nevertheless set out; and the minute they sailed "he became so seasick that he found himself eased of the fever, and began to feel better."[24]

Three pilgrims have left an account of the voyage and the adventures which befell the party in Palestine: Inigo himself in his memoirs, and Peter Fussli, that sturdy Swiss already referred to. Fussli came of a famous Zurich family of bell founders and artillery casters and was entitled to use a bell in his coat of arms. He had fought in the wars from which Switzerland emerged a nation. He seems to have been possessed of foresight, enterprise, and courage; he understood Italian. The third diary was kept by one Philip Hagen, a Strasburgher, who was made a Knight of the Holy Sepulchre in Jerusalem during the pilgrimage. He was wealthy, "neither thrifty nor thriftless"; he knew both Latin and French and had an excellent knowledge of Holy Scripture. In the following chapter, the story of this pilgrimage will be told in diary form, reconstructed from these three sources, with occasional explanatory interpolations.[25]

VII

. . . There was talk of marooning him (Inigo) on some island because he reproved certain filthy and lewd conduct among those aboard ship. . . .   *(Autobiography of St. Ignatius.)*

. . . Beholding the holy city, he was filled with consolation. . . .
                                                                      (Ibid.)

. . . The Provincial (Franciscan) knowing that he had the intention of remaining in the holy places told him that he must make ready to depart next day with the pilgrims . . . that he had authority from the Holy See to send away those whom he would and retain those whom he wished to retain . . . since the Franciscans had so judged and had such authority, Inigo said he would submit to their decision.   *(Ibid.)*

Wednesday, July 15th, 1523: By the grace of God we set sail, between six and seven in the morning. It was a fine strong ship with six sails and magnificent artillery. The ship's master said that we eight pilgrims should have a separate table.

Thursday, July 16th: During the night the wind calmed and the ship stood still; this evening the wind blew up again.

Friday, July 17th: The wind died down again today and we dropped anchor near a place called Revingo, 120 miles from Venice.

Saturday, July 18th: The wind returned, bringing us near to the city; and we got permission to go ashore.

Sunday, July 19th: We heard Mass at the shrine of St. Euphemia and then returned to the ship. We sailed again between 9 and 10 that morning.

Tuesday, July 21st: Eve of St. Mary Magdalen's Day today, when we came to the Slav country. A steep rock rises there near the Gulf of Quarnero; as we neared it, a strong wind came and blew us back fifty miles to a harbor near Pola. There we lay to all night.

Thursday, July 23rd: Favorable winds till midday; then a contrary wind came that blew us back fifty miles to Loreto, where we were that day and the next.

Saturday, July 25th: Day of St. James; for this day and the next we were off Loreto, with little wind.

Sunday, July 26th: St. Anne's Day; in the evening of this day a good wind arose and helped us along. We sailed along to an island called St. Andrea; we were now three hundred miles from Venice. There is a high peaked mountain rising from the sea near that island, somewhat like the Haag at home in Switzerland. The Slav country can be seen to the left. Slow sailing, because of little wind on Tuesday, Wednesday, and Thursday. On Friday, to Apulien.

Saturday, August 1st: Reached Velona, six hundred miles from Venice. Now we shall sail with a very good wind, coming Monday to Zanthe, Tuesday to Mathone, a thousand miles from Venice, they say, and half way to Cyprus.

Wednesday, August 5th: Came to an island named Cerigo. In this ship some lewd and filthy behavior is much in evidence; this the Spanish pilgrim, Inigo, reproved with much severity. His fellow Spaniards advised him to desist, as they had heard those he reprehended talk of having him marooned on some island.

Thursday, August 6th: Fresh water supplies running short, the ship's master advised all passengers to promise an offering of six ducats in honor of the Blessed Virgin Mary that the favorable wind prevail and that the ship be not again becalmed.

Tuesday, August 11th: Passed this day by Rhodes and on Thursday sighted Cyprus; late that night passed by a harbor named Salinen, where the pilgrim ship lay at anchor.

Friday, August 14th: Anchored at Famagusta, a strong, well fortified city. Here they showed us a jug in which Our Lord changed water into wine. Soon there arrived the master of the pilgrim ship, the *Galea*, from Salinen, with one pilgrim. They, having left Venice weeks before us, encountered heavy weather and many storms, and had delayed some days at Crete where the master of the *Galea* was of a mind to leave the thirteen Palestine pilgrims he had aboard, as he thought the group too small to make it worth his while continuing the voyage. We eight pilgrims who came with the Governor on the *Negrona* began to bargain with the master of the *Galea*. Our brothers, the Spaniards, had been advised regarding the next stage of the journey that it was safer to go by Jaffa and avoid Beirut because of the plague in Syria. The Spaniards took up the matter with the master of the *Galea* who said he would see us again; he did, and consented to take those from the *Negrona* from Cyprus to Jaffa and back for twenty ducats apiece, excepting the poor pilgrim (Inigo) whom the master accepted without any other provision save the poor man's trust in God.

Monday, August 17th: We rode along the coast to Old Famagusta—the new city is ten leagues further inland. The walls and towers of the old town are very fine and mounted with excellent cannon. We visited the church of St. Catherine; then we rode on by the coast road through fertile land. We reached Salinen on Tuesday and boarded the *Galea.*

[*The eight pilgrims from the Negrona* had now joined forces with the thirteen on the pilgrim ship. The latter group included the Strasbourg noble, Philip Hagen, one of the diarists; two gentlemen of Lorraine, one of whom brought his servant; nine others, some of them Flemings, some Hollanders. Three of these were from Utrecht: a Canon, the Vicar of Utrecht Cathedral, and a layman; their portrait, which shows them wearing the pilgrim cross and dated with the year of their pilgrimage, 1523, is preserved in Utrecht museum among the works of Jean Scoorel, a renowned portrait painter of the Flemish school.]

Tuesday, August 18th: There was some delay at Salinen, as our baggage had to be put aboard. [This was the not inconsiderable load of provisions brought by the Swiss!] We spent the two days sight-seeing. Not all of us, for the heat was very trying. When we visited the Franciscan convent at Nicosia, a Friar there who had been to the Holy Land warned us that we might expect much greater heat at Jerusalem. In the cool of the evening we went to visit a crucifixion group on a nearby mountain, Mont St. Croix; there the cross of Dismas, the Good Thief, was shown to us. [No doubt it reminded Inigo of the hermit Dom Chanones at Montserrat and his cell, named after the Penitent Thief, where Inigo made his general confession in 1522.]

Wednesday, August 19th: We set sail for Jaffa. A poor wind; becalmed again by Friday. Later, a breeze sprang up and we got on toward Jaffa, but the mariners somehow failed to recognize it, not realizing their mistake until they sighted the minarets of the mosque of Gaza. The master then had to put about, but the wind being contrary we had to drop anchor again. On Monday we made some headway, but at so slow a pace that it took us a full twenty-four hours to cover the nine miles or so we had gone past Jaffa.

Tuesday, August 25th: The watch called to all the pilgrims to come on deck and see that land, our journey's end, the place we so longed to set eyes on. We hurried up and got a clear view of Jaffa. Then we all assembled, standing in the poop while our brothers chanted the *Te Deum* and *Salve Regina:* a tattoo was sounded on the drums and the

ship's trumpeters blew a blast. The master of our ship, taking an interpreter named Steffani, went ashore to ride to Rama to announce our
arrival to the Franciscan Fathers there and other local authorities. The
regulations forbade any of us to leave the ship till they returned with
the guides. Meanwhile a Turkish gentleman, a Mameluke, with his servants, came and inspected us and the ship; the crew entertained him
hospitably. We thanked God for bringing us safe thus far.

Monday, August 31st: At last, after nearly a week's absence, the
master of the *Galea* returned, accompanied by two Friars of St. Francis
and an armed escort of about a hundred men, some of them Turks,
some Arabs. The Moors here are not black skinned. The Friars were
barefoot; one of them, a Hollander, gave us a little sermon in Latin and
Italian and German with all sorts of instructions regarding our visits to
the Holy Places and our conduct while in Palestine; the two Friars
warned us about thieves and robbers.

Tuesday, September 1st: Having at long last obtained permission
to disembark, we followed the Friars and the Spaniards and the rest.
We [the Swiss] took our bed covers with us; it was easy to carry them
on the donkeys and we were glad of them in the nights, which were
cool. The escort was waiting for us with camels and donkeys, and we
had to pay them before starting for Jerusalem. At two in the afternoon
we moved off, mounted on asses, for Rama. There we stayed in the
hospice built by Duke Philip the Good (of Burgundy), where many
traders came selling pullets, bread, fruit, milk, and sweetmeats of
many kinds. We were delayed all that day and the next complying with
further formalities. A caravan of Jewish silk merchants coming out of
Egypt and journeying to Jerusalem said they would travel in our company. We were now a numerous company. As we rode out of Rama, we
saw the vast cavalry encampment of the Emir of that place, with five
hundred pure-bred Arab mounts. We were each furnished with a
passport at Rama. The silk merchants rode camels. All seemed to fear
an attack by Arabs. At a place eight miles from Jerusalem we rested.

[Meanwhile Inigo, both during the sea voyage and the journey to
Jerusalem, was experiencing great interior joy. He had several visions
of Our Lord, which filled him with consolation and renewed his
courage and strength. The form this vision took was of an immense
golden circle or globe. He adds the following incident which does credit
to the devotion of the Spaniards and the traditions of those who mann-
ed Rhodes.]

Friday, September 4th: Very early at dawn we rose and proceeded towards Jerusalem; and when we came within two miles of that Holy City, a noble Spaniard, Diego Manes [this was the Knight Commander of Rhodes], speaking with much devotion, told all the pilgrims that, as soon as we came in sight of the Holy City, it would be a good thing if each man prepared his conscience, keeping silence from then on. All approved of this suggestion and each began to recollect himself; and a little way before coming to the spot from which we could get a view of Jerusalem, we saw two Friars with a cross awaiting us. And beholding the city, this pilgrim [Inigo] was filled with consolation, and the others, too, said that they experienced a joy beyond any they ever had known. The pilgrim felt this same devotion all the time they were there, when visiting the Holy Places. [Here the other diarists resume the narrative.]

Saturday, September 5th: Mass in the Franciscan convent and a sermon on the Last Supper and the Washing of the Feet and the institution of the Blessed Eucharist. The Friar guide took us to the Cenacle where Our Lady and the Apostles received the Holy Ghost. King David is buried beneath; but this part is closed, the Moors not wishing that the Christians should worship over his tomb. Then we were taken to the room where Our Lord appeared to the Apostles on Easter Sunday evening and where, eight days later, St. Thomas placed his hand in Our Lord's side. In the church there, we saw a portion of the pillar where our Savior was scourged. Near that church we saw the place where Our Lady died and where St. John the Evangelist used to celebrate Mass. Also on that Saturday we saw where Our Lord told the Apostles to go and preach the Gospel to all the world . . . and the place where St. Stephen was buried . . . and a place where Our Lady often prayed. On that night we went to the Holy Sepulchre, the chief place for all pilgrims; for within its walls is the summit of Calvary and the tomb of Christ, from which He rose glorious and immortal. This big spiral church was built by the Empress Helena. The Friars had given each of us a rug and a pillow and some food; we left them outside the Holy Sepulchre church and paid seven ducats to our guide before entering. We sang the *Salve Regina;* then a priest, bearing a cross, led our procession until we came to where Our Lord told St. Mary Magdalen: *Do not cling to me thus.* Thence we went to where Our Lord waited while the Jews prepared the cross for Him and later to where the soldiers cast lots for His cloak. We then ascended to St. Helena's chapel and from that to a higher one, each bearing a lighted candle and singing.

This chapel is lit with many lamps, and is called the Church of the Elevation of the Cross. It belongs to the Greeks.

There is a plenary indulgence in this chapel. We went up further still and saw a piece of the stone where Our Lord sat when He was crowned with thorns. Then we took off our shoes and went in procession, with much devotion, up a steep way to Mount Calvary where Christ Our Lord was nailed to the cross; and we saw the hole in which His cross was fixed to the ground. Every man fell on his knees, kissing this spot; some prayed with arms outstretched, some lay crossways on the strip of earth; all wept and sighed, remembering their sins, and thanked Our Lord for His bitter Passion and Death. Then the priests sang *Crux fidelis* and other hymns of the Passion and Crucifixion of our Savior, and told us that in that place there was a plenary indulgence. We kissed the holy spot and said a *Pater Noster* and other prayers. Fifty huge lamps, filled with olive oil, burned there.

[They were then shown several other relics preserved in these chapels and told the traditions associated with the place.]

Then we came to the Holy Sepulchre. The tomb is so wide that four may kneel there at the same time. We rested then until Matins; and a German barefoot Friar, Herr Hugo, gave us Holy Communion in the Holy Sepulchre. On Sunday morning at six we left the Holy Sepulchre, having spent the whole night there, and returned to the Fransicsan convent.

Sunday, September 6th: In the afternoon we visited the Well of Siloe, where Our Lord healed the man born blind. Water still flows from the rock into a thick trench, but Turks wash themselves and their laundry there now. We went on to the house where St. Peter was taken prisoner and from that to a monastery built around the Holy Sepulchre. We saw the place where Abraham wished to offer his son Isaac, and also where Melchisedech offered sacrifice of bread and wine, and the house of Veronica, the place where the women of Jerusalem wept for Our Lord, the house of Simon the leper, the house of Pilate—where there are two stones shown to mark where the words "Ecce Homo" were spoken. The place where Our Lord was scourged is now used by the Turks as a stable. After visiting all the places on the Via Dolorosa, we went to the house of St. Anne, where Our Lady was born. St. Helena built a beautiful church which is still at this spot. We then visited Bethseda. It is dry now. [The pool of Bethseda.]

Monday, September 7th: Visited Mount Sion where we had Mass. Then to Bethany; to the spot where Peter wept after betraying Our Lord; to the Church of the Presentation of Our Lady. Crossing the brook of Cedron—now dry—we saw where Absalom is buried and the tree where Judas hanged himself. We visited the house of Lazarus and Mary and Martha. The Moslems also honor Lazarus. We were at the place where Our Lord taught His Apostles the Our Father. Then we came to Mount Olivet and the place of the Ascension; to the Garden of the Agony. Near this is the tomb of Our Lady.

[*When on Mount Olivet, Inigo was so taken up listening to their guide and endeavoring to keep up with the pilgrims—for so detailed an itinerary had to be done at a fairly fast pace—that he failed to take sufficient note of something he had read in the Vita Christi at Loyola during the days of his convalescence there. Later it will be seen what this omission cost him.*]

Tuesday, September 8th: Visited Bethlehem; saw where the three kings watched the star; also Rachel's grave and the Shepherd's Field. We stayed the night with the Friars there; after supper Herr Hugo, our confessor, took us to many places connected with the flight into Egypt, and the Holy Innocents and the three kings. We saw St. Catherine's Church and where St. Jerome translated the Bible into Latin. A fine church stands here with beautiful marble pillars, each costing a thousand *guildern.* Pilgrims visiting St. Catherine's Church carry a wheel in their insignia, as she was martyred on a wheel.

Wednesday, September 9th: Heard early Mass in Bethlehem where Our Lord was born. Later we visited where St. Philip baptized the eunuch of the Queen of Ethiopia; then the house of Zachary. In the evening we returned to Jerusalem.

Thursday, September 10th: We visited Our Lady's fountain and went again to Mount Olivet. After Vespers in the evening we went to the house of Caiphas, then to where St. Peter denied Our Lord, then to the convent of the Armenians where is the stone which was rolled back from the tomb on Easter Day; we also visited where St. John the Baptist was beheaded.

Friday, September 11th: We saw a place where King David used to go to pray. In the evening we went to the Holy Sepulchre church for our second vigil. On Saturday we rested.

[Meanwhile, Inigo, who intended never to return to Europe, was trying to persuade the Franciscans to allow him to remain.]

For this end he had obtained letters of recommendation to the Father Guardian, whom he acquainted with his resolution of abiding there out of devotion; but he gave no hint of his second motive for remaining, i.e., his wish to be of help to the souls of others; this latter he revealed to none, though he had allowed people to know of his wish to stay in Jerusalem and spend his life visiting the Holy Places. The Father Guardian replied that he did not see how Inigo could remain, because their convent was so poor that he was unable to support the community and was seriously considering sending some of the Friars back to their countries with the pilgrims. The pilgrim, answering, said that he did not want any alms, but only that they would allow him to come there sometimes for confession. Then the Guardian told him that this perhaps would be allowed but that he should await the Provincial's arrival; the latter, who was Superior of all the Franciscan Superiors in Palestine, was just then in Bethlehem. With this promise the pilgrim felt reassured and began to write letters to some spiritually-minded persons in Barcelona.

Alas for his hopes! The evening before the pilgrims were due to leave Jerusalem, Inigo, "having one letter finished and being in the act of writing the other," was summoned to meet the Provincial and Guardian. The Provincial spoke kindly to him, saying that he had heard of his intention of remaining in the Holy Places and had given the matter a good deal of thought; but as he had had former experience of pilgrims who had the same intention, he thought it better to refuse permission. For some who had previously stayed on out of their devotion to the Holy Places had been imprisoned, some killed; and the Franciscans were put to the expense of redeeming their coreligionists out of infidel hands.

So he had decided that Inigo should prepare to leave with the rest.
The pilgrim pleaded that he had come with this intention and with the firm resolve of letting nothing deflect him from carrying out this purpose; and he gave the Provincial to understand that, unless he obliged him to leave under pain of mortal sin, he would not abandon his project. The Provincial then said that he had authority from the Holy See to send away those whom he would, and re-

tain those whom he wished to retain; moreover he had power to excommunicate anyone who disobeyed an order to leave. And in this case his judgment was that the pilgrim must not remain.

Then they wished to show him the bulls with power of excommonication, but the pilgrim said that it was not necessary, for he believed their Reverences; and since they had so decided and had such authority, he would obey them.

To resume the diary; Hagen recorded most of what follows:
Saturday, September 12th: Rested all this day and the Sunday.
Monday, September 14th: Feast of the Holy Cross. Having seen so many Holy Places in and around Jerusalem, all set out for the Jordan. Many Turks, Moors, and pagans rode with us, and Franciscan Friars of the Observance—the whole company numbering about two hundred, of which thirty were guides. We felt rather worried because many Arabs were on the road. We had risen soon after midnight and ridden all night in the dark, our company raising a great din as we clattered along. Once an awful cry was raised that the Arabs were firing on us and we heard gunfire; we had to ride fast over a shockingly stony road to Jericho, where we dismounted, let our donkeys eat and drink, and any pilgrim who had brought food ate it; but just then some Turks and Moors attacked us, taking our food with all the wine and water; they also robbed our money—some of it then, the rest on the way—and struck anyone who showed resistance. But no one dared strike or wound a Turk; if he did, all the pilgrims would be made to pay dearly for it, we were told. At Jericho, we saw the house of Zaccheus to whom Our Lord said: *Come down, quickly!* At Prime we reached the Jordan which is reckoned thirty-six miles from Jerusalem. Some bathed; some washed only face and hands; some swam to the opposite bank. It is not a very big river, but dangerous. While we were thus in the waters of the Jordan, some Turks on horseback—local fellows—made free of our clothes, robbing our pockets. The Turks of our escort rescued us, but the last ones of our group were too late to bathe as we had to ride at once to evade the robbers. We rode back again through Jericho and saw the Dead Sea and visited the desert of Canaan, where Our Lord fasted for forty days. Some Turks were escorting the monks and the two priests and the Spaniards; one of them told us to ride faster; we could not, so he came and beat our donkeys. The heat was frightful and the fellows who should have been escorting us were only plaguing us— they beat and battered us; having taken all our eatables was bad

enough but not even a drop of water did they leave us, and not even for a ducat could one get a morsel of food or a drop of water on that journey. Words fail me and my imagination boggles at the thought of that heat and that ride. It is most improper that pilgrims should be treated in such a manner. We got back to Jerusalem on Tuesday.

Wednesday, September 16: We were due to go to the Holy Sepulchre for our final visit, it being customary for pilgrims to spend three nights there in vigil; but as all our money had been robbed, we could not pay the necessary entrance money. We sent to the master of the *Galea* at Jaffa for some money. This day five hundred Turkish cavalry rode in from Damascus and took over the Jennitzer convent. They gave us an anxious time and we had to take turns keeping watch during the nights. One night they came pounding and hacking on our door with axes and guns trying to force an entry; we reinforced the door with stones. The women and children all roared "Murder" and a most hellish outcry was raised and maintained for so long [by the women and children] that the scamps outside had to fly. Next day they threatened to slit our landlord's throat if he did not admit them and he, being afraid, let them in. They rushed upon me [Philip Hagen] and my companion, dragged me by my beard from one room to another and down the stairs. They then searched our room for wine, to which they are evidently very partial.

Sunday, September 20th: We did some sight-seeing. Then the interpreter came back from Jaffa; we had not enough money to pay him; we lent twenty-eight ducats. [Evidently the money was in some form of promissory note, as next day the interpreter changed it.] On Monday evening we were to spend our last vigil in the Holy Sepulchre; three were to receive knighthood there: Philip Von Hagen, Zoeig Von Krongurl, and Eerhart Ride Von Risal.

Monday, September 21st: Feast of St. Matthew, Apostle and Evangelist. After Compline we went about the Holy Places in the Church of the Holy Sepulchre; many went to confession. At midnight the Franciscan Guardian and the Friars came and called out those who were to become Knights of the Holy Sepulchre. We prepared devoutly and went into the Holy Sepulchre itself, each kneeling apart; having read the conditions and sworn to observe these and the rules, we repeated the latter word for word. I wrote them down with my own hand from Father Guardian's book; when each had sworn his vow, the Guardian girded him with a golden chain; he was also given two golden spurs for

100

his feet and a golden chain for his neck. Then a naked sword was drawn by the Guardian, the pilgrim going on his knees while the Guardian read the blessing from his book over the new knight, confirming him in his new status by the same holy words. The Guardian then struck him three blows of the naked sword on the shoulder, kissed him, and bade him, "Arise, Sir Knight." The Friars then chanted the *Te Deum* and in the morning there was Mass.

Tuesday, September 22nd: After Mass we returned to the convent of the Friars. The interpreter was there, having changed some money. We were to leave that morning but such a crowd came, mostly of the blackguards who had robbed us at the Jordan and those who had tried to break in during the night, that neither the interpreter nor the Guardian thought it safe for us to go and would not let us leave. We stayed all that night and Wednesday. On Wednesday we visited the church of the Sepulchre of Our Lady, which was deep and dark and cool, being underground; this was in the valley of Jehosaphat; we stopped once again at the spot between Bethania and Mount Olivet where the Our Father was first said; then we went back to make our farewells at the Franciscan convent, for we knew that after darkness fell we would slip out of Jerusalem quietly by a side way and take a by-road to Rama.

At this point Inigo, the pauper pilgrim, disgraced himself and earned many reproofs and blows:

> ... He was overpowered by the desire to ascend to Mount Olivet again before leaving, since it was not the will of Our Lord that he should remain in the Holy Place. On that mountain is a rock, the same on which Our Lord stood before ascending into the heavens, and on it the imprints of His feet may still be seen; this was what he longed to return to see. And so, without saying a word to anyone, he slipped away from the other pilgrims and set off alone for Mount Olivet, though anyone venturing there without a Turkish guide runs grave risks indeed. When he got there, the guides would not allow him to enter.

[The Mount and the rock he went to visit were enclosed by the octagonal Church of the Ascension, built by the Crusaders on the ruins of the former rotunda-style church which had been there since the days of St. Jerome in the fourth and fifth centuries. Within the church was an inscribed tablet indicating and commemorating the exact place of the Ascension. Even the Mussulmen did not interfere with this sacred spot, venerated since the earliest days of Christianity.]

He gave the guards a small knife out of his writing case which he carried with him everywhere; and after being allowed to go in and pray, in which prayer he got profound consolation, he got a longing to go to Bethfage; and when there, he could not remember—since he did not take sufficient note of it at Mount Olivet—at which side was the right foot and which the left. And returning there again, I think it was his scissors he forfeited to the guards for permission to re-enter.

When it was discovered in the monastery that the pilgrim had gone off without a guide, the Friars sent diligently in all directions searching for him. And as he was descending from Mount Olivet, a Christian of the Cincture [Syrian Christians who served the Mount Sion monastery and who wore cinctures], a servant of the Friars, came running up to meet him, brandishing a big stick, and making angry gestures at him to come along. When he reached the pilgrim, he gripped him roughly by the arm; but the pilgrim let himself be dragged along easily. The other never loosened his hold; as Inigo went thus, hustled by the Christian of the Cincture, Our Lord gave him very great consolation, the pilgrim having a continuous vision of Christ above him in the air. This lasted until they reached the monastery. He departed thence the next day.

[The Guardian and Provincial, who must have had fears that he meant to disobey their order, would have heaved sighs of relief.]

It would seem from his last sentence that it was already late and that the others had gone on without him; but he did not miss much, for the pilgrim party had to ride hard and fast all night "on a desperately bad and stony road" and their Turkish escort, once clear of Jerusalem, began to fight among themselves for the right to rob the pilgrims. While this row between the horsemen of the escort was going on, some Moors and Arabs slipped up in the darkness and began opening the pilgrims' knapsacks and saddle-bags and helping themselves. The pilgrims, not allowed by law to give any blows in self-defense—no matter how much ill-treatment they received—had to sit on their straw bags on the donkeys' backs, quite unable to do anything to defend themselves. When some pilgrims, probably the Swiss, objected at seeing the rascals taking away their food, the attackers put knives to the objectors' throats and tore their pilgrim hats from their heads. Finally they escaped, only to run into another row further on. This time it was the Turkish escort. Furious because the Arabs had beat them to the robbing of the pilgrims, the Turks wished to avenge themselves on the latter. A debate was held as to whether they should be shot or not; wiser councils prevailing, the escort calmed down. The pilgrims decided that the master of the *Galea* should be made to pay compensation for their losses, he being responsible for their safe-conduct. Peter Fussli reminded Hans Nunegg of the ducats he owed him, and both fell to mourning the loss of their stores of food.

Thursday, September 24th: We rode into Rama, foodless for thirty-six miles. Being absolutely worn out, we sat down hoping to rest a little and ate and drank a little food which some had bought in Jericho. But we had only begun when some Turks rushed upon us and took all our food and wine: they knew we could do nothing, and that one could not buy wine for gold. But we comforted one another saying that we would not have to drink water for long, as the ship's master was due to come next day to get us through to the ship. This all happened outside Rama, and just then a messenger told us that our interpreter had been imprisoned and the Turkish commander wanted a ducat each from us; he said he himself would have to escort us. But he went away on the Friday and left us kicking our heels with nothing to drink but cistern-water for a whole eight days. [Inigo was now with them again.]

Thursday, October 1st: Still at Rama; because of the bad water many of the pilgrims were ill with cramps and all sorts of ailments. At last the master of the *Galea* arrived for us, bringing the authorities of Rama. They made sure we got a strong company of Turks and Moors, both horse and foot, to escort us; which was well, because those other robbers who attacked us formerly had actually gone on ahead, and the scoundrels had pitched their tents and were waiting with guns to waylay us. As the Commander of Rama rode with us, they did not dare to touch us. Arrived in Jaffa; no wine there; a wretched hole of a place. The worthless master of the *Galea* had failed to pay the taxes, so the Turks would not allow us aboard, but drove us all like cattle into a filthy shack, where we were cooped up with the horses and calves already there. We could hear the Moors and Turks outside jeering us and threatening us with all manner of outrages. While we lay in this dirty hole, all of us saying what we thought of that ship's master, along came the same and had the nerve to say to us: "I haven't a ducat. If you are my friends you'll give me forty ducats; if you can't give it, loan it; otherwise you may all have to lie on in this disgusting shack until I sell some of my merchandise and collect some money." (This, we thought to ourselves, was all cheating and villainy on his part.) But for fear of having to stay in that stinking hut and for fear of the threats we had heard made by the desperadoes outside, we made up forty ducats and gave it to him, though not obliged to, for he had broken nearly all the conditions of the contract he made with us in Venice. That same night we were at last allowed to go aboard the ship—after paying every authority at least four times over, but—no one will believe me!—the Turks and Moors tried to get still more off us. Each pilgrim was made to pay something, a *dinar*, or a *reinestal*, or some coin, and then, having got a coin, each of the blackguards would fall back and mingle with the crowd and come up again. What an eye-opener it was! As for that ship's master and interpreter! They were not the slightest help to us. The Commander of Rama made everyone pay him two ducats before entering the boats to pull out to the galley. I [Peter Fussli] did not pay him, nor the master of the ship; the latter owes me money. On Saturday we sailed from Jaffa.

Inigo, being penniless, probably got beaten up each time the highwaymen found that he had nothing for them. They reached Cyprus on October 14th, after a series of misfortunes. Peter of Breda died the first day and was buried at sea. The pilgrims found that the provisions for the return journey, which they had left under lock and key on the ship, had been pillaged by the mariners. Though the pilgrims were five weeks in the Holy Land, the ship's master took on no fresh water nor viands nor victuals of any sort, nor wood for burning; and fires were now necessary. The knight Hagen found the lock of his cabin picked and two ducats worth of wine gone—not a drop left. Added to this the master announced that they were out of their course and, for all he knew, drifting to the coasts of Barbary. He cut the wine ration and in the mornings there was only half a measure of vile and putrid water for each pilgrim; mixing vinegar with this made it less harmful, the pilgrims agreed. The ship sprang a leak, and for ten or twelve days they were in great danger and "the priests and monks in the party warned all to call on God and the beloved saints with great devotion." So they arrived at Cyprus, sailing into Salinen on the morning of October 14.

The eight, including Inigo, who had come to Cyprus on the Governor's ship with Ragazzoni, discovered that he had sailed home to Venice ten days previously, having got tired of waiting for them. Inigo takes up the narrative:

There were three or four ships in the harbor all sailing to Venice; one was Turkish, another a very small ship, the third a very rich, powerful vessel, the property of a rich merchant of Venice. Some of the pilgrims asked the master of this last ship if he wold take the pilgrim; but when he heard that he was penniless, he refused to take him, despite the passengers' entreaties and praise of the pilgrim. The master answered them, "If he's as holy as you say, let him go oversea as Sant' Iago did," or something like that. But the captain of the little ship, when they asked him, took the pilgrim gratis and willingly. They sailed one morning with a favorable wind, but in the evening a tempest struck them so that the three ships were separated just off Cyprus. The grand ship of the Venetian merchant foundered and was lost, though her passengers were saved; the Turkish brig, with all aboard, perished; but the little ship, though much buffeted by the elements, finally made port in Pola, in the Kingdom of Naples.

It was now mid-winter and bitter cold, with snow falling, and the pilgrim had only knee-breeches and shoes, his legs being bare; his doublet of coarse stuff was open and in rags on his shoulders, and he wore a threadbare coat.

Two of his Spanish friends, probably the Knight Commander and his servant, had been on the fine ship that was lost off Cyprus; they were none the worse for their experiences when the small ship took them aboard at Raffani on November 14. They then sailed on but met one storm after another; once their mainmast snapped in two, and the pilgrims woke to hear the sailors roaring, "Jesus, help us! Jesus and Mary help us!" On November 20, the eve of Presentation Day, the knight Philip Hagen got lost. He had gone with other pilgrims to visit a small town (probably an island off Rhodes); they ate a good meal and bought provisions, the knight buying four hens and a large bottle of wine. On their way back, at some point he took a different turning and lost his companions. When he realized his predicament, he hailed two Greek shepherds who were grazing their flocks nearby. Hagen appears to have been a confiding sort of man; he tried to explain to the Greeks,

105

but they walked him a great distance until sleep overcame him and he lay down "saying to myself: 'These good shepherds will stay with me until I wake.' " When he woke up, the hens were still there, but the bottle of wine, his purse and money, his sword, belt, and dagger, even his pilgrim hat, were all missing. "What a gruesome and shocking situation," he writes; "but God was good to me, having saved me from murder; I can't think why those shepherds spared me." Grabbing his four hens, he made off by moonlight, alone, "fearful, until he saw the sea and the ship"; his arrival was a great relief to his friends there who were extremely worried and had promised a pilgrimage for his safe return.

Inigo does not tell us how he completed his journey to Venice, but his brief reference to the intense cold is borne out by Hagen who, with a party, "having decided that they had enough of ships and ships' masters," went overland to Venice, some via Rome, some via Loreto, from Manfradonia, a port some miles north of Otranto. Hagen says, "We all landed on St. Stephen's Day, and let the ship's master get to Venice however he liked; his treatment of us was criminal and increased our sufferings a hundredfold. We had, at one stage, to ride over a mountain named Heartbreak Mountain which was covered with snow. Those who could not keep to the mountain track suffered untold misery and were in danger of being lost in the drifts. In all our lives we never experienced the like of the cold, the frosts, the driving snow, and the fog; sometimes our mounts stuck in drifts and had to be pulled out; we lost scrips, knapsacks, saddlebags, and their contents—much money and jewelry and keepsakes. There was a new Pope since we left—Clement VII. I went by Rome and visited the Pope and kissed the cross on his shoe." Fussli appears to have remained on board, for he keeps a log of places sighted or touched all along the Italian coast. Inigo, if he went ashore, would have gone by Loreto; for all the rest of his life he had a great devotion to that shrine. But he states that "having spent November, December, and half of January at sea, the pilgrim reached Venice in mid-January."

In Venice he met one of his former hosts who gave him gold pieces and a roll of serge, which later Inigo folded and wore across his stomach as a defense against the cold. He now began to consider what he ought to do, his plan of staying in Palestine having come to nothing. At last "it seemed clear to him that before helping souls he should spend some time studying," so he decided to start out again for

Barcelona. He was not very far on the journey from Venice to Genoa when his gold pieces had gone, for the beggars flocked after a man known to be liberal with his money. When he had nothing left and still found quite a crowd of beggars about him, he asked them to pardon him, that he had no more.

Lombardy was again the scene of battle, for Francis I was backing the Milanese against his rival, the Emperor Charles. Inigo met some Spanish soldiers who treated the poor pilgrim from their own land kindly, little dreaming that he was one who knew as much of war as they. Surprised at the itinerary he was following, which would bring him through both French and Imperial lines, they asked him to leave the highway for lesser, safer roads. They even showed him a safe route. But he paid no heed and continued on the highway, before long, as might be expected, finding himself under arrest as a suspect and probable spy. His clothes and belongings were searched and he got nothing back, only his ragged tunic and shoes. Thus clad, he was dragged around the streets, "and he remembered Christ being dragged from one street to another" during the Passion. The thought came to him that perhaps he should change his custom of addressing people as "You," this being how he imagined Christ and His Apostles spoke to their contemporaries, but that he should give the captain to whom they were dragging him some honorable title, such as Lord; immediately, he put the thought from him as a temptation and determined to use no titles, nor to salute this captain or uncover his head in his presence.

When they arrived at the palace where the captain had his quarters, Inigo was left in a hall while the soldiers went up to inform their superior officer. The latter interrogated the prisoner and found him slow to answer, pausing between answers, "with no manners whatsoever"; he took him for a madman and said to the soldiers, "This fellow's a half-wit; give him his things and throw him out." This was done at once. In the street a Spaniard who happened to be passing took compassion on the pilgrim and gave him food and a night's shelter.

The next day he was arrested by the other side—the French. When fetched to their Captain, Inigo was asked where he came from. He replied "Guipuzcoa," whereupon the Captain, exclaiming, "I come from near there—Bayonne," told the soldiers to give him supper and good treatment. This was the first time since he left Loyola that he openly admitted his place of origin. A few days later, after various adventures, he reached Genoa, and there he met an old acquaintance,

Rodrigo Portundo, now ranking as a General of the Spanish Galleys. "The pilgrim knew him when he (Inigo) served in the court of the Catholic King (Ferdinand)." Portundo got him a passage in a ship that was about to sail for Barcelona.

But the pilgrim had to run a last hazard. Andrea Doria, the Genoese pirate, then allied with the French, gave chase to the Spanish flotilla. The galleys just managed to make Barcelona in time and Inigo, landed at the same port from which he had embarked, went to visit his friends, the Rosers. It was mid-Lent, 1524.

The constant references to himself as "the pilgrim" in his life story dictated to Father da Camara show how deeply this long and trying journey to the Holy Land imprinted its pilgrim stamp upon him. He learned something in Jerusalem of the enmity of the infidels who ill-treated the Christians visiting the Holy Places; he must have clearly seen that, even had he obtained permission to remain, there was little hope that either Turks or Arabs would have suffered him to carry out his plan of "doing good to the souls of others" in Jerusalem. It was made very evident to him, both by conditions in Palestine, and the un-equivocal refusal of his request to be allowed to remain there, that—for the time being—God's plan for him was not to be worked out in the Holy Land, much though Inigo would have liked to labor in that vineyard.

VIII

. . . Returning to Barcelona, he began to study with great diligence.
(Autobiography of St. Ignatius.)

. . . After studying for two years, his master suggested to him that he ought to go to Alcala University and attend the Arts Course there; but the pilgrim first asked a Doctor of theology to examine him; the latter, giving the same advice as the master, he (Inigo) therefore set out alone for Alcala. . . .   *(Ibid.)*

. . . the gospel I preach! and in its service I suffer hardship like a criminal, yes, even imprisonment; but there is no imprisoning the word of God. For its sake I am ready to undergo anything; for love of the elect, that they, like us, may win salvation in Jesus Christ, and eternal glory with it . . . in firm resolve, in faith, in patience, in love, in endurance . . . what persecutions I underwent! And yet the Lord brought me through them all safely. And indeed, all those who are resolved to live a holy life in Jesus Christ will meet with persecution.
(Timothy II and III: Epistle for the Mass of St. Ignatius.)

T HE last his Barcelona friends had seen of Inigo was when he left their port for Gaeta, on a pilgrimage to Rome, just a year before. As he had told no one of his intention of going to Jerusalem, nothing was heard of either himself or his whereabouts until Juan Pasqual received a letter from him—one of the two letters the pilgrim was writing the evening the Franciscan Superiors sent for him to tell him that he could not remain in Palestine.

Inigo himself arrived back not very long after his letter, which was perused not only by the recipient and his family but by the Rosers, the Hieronymite nuns, and others who took an interest in him. The Sister Portress at the convent, who had always been very kind to the pilgrim, opened the door to him again at Easter, 1524; he brought a little gift for the community, a small wooden box filled with pebbles and flowers from the various sacred spots he had visited on his pilgrimage to Jerusalem. The Pasqual family prevailed upon him to change his tattered clothes for more respectable looking attire. When he visited Isabel Roser, he told her of his decision to study "so that he might be better able to help the souls of others"; she immediately put him in touch with a professor who taught the rudiments of grammar. Inigo tells that "he consulted with some people at Barcelona as to whether he should study and what subjects and for how long, his whole reason for taking lessons being his intention of either joining some religious order or going as he was (pilgrim fashion) all over the world; but not without first studying."[1] The master, Ardevoll, agreed to take Inigo into his class; Isabel Roser said she would be responsible for his upkeep.

Before commencing, however, Inigo said that he first wished to go to Manresa; he knew a "friar of St. Bernard" (Cistercian) there, a very spiritual man; if this monk agreed to take him, he would be sure of lessons in both spiritual and secular subjects. This was not very complimentary to Ardevoll, and to Isabel Roser it must have sounded ungrateful. But the singleness of purpose of the man was so unmistakable that no offense was given or taken. After a few days, Inigo arrived back from Manresa with the news that the Cistercian had died of the plague which had scourged Manresa during the very weeks he himself was in Palestine, and Master Ardevoll seems to have accepted him without comment, the new boy, aged thirty-three, being duly enrolled as a pupil.

As Inigo had to begin at the beginning, he sat among the youngest scholars and studied with them for two years; though he was eager to learn, his faculties lacked the plastic qualities of younger minds. Isabel Roser bought his books: Latin grammars, Virgil's *Aeneid*, Seneca's *Proverbs*, an anthology of "moral couplets" by a popular writer of the time, the poetic composition of 373 hexameters known as the *Contemptus Mundi*; there was also—to be learned by rote—a "Summary of Doctrine for the Young," another Latin production of 2,624 leonine hexameters, "by means of which," says a modern commentator, "all western Europe, for the space of three centuries, learned Latin." The poor pilgrim must have known a sinking of the heart when he first leafed through this formidable set of volumes; but he was never lacking in courage, so taking up the books Isabel Roser had bought for him, he betook himself to school.[2]

His earliest biographer, Ribadeneira, writes:

> There he began to learn the first principles of grammar, and the fine points of declensions and conjugations. Though his years found them difficult, his desire of pleasing God enkindled within

him the spirit and fervor that enabled him to master them. He did not allow the tedious and thorny tasks, fit only for children, nor the labor they entailed—so little to his natural liking—nor the multitude and variety of rules and laws, nor the obligation of joining in the chant when again and again all repeated the lesson, nor the other puerile exercises given to him, to frighten him off. Indeed, all these together gave him less trouble than the great and many consolations and illuminations which flooded his mind, no matter how much he tried to keep his attention on the lesson.[3]

Finding that these heavenly thoughts were retarding his progress, he again resorted to the self-analysis and introspection he had found so useful in the early days of his conversion. These thoughts, however good and holy, were invading his mind at the wrong time, "always when the choir-work of memorizing started." But he noticed that at Mass and prayer, times when such spiritual illuminations and joys might be expected, they were lacking. Seeing that they came between him and the work to which God had directed him, he concluded that they were a newer, subtler approach of the tempter; it was a lesson to be remembered with the rest. Later he was to crystallize it in a line of a letter written for the benefit of another's soul:

> The enemy cares little whether his words be fair or false, save only that he succeeds in conquering us.[4]

The temptation unmasked, the next step was to overcome it. He made an appointment with his teacher, asking Master Ardevoll to meet him in St.-Mary's-by-the-Sea. There, "both seated," he told how he had discovered what he believed to be the true reason for his slow progress; a distraction that came between him and his lessons—a temptation, masquerading under the guise of spiritual delight; that was what held him back. Henceforth he would take measures to battle with this; he had asked the master to come to the church to listen to his solemn promise:

> I promise never once to be lacking in attention for the next two years, if in that time I find in Barcelona enough bread and water to keep me alive.[5]

He also implored the professor "that he would treat him as the very least in the class, and that he would chastise and flog him hard, each and every time he seemed listless and inattentive at lessons; likewise if he thought him neglectful in the service of God or disinclined to sustain the fight against himself and his enemy the devil." This vigorous action sufficed to rout the temptation; he resumed his studies to such good effect that in 1526 Master Ardevoll thought that his pupil might profitably proceed to Alcala University and attend the Arts course there. Inigo agreed, but stipulated that first he should undergo an examination by a Doctor of Theology. He came through the examination, if not with flying colors, at least with the assurance of an independent authority that he should certainly go on to Alcala.

His own account of these two years in Barcelona takes up little more than a page in the *Acts of St. Ignatius*; beyond briefly stating what has just been related, he gives only two items of information about himself:

> The gastric trouble, which came against him ever since Manresa, and because of which he had taken to wearing shoes, had not recurred since the day he left Venice for Jerusalem. Therefore, when studying in Barcelona, he resumed some of his former penitential practices; he slit the soles of his shoes and by degrees the slit widened until, when the cold of winter came, he wore only the uppers, there being nothing between his feet and the bare ground.[6]

He was all this time lodging in Ines Pasqual's house at the corner of the Street of the Cotton Spinners. The owners had their little shop on the ground floor; Inigo had a poky attic-room, only five feet high, but with a balcony and terrace, where the poor came to him regularly. He still went his rounds begging, not for himself, but for those others who were so glad to receive the "soft, white loaves" baked for him by some noble ladies of the city. For a while he ate only bread and water, but when his Franciscan confessor, Fray Diego, friend of the man who later became St. Peter of Alcantara, commanded him to sit at table and eat whatever the others were eating and to leave off the hairshirt he constantly wore, he obeyed.

Sometimes, when Juan Pasqual was staying in Barcelona, he shared the attic with Inigo; he and two other youths, apprentices to the cotton trade, attested many years later to having frequently witnessed extraordinary wonders. In the room where they had meals together, there was a picture of the Last Supper upon which their guest's gaze was always riveted when eating with them. Sometimes at meals, in the middle of a conversation, he was suddenly raised up into the air. When the transports ceased, he took up the conversation just where he had left off before the rapture. On certain days, as a treat, he told the boys stories of his soldiering days. It is a pity that Juan Pasqual, always so expansive when giving evidence before the tribunal for the canonization, did not recount some of these tales of battle and adventure. In his lengthy deposition, he does, however, tell one story of the trouble which befell Inigo in Barcelona because of his zeal for conversions.

Near the St. Daniel Gate in Barcelona there was a convent of Dominican nuns—the Penitential Sisters of St. Dominic and St. Catherine of Siena. They were popularly known as the Angels, possibly from their white habits. Some seven years previously, this community seceded from the Order of Preachers and placed themselves under the jurisdiction of the ordinary of the diocese. The Dominican Father Provincial, hitherto responsible for the convent, must have heaved a sigh of relief; the real reason for the defection of the Angels was their unwillingness to observe the Rule of St. Dominic, and the offense they took when their brethren, the Dominican Fathers, reproached them for their laxity. The bishop soon found that he had a most unedifying community in the Angels and sent to Valencia for two Dominican nuns from a convent where the rule was strictly observed, hoping that they could restore some semblance not only of observance but of seemliness. All in vain. Soon Barcelona had two Dominican convents, which the citizens at once named the New Angels and the Old Angels.[7]

The latter were indeed the scandal of the town; the cloister was an enclosure only in name, each nun's visitors and relatives having the run of the house; there were gay parties given in the Sisters' cells and some callers, far from angelic, came at all hours of the day and night. Inigo heard of this sorry state of affairs, possibly through the Pasqual family who were related to the Dominican Father Provincial. He prayed and did penance for a long time, asking God to direct him how best to help these nuns—

—his heart being torn with pity for them, both because of the bad name they had earned for themselves and because they seemed to have no one to tell them what all Barcelona was saying about the Old Angels. As things were getting worse daily, he finally decided to go and tell them a few home truths.[8]

So he began "visiting the convent every day, neither rain, sun, nor great heat keeping him away." At first they probably laughed at him, if their callers did not throw him out; but he kept returning, with "prayers, penances, and little lectures," for quite some time. At last the Old Angels, coming to their senses, saw themselves as others saw them; "they told their visitors and suitors—the cause of all the dishonor and bad standing of that convent—to clear out, and with them they banished the many frivolities and vanities that caused so much scandal." They lived up to their order's title—the Penitential Sisters—ever after.[9]

The Old Angels were converted. Inigo was very happy. But the gentlemen who had been sent packing, all because of a penniless student's words, were neither converted nor happy. One of them, "a personage of quality," owned a negro slave. Determined to be revenged on the man who caused such a change in the nuns, this man-about-town and a few of his friends who shared his grudge against Inigo sent the slave to waylay and attack the pilgrim one evening when he was returning from the convent. The negro did his work well, flogging his victim cruelly and then bludgeoning him until he lay half dead on the road. Some millers found him lying unconscious in a ditch and took him to the Pasqual house. For five days he lay between life and death; he received the last sacraments; so bruised was his body that he could not bear to be touched. After two months in bed, he was able to go about again, and Ines Pasqual came begging him not to venture near the Old Angels any more; he replied that he could not imagine anything more delectable than to be killed for the love and honor of Christ and one's neighbor.[10]

"There is not a stick or stone in my house" declared Juan Pasqual, with justifiable pride, "but could be considered as a relic of that holy man; he sat on our chairs and benches; he slept in our attic; he ate at our table and used our delft. He had at his disposal the little library of my uncle, Canon Pujol. How often at night I feigned sleep and watched him at his prayers and devotion. If I forgot the pretense and moved, he was off his knees in a flash, saying to me, 'Are you not asleep yet, my son? Go to sleep, Juan. Go to sleep.' "[11]

As regards his reading, apart from textbooks, he seems to have been by this time a man of one book. He carried the *Imitation of Christ* with him everywhere and at all times. "So well did he imbibe and assimilate the spirit of a Kempis," says Ribadeneira, "that the life of our holy Father Founder was once described to me by a servant of God who knew him as the living and perfect portrayal of all that book contains."[12]

In Barcelona he gathered a few followers—three men with Castilian surnames, de Sa, de Caceres, and Arteaga. Later they followed him to Alcala. One letter is extant which Inigo wrote during these two years in Barcelona. It was to Ines Pasqual in Manresa, and ended:

> A pilgrim named Calixto is in Manresa. I wish you would unburden your mind to him; I assure you that there is more in him than meets the eye.
>
> And so, for love of Our Lord, let us take courage and make great efforts to serve Him, since we owe Him so much. How very soon we tire of His gifts and refuse them, though He never tires of giving them to us.
>
> Pray that Our Lady may intercede with her Son and Lord for us sinners, to obtain His grace for us in all our work and our trials, so that our souls, so sad and enfeebled, may wax strong and joyous to praise Him.
>
> From Barcelona. Day of St. Nicholas, 1525.
>
> The poor pilgrim, Inigo.[13]

The pilgrim set off from Barcelona alone, some time between March and August in 1526; he had a journey of almost 250 miles to traverse. The University of Alcala, young in years, was already venerable in traditions of scholarship; it was Cardinal Cisnero's greatest monument. When Francis I was taken to Spain, the prisoner of the Emperor Charles after the rout of Pavia, he spent three days in Alcala; seeing the procession of several thousand students coming out to escort him into the town, he exclaimed: "It has taken centuries and dynasties to give France the University of Paris, the pride of our kingdom; the same has been accomplished here by one Spanish Friar within a generation." The first stone had been laid in 1498; and the university was established in 1513, its faculties including theology, philosophy, canon law, moral philosophy; rhetoric, grammar, mathematics, medicine, anatomy, and surgery. Thanks to the Cardinal, who used the revenues of his primatial see for the purpose, and to Queen Isabella, always eager to forward learning, munificent provision was made for the free education and upkeep of poor students, of which there were always a great many. The printing presses of Alcala University, having won international renown with the six volumes of the polyglot Bible produced

115

between 1514 and 1517, continued to turn out numerous books of devotion, plain chant, and popular works on agriculture, interspersed at intervals with more notable works like Tostado's Commentaries on the Bible and de Vegara's Greek-Latin edition of Aristotle.

To this banquet hall of learning came "the poor pilgrim," and he proceeded to sample as many classes as possible, seemingly naive enough to imagine that he could shorten his scholastic career by doing all the courses at the same time. The courses had their sub-divisions; and Inigo tried to attend as many lectures as possible. Too many subjects and these too badly chosen to enable him either to lay proper foundations for any of the sciences or to assimilate information in any ordered sequence; but he does not seem to have had anyone to advise him that this diverse mental diet, with so many novel and abstract ideas, was not advisable for one of his scant education.

During his first couple of weeks in the university town he went about begging; but Alcala was not Barcelona. The students of Ximenes' great foundation were no more affluent than their fellows elsewhere; then, as now, undergraduates offered a poor prospect to a man seeking alms. It was the custom to hoot and jeer able-bodied beggars who appeared in the streets, so Inigo was made the butt of "a cleric and others"; finally, a student from Vitoria, a town halfway between Najera and Loyola, rescued the unfortunate man whom his fellow students were baiting. He sought out the pilgrim and "gave him his first alms in Alcala." The provost of the new Antezana Hospital, who saw Inigo "surrounded by a ring of lazy loungers," went to his aid and brought him to the hospital, where he received "food and drink, a candle and a bed."[14] The pilgrim himself says little of his studies, beyond indicating the courses he followed:

> In the year 1526 he arrived at Alcala and studied the Terminos (Sumulas) of de Soto, the Physics of Albert, and the Master of the Sentences (Peter the Lombard). While in Alcala, he gave the Exercises to some and taught Christian doctrine and thus gained some glory for God. And many persons there were who obtained great knowledge and joy of spiritual things; and others had various temptations, one, for instance, who, wishing to discipline himself, could not do so, as though his hand were held and other similar things, which caused rumors to run around the place all the more because of the crowds who gathered in great numbers

wherever he wished to teach the Christian doctrine. From the beginning of his stay in Alcala he knew Don Diego de Eguia, who was staying in the house of his brother the printer, and who, being well off, gave the pilgrim many alms for the poor and kept his three companions in the house. Once when the pilgrim came to him asking alms for some needy people, Don Diego said that he had no money, but opening a chest he gave some bedhangings of various colors, some candlesticks and other similar things, which the pilgrim wrapped in a cloth and carried away on his shoulders for the relief of the poor.[15]

The brothers he mentions, the Eguias, though from Navarre, were Guipuzcoans, and second cousins to a young Navarrese student then in Paris University—Francis Xavier. Don Diego was a priest; he later became a Jesuit and was for many years the confessor of St. Ignatius. In fact, Alcala was to prove a most fruitful source of vocations for the Company of Jesus. The three companions of Inigo who were lodged with the Diegos were not recruited at Alcala, but at Barcelona. When there, Inigo got the idea of assembling some companions to work out the plan he had in mind to help in the reformation of some of the defects so obvious in the manner in which God was served; he sought men who should be as "the trumpeters of Jesus Christ." Three joined him in Barcelona and followed him on to Alcala where a fourth asked to be admitted to their company.

> But this company of his, as though born before its time, did not last long. For although the Lord visited them with admirable fervor and gifts as long as they remained with Inigo, between the afflictions that befell and his departure from Spain, they separated from him and returned to the world, ending up very differently from the way in which they began.[16]

Arteaga became a bishop in the Indies; he died of poison which a servant gave him in mistake for medicine. Calixto de Sa, the same whom Inigo recommended to Ines Pasqual as "having more in him than meets the eye," suddenly finding himself catapulted among the great and the wealthy, seems to have forgotten the sound of the trumpet he was to blow for Christ; after two years in the Indies he returned "so rich," recounts Inigo, "that those who had formerly known him as a poor student never ceased to marvel." Caceres eventually went home to his native Segovia and there "commenced to live a life that showed how completely he had forgotten his former ideals." The fourth, a French youth, Juan Reynald, who joined the group in Alcala, became a Franciscan in Salamanca.

It will be recalled that St. Ignatius once confessed to having been plagued with temptations to vainglory for two years after his conversion; it was to conquer these insidious temptations that he concealed his identity, successfully passing for a nobody in the company of strangers and chance acquaintances. But at Alcala it was no longer possible for him to preserve his anonymity. He was back in Castile, and among the student body there must have been some who knew him at Arevalo or Madrigalejo or the other Castilian towns where the gentlemen of the household of Juan Velazquez—Inigo de Loyola among them—dallied as long as the Court remained. At Alcala, too, besides his friends the Eguias there were many other Guipuzcoans. Some were students; some were "courtiers of courtiers"—holding positions not unlike that Inigo had held with the Velazquez household—in various noble houses of Castile; and others came to Alcala for business reasons, usually at the time of the great fairs in August.

In 1526, Martin Saez de Goyas, a wealthy man of Azpeitia, happened to be in Alcala for the August fairs. One of the sights of the town was the vast torrent of students that poured into the streets and plazas when lectures ended in the university. Strangers stood to look at this, for them, unusual spectacle, and to listen to the various languages and dialects spoken by the students. The Azpeitian, listening to the babble of voices all around him and looking at the scholars—each wearing the color of his own particular college—suddenly noticed one student wearing a most unusual gown, a sort of imitation religious habit. Looking again, he thought that the face seemed strangely familiar; the bearded student looked a thinner, older Inigo de Loyola. Martin de Goyas could not be quite sure. The fellow was the same height as Inigo; he limped a little, too; but there was a big difference between the ungainly garment he now wore and the rich attire the dashing captain used to affect when riding through Azpeitia. No one had seen Inigo since he left the *Casa-Torre* more than four years previously; no one had heard anything of him in the interim. If his neighbor from Azpeitia had made no mistake and if this were really Inigo, what a tale Martin Saez would bring back to the family of the *Casa-Torre*.

Determined to keep his quarry in sight, he followed the student until he went into a small, poor house. He came out again after a few minutes and went along the street. Martin Saez at once called to the house and asked the owner, "an honorable widow," if his friend Inigo had not just called there and if she knew where he was staying. She replied that she did not know the name of the man who had just left nor where he had gone, "but every day he calls to give me alms." De Goyas, who probably added an alms to what Inigo had given, told the widow that when her benefactor called on the morrow she was to say to him: "If you need clothes, money, a horse, or anything else, you have only to ask Martin Saez de Goyas." The poor woman delivered the message verbatim on the following day, but the kind student did not appear overjoyed; in fact, he thanked her rather abruptly and made a quick exit, telling her that from this time on he would commend her needs to God, as he feared he could not call any more.

But his compatriot was not so easily put off. He did not leave Alcala "until he met and spoke with Inigo and got a letter from him to take home to Martin Garcia."[17] This letter was not preserved, but it is easy to imagine the various reactions with which it was read by Inigo's family. It was probably brief and laconic; the witness who testified to the incident just related said that "among other things Inigo told Martin Garcia that they would be reunited in Heaven." The letter made it clear to his family that he had no intention of ever returning home. But although he did not mean to visit Iraurgi any more, Inigo was to see Azpeitia—and his brother Don Martin of the *Casa-Torre* of Loyola—again.

The pilgrim and his four companions in their unusual sackcloth gowns soon became a familiar sight in the streets of Alcala. Wherever they were, crowds gathered; especially around Inigo, listening to him teaching Christian doctrine; his little homilies began to be quoted; the Spiritual Exercises which some people had done under his direction were discussed. So were his method-for-examining-conscience, his method-for-making-prayer, his directions-for-making-a-choice, his-test-for-discovering-which-spirit-moved-one. One day his friend, Don Diego, took Inigo aside and told him that the Inquisitors from Toledo had come to Alcala; people said that they were there to look into the doctrine and the activities of the "sackcloth fellows," as Inigo and his friends were called. Don Diego had heard something even more serious. The companions were under suspicion of being members of the *Illuminati*. The pilgrim had been on his way to Palestine when that heretical sect had sprung up in the wealthy seaport cities of Seville and Cadiz. Their teachings had been condemned, for they held that interior prayer sufficed for salvation; by this means alone, they claimed, souls could arrive at so sublime a state that good works, the sacraments, and even the commandments could be ignored. Don Diego was distinctly perturbed at the rumors he had heard. Some had said that Inigo and the others were "for the butcher."

But the visitors came and went, and Inigo was not summoned before them. It was nothing out of the ordinary for the Inquisitors to visit university towns, particularly those with their own printing presses like Alcala. It may not be out of place, before coming to Inigo's eventual encounters with the Inquisition, to quote some comments on that body by a non-Catholic historian, R. Trevor Davies, in his book *The Golden Century of Spain*. In his preface, Mr. Davies says that he has attempted "to steer an even, though immensely difficult, course between the Scylla of Protestant, Liberal, and Anticlerical prepossessions, and the Charybdis of Roman Catholic partisanship, to give definite facts and figures instead of the wild surmise that so often supplants them in facile generalizations about Spanish history."

"Judged by the standards of the times, the Spanish Inquisition was neither cruel nor unjust in its procedure and its penalties. In many ways it was more just and humane than almost any other tribunal in Europe. . . . A conviction could not be obtained without the testimony of seven witnesses, two of whom had to be in substantial agreement. . . . The accused was allowed the assistance of trained lawyers and an advocate to save him from making any false step through ignorance. . . . He had the right to refuse any judge suspected of prejudice. . . . To protect him from the effects of private animosity, he was allowed to make a list of all persons whom he believed to be his enemies; and should any of his accusers' names be found on this list, their evidence would be completely rejected. False accusations were subject to severest penalties. Prisoners awaiting trial were comfortably lodged, prisons frequently inspected, and complaints received attention. Unlike most other tribunals of the time, the Inquisition was sparing in the use of torture, and no torture was used likely to cause permanent injury."

There were three kinds of prisons for those arrested by order of the Inquisition: the first for offenses of a moral nature—not strictly against the faith; the second for officers of the Inquisition who had committed offenses in the discharge of their duties; the third, the "secret" prisons, for those accused of offenses against the Faith. [The number of persons burned alive—the penalty for a heretic who, having repented, had relapsed into error—was, says Mr. Davies, surprisingly small in Spain, smaller perhaps than in other countries such as England, where those—even women—convicted of high treason were burned alive.] The punishment known as wearing the "sanbenito"—a large yellow robe, embroidered with red St. Andrew's crosses and other symbols—was the most dreaded penalty of all, for the wearer was liable to be insulted, if not lynched, when he appeared in public. Worse still, after having been worn for the prescribed period, the garment was hung in the parish church and kept there forever, bringing the stigma of "damned heretic" to all descendants of its wearer. To have been known as a Quisling or Fifth Columnist in World War II, to have won the notorious title of Informer or Land-grabber in Ireland in times now happily past, was nothing to the shame suffered by the family of a Spaniard who had worn the sanbenito.

If a person disappeared without trace, remaining unheard of for a long time, his relatives were rather slow to make inquiries for him. The awful possibility of his having been arrested and thrown into the "secret" prisons, from which he might emerge wearing the sanbenito, deterred relatives from searching for a missing person. Remembering Inigo's sudden penchant for discussing religious matters during his last months in the Casa-Torre, one wonders if the Loyola family, hearing no news of him for four years, had feared the worst and made no move to inquire about his whereabouts.

Naturally, the sight of a few students going about Alcala in peculiar garb, giving instructions and speaking on subjects that came within the scope of ordained priests and trained theologians, aroused the interest if not the suspicions of the Holy Office. The first visit of the Inquisitors was made in the second half of November, 1526, but nothing happened just then. Shortly afterwards, the Vicar-Inquisitor, Figueroa, arrived in Alcala; and Inigo and his four friends were summoned before him. He told them that he had investigations made into their way of life, but that the Inquisitors had found no fault either in what they taught or in their manner of life; and they could continue as they were. However, as they were not religious, the Vicar advised them not to dress alike; Inigo and Arteaga should wear black, Calixto and Caceres "lion color," and the French boy Juanico could keep what he was wearing. Inigo gave a guarantee that these orders would be carried out. "But," he added, "I do not know what good comes of all these inquiries; the other day, a priest refused one of us Holy Communion because he receives weekly; and he was reluctant to allow me to receive. We are anxious to know if any heresy has been found in us." "No," replied the Vicar, "if there were, you would have been burned." "Yes," rejoined the pilgrim, "and you also, if they found any taint of heresy in you."[18]

The gowns were "tinted, as commanded," and fifteen or twenty days later Inigo was told by the Vicar not to go barefoot, but to wear shoes. It was then December, and the winters are cold in Castile. This order was likewise obeyed at once. Three months later, on March 6, 1527, the Vicar returned and instituted a further inquiry concerning the five companions. Inigo heard that a new charge had been brought against him. A "lady of quality, a married woman," her mother and her grandmother were brought before the Inquisitor, beginning with the oldest lady, "to declare on oath and in secret what Inigo de Loyola had been teaching them." The three told about the Spiritual Exercises; how the pilgrim had taught them "to examine their consciences on the commandments, the mortal sins, the five senses, and the powers of the soul; they spoke well and testified by the Gospels and by St. Paul and other saints; and they said that they made an examination of conscience twice daily, recalling, while kneeling before some holy picture or image, in what they had sinned; he had also advised them to confess every eight days and to receive Holy Communion also, once a week."

[St. Ignatius, in his own account of this, tells how the Vicar had been informed that "a married lady of high rank was going to visit the pilgrim in the mornings, between dark and day, wearing a mantilla such as the ladies of Alcala wore out-of-doors; and that in the hospital she discarded the mantilla and went to the pilgrim's room." The Inquisitor disdained to follow up the covert suggestion conveyed in this information, by either question or reference. The three ladies were dismissed; Inigo and the companions were not even called. But they were not to escape altogether. He himself relates what happened:

After another four months or so, the pilgrim now being lodged in a small house outside the hospital, an officer came to his door one day, called him, and said "You there! Come a little way with me." And he left him in the prison, saying, "Don't leave this place until you get orders to do so." It was early summer and his imprisonment was not harsh, many coming to visit him there—among them Miona, later his confessor. He was allowed to teach and give the Exercises just the same as when he had been free. Although some came offering to act as his advocate and procurator, he would not accept their services. One lady in particular, Dona Teresa de Cardenas (mother of the Duke of Maqueda), sent visitors to him on several occasions, offering to obtain his release; but this offer he did not accept either, but said each time: "He for whose love I entered this place will bring me forth, if it pleases Him." He remained there for seventeen days without being told why he had been imprisoned or being brought for examination. Finally Figureroa came to the prison and examined him concerning many things, even asking him if he observed the Sabbath. Also, if he knew a certain mother and daughter. The pilgrim replying that he did, the Vicar asked if he knew before these two women left Alcala that they meant to undertake the journey they had embarked on. He (Inigo) replied no, by the oath just administered to him. Whereupon the Vicar clapped him on the shoulder to show how glad he was and said, "That was the reason why you were thrown into this place. . . ."

Among the pilgrim's followers were a mother and daughter, both widows, and the daughter very young and beautiful. They had made notable spiritual progress, especially the daughter; and, although of high estate, they had gone on foot to the Veronica of Jaen; I cannot say whether they went alone and whether they begged their way there or no. This gave rise to great talk in Alcala. And their guardian, Doctor Ciruelo, charged the prisoner with having induced them to do this and had him arrested for it. Hearing this from the Vicar the prisoner said, "Would you like me to tell you more about this?" "Yes," said the other. "Well," said the prisoner, "you know that these two women often came to me, insisting that their wish was to travel the world ministering to the poor now in one hospital, now in another; and I always tried to dissuade them from this project, the daughter being so youthful and so fair, etc.; and I told them they could fulfil their desire in Alcala,

123

by visiting the poor and by accompanying the Most Holy Sacrament." These talks over, Figueroa went to the notary and had all
transcribed.[19]

The query concerning the Sabbath was to see if Inigo were a Jew.
His reply is on record; it has a genuine Loyolan ring: "I keep the Saturdays always in honor of Our Lady; the feasts of other faiths I do not
know; in my native place we have no Jews." The pilgrim was arrested
on April 21, Easter Sunday. April 19 was the day of the yearly
pilgrimage to Jaen; there, every Good Friday, a portion of the towel
with which Veronica wiped our Lord's face was exposed for veneration. Jaen was about sixty leagues from Alcala, so the ladies would
have started their long trek south on Palm Sunday, if not earlier. Inigo
was held until they returned, to see if they could bear out his statement
that he had not encouraged such a pilgrimage. Unfortunately, when
they had finished one pilgrimage they began another, and went almost
as far again in a westerly direction to Guadalupe, not returning to.
Alcala until May 22. They were interrogated immediately and said that
they had visited the two shrines mentioned, but against the advice of
Inigo; they had heard him exhort people to go to confession and Holy
Communion weekly; they knew him and had spoken with him occasionally; he had given them little talks on St. Joseph, St. Anne, and other
saints. They thought him a "very good man and a servant of God." The
prisoner was released on June 1st.[20]

The text of the trial of Inigo at Alcala is available. It is not without
interest in the light it casts on the life of central Spain in 1527. Fray
Rubio, a Franciscan, went one day to borrow a peck of bran from
Isabella, whose nickname was the One-Forever-Praying; but Isabella,
with others, was listening to a barefoot man who was seated in a chair
speaking to them. She said to Fray Rubio, "Don't disturb us, Father, we
are busy." Forced to go further in quest of the bran, the Franciscan
was hardly in a very good humor when, later the same evening, he met
Isabella again; she approached him and said, "Please don't think
anything scandalous was going on today; that man we were listening to
is a saint."

A local *beata*, Beatrice Ramirez, said she met Inigo in the shop of
Davila, the baker; the baker and his wife, a wine merchant and his
wife, and some other women were there listening to him. He wore a
dark tunic and went barefoot; she had heard it said that he was of no-

ble birth; she had begged cloth from some rich ladies to give to Inigo and his companions; she had given Calixto and the French boy a woolen pillow each, and sent gifts of pork and grapes to the five occasionally. The hospital attendant and his wife testified that married men, students, friars, women, and girls used to visit the hospital to hear Inigo; the pilgrim used to tell the attendant not to admit visitors as he had to study, but on feast days people came in crowds, usually very early in the morning. The women who came in the morning wore mantillas; they were all well known and of excellent character, except, perhaps, the baker's wife, who had been "a woman of the world" before Davila married her.

At the second session in the following March, many of the women who had gone to hear "the sackcloth fellows" were interrogated. The Inquisitors must have felt sorry for themselves and rather sympathetic towards Inigo when the widow Benavente got into the witness box. In telling of all who went to hear the preachers, she told the history of half Alcala and gabbled inconsequently about everyone and everything; "Maria Dias was there, and one who is married to Francisco, the weaver; and a friend of hers, a girl who is staying with the wife of Fernando Dias now; that woman having just had a baby, and recently widowed, too; and the servant of Loranca, the Chaplain of St. Juste, was there; and her sister, Ines; I think Ines works in the house of Luis Arenas. And a servant of Luisa Velazquez, the furnace stoker, and another Maria, and Maria Ocana, the one who, being widowed wished to hang herself, only I cut the cord from her neck; and other women, and my daughter Ana, and Leonor who is my companion" and so on, until the Vicar Figueroa must have had a pain in the head and the notary a cramp in the hand.[21]

In the third session, particular attention was paid to what Inigo taught. Besides advising weekly confession and Communion, and the examination of conscience twice daily, he taught them how to meditate, using the three powers of the soul; also different methods for vocal prayer. He gave instructions on the commandments, not forgetting an injunction against backbiting; he told them how to act in time of temptation and distinguished between mortal and venial sin: In this third session it came to light that some of the women attending these religious lessons got fits of melancholy, and some had long fainting fits. The witnesses had agreed that the worst case of fainting had been that of a woman who formerly led an evil life. This was a little too like the phenomena associated with the *Illuminati* group-meetings to be wholesome, so Figueroa left the Inquisition Tribunal and went to the prison to see Inigo again. The prisoner said that it was true; five or six of the women who listened to his talks were thus affected. He thought that it was because of the strenuous efforts these might have needed to make a break with the past; in the case of a person starting to lead a reformed life (and though he did not say so to the Vicar, none knew better than Inigo what he was speaking of!) natural repugnance for the change one made, the restrictions one had to place on oneself, and the redoubled attacks of the demon when a soul tried to lead a good life after forsaking evil ways—all these things could, he thought, account for the fainting and hysteria.

It is pleasant to note that his imprisonment in Alcala seems, if anything, to have increased his following and his popularity. The students came in throngs to listen to the pilgrim; even an occasional professor turned up. One eminent lecturer, Dr. Naveros, was so enthralled one evening that he was late for his lecture. On arriving before his assembled students, he began by saying: "*Vidi Paulum in vinculis;* I have seen Paul in chains."

While Inigo was in prison, one of the companions, Calixto, was in Segovia, where he fell very ill. During his convalescence, he heard of Inigo's trouble and at once journeyed back to Alcala and "put himself into the prison." Inigo advised him to go first to the Vicar; the latter received him well and said that he had better remain in the prison until the two women on pilgrimage arrived home, to confirm the statemnts of Inigo. Calixto, however, was not sufficiently recovered from his illness to be able to bear even the mild form of imprisonment the pilgrim was enduring, so the latter sent for a doctor, a friend of his, and managed to secure his companion's release.

When on June 1st a notary came to read the sentence of liberation to Inigo, he told him that he and his friends must dress like the other students; they were forbidden to instruct others in the faith, until after four years (by which time they would have studied more), as they were not learned. "Because," adds Ignatius, "the truth of the matter was that the pilgrim, though he knew a bit more than the others, had no foundation, which he always used to state straightaway any time the Inquisitors examined him." The order of the Vicar that the companions were to dress like the other students could not be obeyed at once, as they had no money. When Inigo pointed this out, Figueroa sent a well known man to go through Alcala with them and ask for alms.

Now that he was forbidden to help souls for four years, Inigo was rather doubtful as to what he should do; the only reason given prohibiting him from his apostolate was "that he had not studied enough." Finally, he decided to go to the Archbishop of Toledo, then in Valladolid, and place the whole affair before him. With Inigo, to decide was to do. The primate was in Valladolid for the christening of the Emperor's heir, Prince Philip—later Philip II—on June 5; he was still there when Inigo arrived a few weeks later.

> He gave the Archibishop a faithful account of all that had happened and said that, although not in His Grace's jurisdiction, he would abide by his decision. The prelate received him well, heard him, and, understanding that he wished to go to Salamanca, said that he himself had a college and friends in that city; he offered to befriend him there and, when he was leaving, gave him four *escudos*.[22]

It was full summer as the companions trudged into Salamanca, that city of learning which was to Spain what Oxford was to England, Bologna to Italy, Paris to France. Its history went back to Hannibal and the pre-Christian centuries; its bridge over the Tormes was built by the Romans who made the great road that ran through the town, the old road connecting Cadiz with the north. The town is on the heights overlooking the right bank of the river. The center of the old town in Inigo's time, as of the larger Salamanca of today, was the Plaza Major; from this square ran four roads. Taking the street leading west, they came to the new college, just completed that year, with its magnificent Renaissance doorway. Later the college became the Irish College, a refuge for the Irish seminarists who could not study for the priesthood in their own land during the centuries of persecution; quite recently it has been taken over once again by the Spanish authorities.

In Salamanca the pilgrim again gravitated to the Dominicans, thinking no doubt of the many kindnesses they had shown him during his Manresan year. But the Fathers in Salamanca were teachers and scholars of prestige in a town full of doctors and schools, whereas those he had known in Manresa were priests whose main preoccupation was the care of souls in a small out-of-the-way town. Among the Salamanca colleges, the Dominican College of St. Stephen was preeminent and, in a town where several thousand students were congregated—a susceptible body for any germs of heresy that might be in the environment or picked up by contact—the sons of St. Dominic kept a vigilant eye on anyone whose speech or conduct showed any singularity. Needless to say, Inigo was soon noticed; he used to pray in their church and went to confession there. One day after confession, a Dominican invited him to dine with the community; they wished to speak with him and, the Father added, "the pilgrim might expect many questions."[23]

On the following Sunday evening, Inigo and Calixto arrived to keep their dinner appointment. The sub-Prior pointed to Calixto who cut a sorry looking figure, "being very tall and dressed in a very short tunic of coarse cloth; he had a staff in his hand and a very wide sombrero on his head and buskins that reached halfway up his thighs." Why did he wear such attire, the Dominican asked. Inigo explained that they had been imprisoned in Alcala (he certainly seems to have been looking for trouble!) and there they had been told to dress like scholars, and the robes they got were heavy, so Calixto, because of the heat of Salamanca (often 100 degrees Fahrenheit in summer), had given his to a poor priest. The interrogator seems to have had no sense of humor; "he showed that he was not pleased and muttered between his teeth, 'Charity begins at home.'" After the meal they were invited to a chapel. There the Father acting as Prior in the latter's absence asked some questions. What had the companions studied? What did they preach? How, not having studied, did they presume to preach? As they had not the requisite training they must have had heavenly illumination to dare to preach and instruct others. What revelations had they received from the Holy Spirit?

This was serious. Inigo thought silence would be the best course and said that he would prefer to answer no more questions. "No more to be said!" echoed the Dominican, "when Erasmus and so many others are deceiving the world with a multitude of errors: and you don't wish to say what you teach!"

"Father," replied Inigo, "I will say no more than what I have said, save only before Superiors who can oblige me to answer."

Seeing that his guest meant to keep silence, the sub-Prior and the other Dominicans, saying, "Well, we have ways of making you speak. Stay here," went out and, locking the two suspects into the chapel, hastened away to the Salamanca Inquisitors to inquire what should be done. For three days Inigo and Calixto were held in St. Stephen's Priory; they dined with the Dominicans and afterwards the Fathers visited them in their cell where Inigo held his usual little talks; "and some of the Dominicans were for and some against them."

At the end of three days the notary took them away and the Alcala story repeated itself, only the Salamanca prison was far different. Inigo describes it:

> Not the lower prison where criminals were placed, but a high cell, old and, because it had not been used for a long time, very dirty. Both were fastened with one chain, ankle to ankle. The chain was about a dozen hands long, and fastened to a stake in the center of the room. . . . That night they spent in vigil, but next day, when people in the city heard of their imprisonment, bedding was sent in to them, and all necessities; and, as was his wont, the pilgrim spoke to their numerous visitors of God and holy things.[24]

The Bachelor Frias examined Inigo first, taking away all his books including the *Exercises* for examination. Later a tribunal of Inquisitors and professors, eight in all, questioned him at length on the Exercises, the Blessed Trinity, the Blessed Sacrament, and the Commandments. One of his visitors was a Mendoza who later became Bishop of Burgos; when this friendly visitor asked him how he was and whether he suffered much in his prison cell, Inigo replied with a flash of the old Loyola spirit: "To you I repeat what I said to a lady earlier today who pitied me to see me imprisoned. By compassionating me you show that you do not wish to be in bonds for the love of God. I tell you that Salamanca does not contain enough bars or fetters to satisfy my desire for them—for the love of God."

Around this time a prison break was made, all prisoners escaping. But Inigo and the companions remained, causing a nine-days' wonder in Salamanca. To mark such an unheard of renunciation of liberty, the prisoners were given "the whole of an adjoining palace for their accommodation." Three weeks later they were told by the Inquisitors that no fault was found with their life and teaching; they could continue to teach and speak of spiritual things, provided that they did not define what was mortal and what was venial sin. Inigo protested his obedience, but at the same time remarked that "without condemning him, they had shut his mouth." And "despite the affectionate demonstrations of the Bachelor Frias, the pilgrim would say no more, only that he would obey as long as he was in Salamanca."

They were released from prison at once; but "they found great difficulty in being of any help to souls, since the door was closed to them by this prohibition of not being allowed to say when a sin was mortal or venial." So Inigo determined to go to Paris to study.

> When he had formerly been deliberating at Barcelona whether he should study and for how long, and what subjects, his whole idea was that, after having studied, he would either enter some religious order or go as a pilgrim throughout the world. And whenever he thought of entering an order, he wished to join some lax, little-reformed order; in such a one he could suffer more; also he thought that by doing so, God might enable him to be of assistance to others. For God used to give him great confidence that he would be enabled to suffer any affronts and injuries that might there be offered him.[25]

The French boy, Reynald, was the first to leave the company; he entered the Franciscans in Salamanca either before Inigo left that town or soon afterwards. The other three agreed to follow the chief pilgrim to Paris; he was to go on ahead and make arrangements. "Many leading persons" in Salamanca "tried to dissuade him from leaving the city; but in less than three weeks after being set at liberty, Inigo set off alone, with his books strapped on to a little donkey."

> And arriving at Barcelona, all who knew him in the city remonstrated with him, begging him not to proceed to France, because of the war then being waged, giving him instances—with full details—of the atrocities, such as impaling, being committed on the Spaniards by the French. But he felt not the slightest fear.[26]

His stay in Salamanca had been short, barely two months, and he had made no progress in his studies. Indeed, from the educational viewpoint, his fifteen months in Alcala and his two in Salamanca were a dead loss. Between the time he spent in prison and attending the various sittings of the Inquisition, and the amount of time he spent in "helping souls," little time remained for intellectual pursuits; and, as has been seen, his attempt at Alcala to assimilate too much learning all at once ended in his failure to lay the proper foundations for any one science. He was now about to leave Spain for France, where there was every likelihood of his being arrested as a spy or killed as an undesirable alien; unless he had picked up a few phrases from Queen Germaine and her following in the old days in Castile, it is unlikely that he could speak French. He had no money and had to spend from late autumn to January in Barcelona, begging enough to pay his fees in the great international university where he now hoped to study. The evidence of Juan Pasqual tells us of how Inigo left Barcelona:

> He said farewell to all of us; to my mother and all in our house, to me and to all Barcelona, with many tears on his part and on ours. My mother had done what she could to provide him with what was needful for his journey, and several devout ladies also helped him.[27]

The mother and son accompanied him as far as the church of St. Andrew, three miles outside the city, one day early in the new year of 1528; they had known him from the March of 1523; they never forgot him, or he them. Soon after arriving in Paris, the pilgrim wrote to Ines Pasqual to allay the anxiety she and his friends felt on account of the perils he ran in that winter journey through enemy country.

In the evidence of the witnesses for St. Ignatius' canonization, as in the brief memoirs of the Founder written by Fathers who knew him and in the earliest lives of the saint, it is extraordinary how often he is shown as a man easily moved to laughter and tears. "There is," says Father de Iriarte, one of Spain's leading psychologists, in his study of the appearance and character of St. Ignatius, "something almost childish in the frequency and spontaneity of his tears. They well up on the simplest excuse; when he hears of the poor beggar to whom he gave his clothes being arrested at Manresa; when people came to bid him farewell or when he bade God-speed to those who loved him—whether they were the acquaintances and benefactors and friends of Manresa and Barcelona or his own sons and Companions that went, at his behest, to the ends of the earth; when he heard the confession of young Ribadeneira (the fourteen-year-old page who became a Jesuit novice); when at his favorite recreation of contemplating the starry heavens; and—always—from the time of his conversion until his death, he wept during his prayers; in fact, the absence of tears during prayer rather disturbed and saddened him, as if the normal rhythm of his life had been someway altered. He had to be dispensed from saying the divine office and even prohibited by order of the doctor from thinking too much of the heavenly life, for his holy tears, always so ready to overflow, menaced his eyesight, and blindness was imminent."[28]

That his laughter was as ready and spontaneous as his tears is not so evident in the first half of his life; it is more noticeable in his later years. But people are not attracted by men who seldom laugh, and in view of the attraction of Inigo for so many persons of such varying walks of life in his years at Barcelona, at Alcala, and at Salamanca, it must be concluded that this personal magnetism emanated from the ready smile, from the friendly word and gesture that denotes the warm heart.

. . . with favorable weather and good health, praise be to God, I arrived in this city of Paris on the second day of February, where I am studying until the Lord wills otherwise. I was hoping that you would write . . . .

Many remembrances to Juan, and tell him to be always an obedient son, for by so doing he will live many days on earth and hereafter will have life eternal in heaven . . . . Remember me to your good neighbor; tell her that her gifts arrived safely here; for the sake of God Our Lord, I will never forget the affection and good-will shown me. May the Lord of All, who by His Infinite Goodness dwells within us, repay you, so that His holy Will and Pleasure may always be accomplished in us. From Paris, third of March, Year 1528.   Poor in goodness,

Inigo.
(Letter of St. Ignatius to Ines Pasqual.)

He found a lodging with some Spaniards and studied the humanities at the Montaigu College. And because he had made too much haste with his studies hitherto, he found himself sadly lacking in the fundamentals, so he began in the boys' class, progressing on the Paris system.

(Autobiography of St. Ignatius.)

. . . "When the master gives me an order, I will think that it is Christ who commands me; when any of the others bids me to do something, I will take it as an order from St. Peter."

(Ibid.)

He used to hold conversations with Master Peter Favre and Master Francis Xavier, whom he gained for the service of God by means of the Exercises . . . . And he passed in the Arts Course and studied Theology for some years and gained the Companions . . .   *(Ibid.)*

IN PARIS, Inigo was inscribed on the University register as Ignatius of Loyola, from the diocese of Pamplona. His motive in going there was twofold; he now realized the mistake he had made in undertaking too much at Alcala and saw the necessity of laying a good foundation. He would have to begin all over again. Though the prospect would have daunted younger men, the pilgrim, despite his thirty-seven years, was not discouraged. "He was a man who would begin a thousand times, when he was sure of his goal, regretting neither the time hitherto lost nor the new labor upon which he had to embark."[1] Great as was the fame of Salamanca and Alcala, they were not comparable with Paris as centers of universal culture. In Paris he would begin again a more ordered, systematic course of studies; there he would mingle with men of learning from all over Europe. Father Lainez gives another reason for Inigo's choice of Paris University: "Because he did not know French, in Paris he would be unable to give talks to people (on spiritual matters) and so would be less impeded and able to go on with his studies."[2]

The Paris of 1528 was already a great city. On the south bank, left of the Seine, some sixty colleges with their thousands of students fitted somehow into the huddle of convents, churches, hostels, lodging houses, shops, and taverns which clustered around the hill that had known, long centuries before, the holy footsteps of St. Genevieve, the city's gentle patroness. The glories of Paris University during the thirteenth and fourteenth centuries were slightly dimmed by Inigo's time, but there were four faculties: theology, with which science the Sorbonne came to be particularly identified in that century; the decrees, or canon law; medicine; and the arts, or philosophy, by far the greater number of students—and the less serious element—enrolling in the last. There were four great "national" divisions: the Gallic, composed of Italians, Spanish, Portuguese, and the inhabitants of east, central, and southern France; the English or German, for the English, Scots, German, Alsatians, and Swiss; the Norman, for natives of Normandy, Brittany, Anjou, and Mans; and the Picard, for students from the Artois and the Walloons. On all sides one heard "the noisy brawl of the Town, its sights, sounds, and life, its slang, its thieves' patter, foreign oaths left over from the wars, Latin of the University and the Church, rude jokes of the tavern, the drone of the Schools, scraps of street songs ('My sweet love'—'Open your eyes, Guillemette'), country patois, the mincing affectations of the genteel . . . the swish of the comb through the threads, the crackling of the log fire, the rhythmic chopping of the knife on wood . . . the tramp of the Watch, the stumbling along the cobbles, the word of command, the rasp of halberds poked beneath the stalls, the grunted exchanges, and over all the vast murmur of the Town . . ."[3]

On the feast of the Purification of Our Lady, 1522, into this city trudged Inigo, his hand on the bridle of the little donkey that carried his few books. In a house where some Spaniards were lodging, room was made for him. An early and welcome surprise was a gift from Isabel

Roser of Barcelona, who sent him a bill of exchange which realized twenty-five gold crowns. He gave it to one of his fellow lodgers to mind, but, when he went later to draw some coins to meet expenses, his compatriot had spent the money and had no means of repaying it.

And so by Easter the pilgrim was penniless, because this fellow had squandered his money; and he was forced to beg, and even to leave his lodging. He obtained admittance into the St. Jacques Hospital, beyond the Innocents [a famous church and cemetery]. This was most inconvenient for a student, as the hospital was a good way from Montaigu College; to be sure of finding the door open each night, he had to leave and come home at the first stroke of the Ave Maria [6 p.m.], and in the mornings he had to set out before dawn; even so he missed some lectures. It was also a hindrance to have to take time to beg his support. . . . As it was now five years since he had had any trouble from his gastric ailment, he resumed his major penances and fasts. Things went on like this for some time until, seeing that he was making little progress in his studies, he began to consider some solution for his difficulties; noticing that some students served in the colleges and houses of the professors, he resolved to seek a master.[4]

His college, the Montaigu, had an unenviable reputation for squalor and a notoriously mean table. Nevertheless, most of its students not only survived its stale herrings, staler eggs, and rancid butter, but did better than students of other colleges at the examinations; it was undeniably the best college of Paris University in the early sixteenth century. It gave Europe, among other scholars, the humanists Erasmus and Luis Vives.

The Montaigu's daily schedule ran as follows:

Morning	Evening
4 a.m.-6 a.m.—Rise. Class.	3 p.m.-5 p.m.—Class.
6 a.m.—Mass.	5 p.m.—Vespers.
8 a.m.-10 a.m.—Class.	5 p.m.-6 p.m.—Debates.
10 a.m.-11 a.m.—Debates.	6 p.m.—Supper and Debates.
11 a.m.—Dinner.	7:30 p.m.—Compline.
12 (noon)—Debates.	8 p.m.—Retire.

The loss of his money was a hard blow. It meant that he had to rise an hour or more earlier than the other students, it caused him to miss the evening debates, and it involved a good deal of walking between his lodging and the Montaigu—a considerable hardship for a man with a limp. In an endeavor to solve his difficulties, he tried hard to find a professor who needed a servant, which master he meant to serve as he would Christ; but, try as he would, he failed to get employment in any of the colleges; there were plenty of young, able students, not handicapped by lameness and ignorance of French, ready to snap up all such vacancies as they occured.

Finally, being penniless and unable to find employment in a college, he was advised by a Spanish friar to go each year—even if it meant losing two months from his studies—to Flanders and gather there sufficient alms to keep him for the rest of the year. After praying about this, it seemed to him a good idea. So following the friar's advice, he collected each year in Flanders enough to help tide him over; and one year, he went on from Flanders to England, receiving in that country more alms than in all the former years.[5]

As the Spanish had complained on the accession of Charles that Flemings were coming in droves to the peninsula, seeking a livelihood there, so now the inhabitants of Antwerp and Bruges and other cities in the Lowlands might complain of how colonies of Spanish merchants had set up in business among them, becoming men of wealth and substance within a short time. Among these Spaniards Inigo needed no French; on his first begging expedition, probably in the Lent of 1529, he met a Guipuzcoan acquaintance who told him that "it was wrong and shameful to dishonor his lineage by going about begging." The reproach caused the pilgrim some scruples, for he wrote to "certain Doctors of the Sorbonne" putting the question to them; having received the unanimous decision that there was nothing wrong in what he was doing, he continued begging until one rich merchant, married to the sister of a theology professor—a friend of Inigo's—in the Sorbonne, took the poor student into his home and lodged him there.

While in Bruges, during the Lenten season, Inigo was invited to dinner by no less a person than Luis Vives, the humanist scholar, who not long before had returned from Oxford where he had been reading history. Vives, friend of Erasmus and Sir Thomas More, the English Chancellor, had an outstanding record; Spanish by birth and upbringing, he was a scholar of Paris University, a Montaigu man; a close associate of Erasmus of Rotterdam; a leading humanist thinker and writer, enjoying international fame. During his years in England, from 1523 to 1528, he had been asked by King Henry VIII and the Queen, Catherine of Aragon, to draw up a plan of studies for their daughter, the little princess, Mary Tudor.

Like many a lover of learning, Vives was in perpetual financial straits. When Inigo made his acquaintance, Vives was again poor, for he had lost King Henry's favor at the same time and in the same manner as his good friends, Thomas More, Bishop Fisher of Rochester, and the powerful Wolsey, on the question of the royal divorce. He was writing fast and concentratedly, being engaged in 1529 on a treatise concerning the life of Christians under Turkish rule, while he had just completed four books on concord and discord. When he heard that a poor student of the Montaigu was in Bruges—a man who had served under Najera and fought for the emperor, who had travelled to Palestine and could be expected to know a little of how the Turks treated the Christians—he naturally wished to meet Inigo, so he invited him to dine.[6]

Although poor, Vives lived in a house put at his disposal and comfortably furnished by a wealthy compatriot. Like his friend, More, he was exceedingly abstemious, drinking only water. At the dinner, perhaps apologizing for the Lenten fare, the scholar passed some rather disparaging remarks concerning the Church's legislation regarding fast and abstinence. Fast day dishes, well cooked and seasoned could be, he declared, as palatable as meals at which meats were served. To this Inigo replied that those who went in for pampering the sense of taste showed little appreciation of penance; because most men did not take kindly to penance, prescribed by the Church as an aid to mortification, rules were necessary to ensure that all got some fast and abstinence, that salutary spiritual tonic. How these two could have discoursed on poverty—Vives poor in worldly goods, but rich in learning and principle, a man of integrity; Inigo, poor in money and learning, but already having laid up treasure where neither rust nor moth can consume, nor thieves steal! They could have exchanged reminiscenses of the monarchs both had known and served. But no record of the conversation, save the remarks about the Lenten fast, remains.

In Antwerp, a noble Castilian received Inigo hospitably into his house; after his third trip to Flanders to solicit alms, this merchant saved the pilgrim any further journeys, sending him a bill of exchange regularly. Vives, or any of the Spanish merchants in Antwerp, Louvain, or

Bruges, could have given Inigo some London addresses; the English capital also had its Spanish colony, many Spanish merchants residing in the streets adjacent to the Tower and not far from St. Paul's. The pilgrim left no record of his impressions of the England of good King Hal. The Spaniards and others he met in London were generous; from them he received "more alms than in any of the other years."

Meanwhile, Ines Pasqual continued collecting among his Manresa and Barcelona friends and sent him a hundred escudos a year; this, with the alms sent regularly from 1531 onwards by his friends in Flanders, relieved him from having to break his studies to beg sufficient to keep him. He was, therefore, able to give all the time he wished to study; but even these first three difficult years had seen him make progress in the schools; after spending a year and a half in the Montaigu, mostly in the study of Latin grammar and classical texts, with, perhaps, an introduction to rhetoric, Inigo passed on to the College of St. Barbara—the Ste. Barbe—on November 1st, 1529, there to begin the Arts or Philosophy course.

This course took three years; before Christmas, 1532, he got his Bachelor's degree in Arts; in March, 1533, he obtained his Licentiate; the following year in Easter week he took his Master's degree, though he had some scruple about doing this examination. The students' slang for this final—probably because it was the rock on which so many promising scholars foundered—was "taking the rock." One had to incur considerable expenses in connection with the examination and, in view of his profession of evangelical poverty, Inigo asked his professor for advice as to whether he should "take the rock" or not. The latter told him to do the examination, regardless of the comments his expenditure might invite. Even the Licentiate examination and conferring was an expensive business; the beadles had to be tipped, the students had to be wined and dined, and there were gifts to the various masters in the colleges. It is not surprising that on June 13th, 1533, the Licentiate Ignatius Loyola is penning an anxious note to the reliable Ines Pasqual, to be followed by a second cri de coeur to another Barcelona friend for money. To the good Ines he writes:

> May the grace and love of Christ Our Lord always favor and aid us. It is now just a year since Doctor Benet, glory to his soul, brought me a letter from you, with alms and provisions. Your letter and all he told me showed how much diligence and good will you expend on my

behalf—as always; and of the future, too, you offered to relieve me of the worry for providing for myself, as you have done in the past. May God Our Lord, that true Senor for whose love and reverence you do this, repay you.

Although I replied to that letter, I now write this, partly because you like to get a letter from me, and partly to procure that my studies may be yet more advanced. Because, this Lent, I got my Master's degree and alas! I had to incur expenses more than I could meet and unavoidable ones; so I am now in much debt; and I greatly need that God should help me. Therefore, I wrote to *la Sepilla* [Ana de Rocaberti, another Barcelona benefactress] who, in a letter, made a handsome offer of assistance, begging me to tell her my needs. I wrote to Isabel Roser, too, but I did not ask her for any help, as in a letter I had from her she tells me not to wonder if she does not provide for me as hitherto, and as she would wish, she herself being now in needy circumstances. And I can indeed believe her, for I can say with justice that she has done more for me than her means allowed, and so I owe her more than I can ever repay. Better not to let her know at all of my present straits, for she would only grieve at not being able to help me.

When I left Barcelona, the wife of Monsieur Gralla made many offers to help me in my studies, and she has kept her word. Also Dona Isabel de Tosa and Dona Aldonza de Cardona; this latter lady sent me aid. To these three I am not writing, as I do not wish to be too importunate; tell them I wish to be remembered to them. As for la Gralla, I think that if you told her she would wish to subscribe to the alms collected for me. In her case, as in the others, do whatever you think best; your decision in the matter will be the best one as far as I am concerned, and the decision with which I will always be contented; for in the future, as in the past, I am your debtor. The bearer of this will give you more news of all that goes on here; you may trust him as you would myself. I would be delighted if you would write and tell me how things are with your son, Juan—my old friend and my truly beloved brother in the Lord, who is our everlasting judge; for you know well that I cannot but rejoice when I hear of Juan's well-being, and grieve to hear the opposite. May God Our Lord give him the grace to know Him perfectly, and to experience the indwelling of His divine majesty in his soul, so that, captivated by God's love and grace, Juan may be detached from all the creatures of this world.

I conclude, praying God Our Lord, by His infinite goodness, to make you in this life as that blessed mother who had St. Augustine for her son [St. Monica].

Remember me a great deal to all your neighbors, whom I know and love in Christ Our Lord.

From Paris, XIII June, the year 1533.

Poor in goodness,
Inigo[7]

When he finished philosophy, he began theology—in 1533—attending the Dominican college of St. Jacques; but owing to various bouts of fever, he was unable to complete either of his two courses. A year later, in Bologna, he tried again to resume the theological course, and again later in Venice. "But," says Father Astrain, "these isolated studies could not have amounted to much." Father Lainez sums up the eleven years Ignatius Loyola devoted to study, from March, 1524 to April, 1535, in these words:

As for his studies, although he had perhaps more impediments than anyone of his time, or even since, he had as much diligence or more, other things being equal, than his contemporaries, and made fair progress in letters, which he showed when answering in public at the time he and his co-disciples gave talks and lectures.[8]

So much for his studies. During his years in Paris, Inigo found that the philosophy classes brought the same temptations which had assailed him in Barcelona when first he joined Ardevoll's grammar class; spiritual thoughts and consolations came to him at the wrong time—when he should have had his mind on the subject under discussion. He took the same means to vanquish the temptation, pledging his attention to the Master in the Ste. Barbe who, doubtless, never before or after had a student who made such a confession or such a promise.

As early as 1529, while he was yet doing his preliminary studies at the Montaigu, he talked about spiritual things and gave the Exercises to three Spaniards, one a Bachelor of the Sorbonne. The three were new men when they had completed their thirty days' retreat—so much so that, following the Gospel injunction, they gave away all they had, even their books, to the poor. Like Inigo, they lodged in the hospital and begged from door to door. This news ran like wildfire among the student body, then numbering between twelve and sixteen thousand. The three converts being all Spaniards, the students of the Spanish colony in Paris were particularly agitated, especially in regard to the Sorbonne man who, to the pride of those who came from beyond the Pyrenees, had been appointed assistant lecturer in theology in that college the previous year. Inigo tells about the uproar:

> A great hubbub arose in the unversity about this matter, as these three were very well known and two of them distinguished in the schools; and soon the Spanish students began to attack the two Masters and, being unable to convince them by argument to return to the university, a great mob of students went armed to the hospital one day and dragged them out by force.
>
> When they arrived at the university, a compromise was made, which was that, when the three had finally completed their courses, they could then go ahead with their plans. Afterwards de Castro, the Bachelor [of the Sorbonne], returned to Spain and became a preacher in Burgos [his native city]; after some time he entered the Carthusian order at Valencia. The other master set out to go on a pilgrimage to Jerusalem on foot; an army captain, a relative of his, chancing to meet him as he went, pilgrim fashion, through Italy, had him brought before the pope and ordered to return to Spain. But this took place some years later.[9]

The date of the uproar in the university was around mid-summer, 1529, the year when Inigo had been to Flanders for the first time and met Vives. When questions were asked as to who or what was responsible for the change in the three Spanish students, two of whom had already graduated and were preparing to "take the rock," the answer was—Inigo of Loyola and his Spiritual Exercises. So, as in Alcala and Salamanca, another storm of persecution blew up about the pilgrim. Don de Gouvea, Rector of the Ste. Barbe—a college which always had many Spanish and Portuguese students—was particularly incensed; one of the three who had done the Exercises had been studying in the Ste. Barbe. The rector declared that "Inigo de Loyola had made a madman out of him [the student], and the first time the pilgrim showed his face at the Ste. Barbe, the rector would 'give him a hall' for seducing the scholars."

"To give a hall" was the university term for a public flogging; the offender had to appear, stripped to the waist, before his assembled college and go up and down between a double file of the masters who administered a severe flogging with canes. It was so serious a punishment that it was reserved for "those who raised disturbances and who were known to have pernicious habits." The principal of the college would order the doors to be closed and the college bell to be tolled solemnly; all the students assembled while the masters, grasping their rods or swishing them through the air, awaited the delinquent. Ribadeneira gives an interesting account of this incident:

All the preparation for the flogging having been arranged, someone told Inigo what was afoot, warning him to beware. But he rather rejoiced, not wishing to lose so good a chance of suffering and overcoming himself. And so, without losing any time, he presented himself at the college, where this ignominious trial awaited him.

Then he experienced a refusal within him; the body jibbed at this obstacle he asked it to surmount; he went deathly pale and trembled from head to foot. But taking himself in hand, he told himself: "What's this? You would kick against the goad, would you? I tell you, Sir Ass, this time you'll get your vanity well walloped. I'll see to it that you'll be made dance." Having thus lectured poor Brother Ass, the whitefaced Inigo went to the college. And the moment he arrived, the doors were shut, the bell was rung, and all the students assembled; and the masters came with the rods used for flogging in Paris; the allegations were made and all present agreed that he deserved this rigorous punishment. . . .In that hour, two spirits were in combat in the soul of Inigo, which, though seemingly contrary, directed him to the same end. The love of God and a burning desire to suffer pains and insults for the sake of the name of Jesus Christ, moved him to offer himself joyfully to the infamy and the flogging; on the other hand, the self-same love of God, coupled with love of his neighbor and zeal for souls, told him otherwise. "It is good for me to suffer thus," he told himself; "but how about its effect on those just begun to live a new life? Will the sight of this make them turn back from the road to heaven; they who have gone only a little way? To be made a fool of for Christ is an honor for a Christian. Which must I consider—the love of God as seen in my neighbor's needs or the love of God as seen in my own need?" After weighing the matter for some time, he finally decided first to offer God his desire to suffer the punishment and then to see if he could do anything to save scandalizing the weaker brethren.

So he went to the Doctor de Gouvea, still in his apartments, and told him all this matter which so agitated his soul, saying that nothing in life was as sweet to him as to suffer for Christ, which he had already experience of—even to imprisonment and chains; but he feared for the weakness of some beginner, still of little and tender virtue.[10]

After a while, the waiting students and faculty saw the rector and Inigo come into the dining hall together arm in arm, and Doctor de Gouvea addressed all present, saying that he wished to apologize publicly to Inigo for having too lightly given ear to those who had come complaining of him. Though he probably took the new student of Ste. Barbe to task privately for his zealous out-of-class activities, the rector remained his staunch friend from then on. Eventually de Gouvea was the means of recommending the members of the newly formed Company of Jesus to King John III of Portugal and, through him, to the pope, as men who should be given the Indies and the vast expanse of the farther Orient as a fitting field for their zeal.

Another story concerning Inigo's subjugation of natural fear is told by himself. One day a doctor named Frago and Inigo entered a house where several deaths had taken place within a short space of time; Frago wished to ascertain if it were the plague or not. They brought with them "a woman very knowledgeable in the matter," and the moment they entered she pronounced the sick persons plague-stricken. Inigo, in the act of consoling one of the poor sufferers, took him by the hand. That evening, his own hand began to pain him violently, and "his imagination ran riot, persuading him that he had contracted the plague." He became terrified. He finally overcame his panic when "with a great effort of will, he thrust his hand into his mouth, saying: 'If you have the plague in the hand, have it also in the mouth!'" This forceful action—not good from the hygienic but excellent from the psychological standpoint—"calmed his imagination and the pain in the hand vanished." There was an aftermath, however: when he got back to the Ste. Barbe, and his fellow students heard where he had been, all fled; "he was locked out of most of the rooms and had to spend some days out of the Ste. Barbe."[11]

Father de Iriarte, S.J., whose psychological studies on Saint Ignatius have been already mentioned, refers to his propensity for changing color and quotes several witnesses on the subject. One said, "He used to blush sometimes like a young girl." Another: "I saw him sometimes when at table, if the conversation turned to spiritual matters, his face would suddenly flush as though he were burning hot." "When praying, often his ardor was such that even his face reddened; and we used to start, thinking that he had got a rash." "I remember one day when he preached, his force and spiritual fervor were so great that in some way he seemed enkindled by the fire of charity, and even his hearers were set aflame in their hearts, so that when he fell silent his very appearance inspired all present with the love of God." Inigo paled and trembled at the thought of the punishment awaiting him in the College Ste. Barbe; he panicked, fearing contagion, when he touched a man smitten with plague; but there is another more notable instance of this sudden access of fear. He himself relates the incident:

> The Spaniard, the fellow lodger to whom he had entrusted his money on arriving in Paris and who had spent it, was setting sail for Spain from Rouen; and having to wait in that port, he fell ill; and the pilgrim received a letter from him telling him this and straightaway he [Inigo] got the wish to go visit and aid him; he thought, too, that through such a meeting he might gain the other so that, leaving the world, he would dedicate himself entirely to the service of God. To obtain this, he got the wish to go the twenty-eight leagues between Paris and Rouen walking and barefooted, without eating or drinking. And going to pray about this, a great fear seized him. At last he went to St. Dominic's church and there made the resolution to go in the manner just described; the great fear he had that his project might be tempting God left him for the time being.

> The following day (the morning he was to leave) he got up at dawn; and, as he dressed, such a terror took hold of him that he was hardly able to put on his clothes. Despite his repugnance, however, he left the house and was even out of Paris before sunrise. But the dread persisted all the way to Argenteuil which is a castle three leagues from Paris on the Rouen road, where there is a relic of portion of our Savior's garment. Great was his spiritual travail as he went by the castle; as he climbed up out of the valley, his fear began to pass away and great consolations and spiritual strength came to

him, so that he began to shout for very joy, speaking with God as he walked past the fields. And he spent that night with a poor beggar in a hospital, having covered fourteen leagues in that one day. On the next night he slept in a straw hut and on the third reached Rouen, being all the time without eating or drinking and going barefoot as he had determined. In Rouen he consoled the sick man and helped him, putting him on the ship for Spain and giving letters for the companions who were in Salamanca: Calixto, Caceres, and Arteaga.[12]

Father Iriarte makes the point that Inigo had the sort of temperament that tended to ricochet from one emotional extreme to the other. His fear overcome, he becomes so exultant that he has to cry his happiness aloud as he goes along. On the other hand, when on the evening of Saturday, May 25, 1555, word was brought to Ignatius that Cardinal Carafa, always anxious to merge the Jesuit and Theatine Orders, had been elcted pope, "Our Father's color changed and his whole countenance, and he told some of the older Fathers afterwards that his bones shook in their sockets; nevertheless he rose, without saying a word, and went to the chapel, to come back shortly afterwards all smiles and contented looking." The legend of the iron Ignatius, a stranger to all emotion, is after all but a legend. Notwithstanding his self-control, the quick blood mantling his face or ebbing back to the heart, the ready smile and the readier tear, the sudden plunge into gloom, the swifter upthrust into joy and gaiety, told only too readily and too openly his feelings.[13]

After 1529, when his philosophy course had begun, he did not seek to discuss spiritual things with others or to give the Exercises; he contented himself with keeping and helping those who had already been in contact with him "for he wished to devote himself to his studies." From this time onwards, the giving of the Spiritual Exercises—and the persecutions that usually ensued—took place only in vacation periods. Ribadeneira tells of how in midwinter, probably during the Christmas holidays, Inigo stood in a frozen pond one night waiting for a certain reprobate to pass on his way to an illicit assignation; the water was to his neck. The gay Lothario must have got the fright of his life when a voice spoke from the pond, admonishing him and his ways; when he heard that the severe penance had been undertaken for his sake, he "turned over a new leaf, changing his life."

A doctor of theology, whom Inigo had been particularly anxious to gain for God, proved a difficult catch; he tried every means he knew to persuade him to do the Exercises, but the theologian always had some excuse. One day when the pilgrim called to see him, he found the doctor playing a game of billiards. Either to excuse himself, or to get rid of Inigo, he immediately began to insist that the caller should take a hand. The other apologized, saying that he neither knew how to play nor had he any money to wager. But the doctor only insisted the more and would take no refusal; finally Inigo said to him "Senor, I will do as you ask; I will play, but on this condition—that we play fair and that, if you win, I will do whatever you ask me for thirty days, and if I win, you will do as I ask for thirty days." That took some of the wind out of the doctor's sails; still he could not but agree—he was the one who had been hankering for a game. Inigo, "who never had as much as held a billiard cue in his life, much less played a game, played as if he had done nothing but play billiards from the day he was born, not giving the doctor as much as one game." And every now and again he would say to his opponent, "Senor Doctor, the finger pushing this cue is not Inigo's but God's. He's playing for a big stake—you." The inevitable happened; the theologian did the Exercises, changed his life, and did much for the glory of God.[14]

When Inigo got back from his journey to Rouen in the September of 1529, he heard that the Inquisitor of Paris, Master Mateo Ory, a Dominican of the convent of St. Jacques, was instituting inquiries about him, on account of the professors, students, and others who had been making such extraordinary changes in their manner of living since they had come under the pilgrim's instruction.

By now Inigo was well acquainted with the procedure of the Inquisition; he had no wish for proceedings to be dragged out and to find himself missing further classes. This time he went looking for the Inquisitor, telling him that he was there to answer all inquiries; the only favor he asked was that the matter should be dispatched promptly to enable him to start his Arts and Philosophy course on October 1. The Inquisitor was Spanish, for there was no Inquisition in France; he told Inigo the things he had heard about him, but let him go free.[15]

On the last day of September, Inigo came knocking at the doors of Ste. Barbe. Although he had, thanks to his first journey to Flanders, a little money laid by for the current year's expenses, it did not amount to much and he could not pay for any but the cheapest accommodation. In the Ste. Barbe he found two other students no richer than himself; they were two young men of twenty-three, already Bachelors of Arts and preparing for the Licentiate examinations. The excitement in the College

Ste. Barbe caused by the preparations for the "hall," and the further excitement caused when the rector called off the punishment and publicly exonerated and reinstated Inigo, had hardly died down when the newcomer moved into the room he was to share with the two Ste. Barbe men. He was not unknown to his roommates, having provided a topic for discussion not only that day but for some time previously in both the Ste. Barbe and the Montaigu, two colleges separated only by the dark, noisome alley known as the Street of the Dogs.

The pair who were to share their already cramped quarters with the pilgrim had been close friends for a considerable time, although their origin and temperaments were very dissimilar. Peter Favre was the son of a Savoy shepherd; gentle and guileless, from his childhood he had always been inclined to both prayer and study, having quite a flair for Greek. He owed his place in the Ste. Barbe to the good offices of his uncle, a Carthusian Prior; at an early stage in his college career he had won such a name for his proficiency in Greek that the masters "when in some doubt as to how a certain passage in Aristotle should be rendered, referred the matter to Master Peter Favre."[16]

The other occupant of the room, Francis de Jassu of Xavier, was the youngest sprig of an impoverished but noble family of Navarre. His home, a sturdy fortress in lonely, remote uplands about ten leagues from Pamplona, was but a day's ride from Loyola. His brothers had fought in the same war and, as likely as not, in the same siege in which Inigo of Loyola had stopped the cannon ball that changed the whole direction of his life. But the Xaviers were on the other side—they had fought with the French in the bid to restore the d'Albret dynasty to the throne of Navarre. Like other loyalist families of that province, so long a bone of contention between France and Spain, they had staked their all on victory. Like their king, d'Albret, they had lost. When Inigo of Loyola and Francis of Xavier faced one another in the little room they were henceforth to share, neither could have been unaware of the other's antecedents.[17]

There is some evidence that Xavier was decidedly cool towards Inigo in the beginning. As Francis was by nature a friendly fellow, this hostile attitude in the case of Inigo invites comment. An easy and ready-made explanation would be to say that the sight of the Guipuzcoan, with his slight limp, immediately reminded the other of the ruin the wars of the previous decade had brought to the Xavier family, and of a further and more personal misfortune stemming from the same source—the constant penury of Francis. But such an explanation implies that the young graduate of twenty-three was so immature as to hold Inigo partly to blame for the decline of the Xavier fortunes; it also suggests that Francis Xavier, whose purse did not permit him to live up to his claims to noble lineage, suffered from that modern malady, frustration. Neither implication rings true. Xavier was high-spirited and merry; he was impulsive and generous to a fault; he was rather vain and ambitious; but he was certainly not frustrated—despite his indigence. And after having spent three years in a metropolis that stood at a crossroads of Europe, after having studied in a university in which learning meant more than the ability to pass examinations and thought more than the acquisition of information, it is not likely that he was so naive as to identify Inigo with the loss of that prosperity which the Xaviers had enjoyed before the wars of Navarre.

A more likely reason for Xavier's hostility towards the pilgrim—if there was any real hostility, for the earlier biographers make no mention of it—was Favre's reaction to Inigo. The new student, although almost twenty years older than his room companions, was far behind them in his studies; Favre undertook to coach him. The Savoyard was just then suffering from scruples and uncertainties of all sorts. Should he become a doctor, a lawyer, a master in one of the colleges? Should he get married and found a family? Should he become a priest and pastor of souls? Or should he, perhaps, abandon his studies altogether, fly the world, and live as a hermit? Being of a very reserved nature, Favre had found no one in whom he could confide. But after a few sessions spent helping the pilgrim, who was grateful for any aid in his wrestlings with Aristotle, the tutor came to think that here was a man to whom he might unburden himself. Inigo's very gaze invited confidences. Not for nothing did one who met him in 1535 attest, many years later before the canonization tribunal: "He had such a gracious way with everyone that each man said to himself 'Here is one who understands me.' . . . All in our town loved him." And another stated: "When anyone disclosed his mind to Ignatius, telling him of his faults and weaknesses, it was as though he robbed his heart, for from then on he was doubly fond of such a one and particularly interested in all his affairs."[18]

Before long the grind was interrupted while Favre told Inigo of his troubles. He was advised to make a general confession, and then to follow Inigo's plan of life—weekly confession and Communion, daily examinations of conscience, prayer and such penances as his confessor

148

might advise and which would not be detrimental to his health or his studies. Although Favre took his Licentiate examination in 1530, he did not "take the rock" until 1534; his delay was probably due to the difficulty in gathering sufficient money to defray the expenses connected with the final examination. As his services to Inigo can hardly have proved a lucrative occupation, it is to be hoped that he found some wealthier students weak in Greek and unable to grasp Aristotle.

In his *Memoriale*, Favre mentions that the pilgrim helped him in many ways and that he assisted him "to conquer the agitation his neighbor's defects caused him."[19] Father Brodrick observes truly that "the neighbor nearest to Favre and most likely to rile him was the man from Navarre." This indicates that Xavier's objection to Inigo was because of his spiritual zeal; there is no documentary evidence which suggests that Francis changed his room at the Ste. Barbe for some time after the prilgrim went to lodge there. In any case, an athlete of no mean repute in the playing fields like Xavier would have had little use for a forty-year-old scholar, already gone bald at the temples, too small for vaulting, and at a very obvious disadvantage for running, *pelota* playing, and javelin throwing—the four sports in which the other excelled. Handsome, sociable, fond of gaiety, popular not only on the *Pre-aux-clercs*—the meadows by the Seine where the students gathered for the sports and contests—but in the taverns and the halls, Francis had no intention of missing the masques and carnivals and fairs that succeeded one another in the round of the Paris year for "spiritual conversations" such as now engrossed his old friend Peter Favre and the newcomer to their room.

So the young man from Navarre continued to do the rounds of the town with the boys of Ste. Barbe. There were nightly expeditions after the lights had been doused and the doors locked and when the rector and beadles were safely in bed. Some of these roisterings meant a tour of the taverns; a dance in the *Devil's Pet* or the *Red Apple*; a chorus in the *Men-at-Arms* or the *Brimming Goblet*; a fight with the Montaigu fellows in the *Wooden Sword*. When money was scarce, which was often, the penniless of the various colleges went about in droves, yelling appropriate nicknames when a band from another college or "nation" was encountered in a dark street. It was not a very scholarly pastime, but good fun and the cause of many a scrimmage between "the proud Spaniards, the fickle Bretons, the soft-as-butter Flemings, the mean, malicious Lombards, the drunken English, the mad and gluttonous Germans, the porridge-eating Scots and Irish, the cruel, tyrannical Sicilians, the Roman nail-biters—seething to start a row—the turncoat Picards, knaves, traitors, and fair-weather friends."[20]

Francis took part in these surreptitious excursions, in the battles waged first with tongues and then with fists and stones. He enjoyed the running and dodging from one dark corner to the next when the sergeants of the Chatelet—foot and horse—came at the cry of the Watch to run the tipsy, roaring students into one of the city prisons. Sometimes the scholars' nocturnal outings ended in antics far from innocent. Francis was to confess later the repugnance and terror he felt at sight of the diseases contracted by students and by a master "who accompanied and encouraged them"; fear, not love of virtue, kept him chaste and deterred him from the worst excesses of his "crowd." "But," adds Pere Dudon, "being somewhat bespattered from his contact with these scandals, and eager to follow the mirage of human glory towards which his imagination and ambition ever urged him, he was, unlike Favre, a long time before he would listen to Inigo telling the austere message of the Gospel."[21]

Though the pilgrim was not a first-rate scholar, he was a good judge of men. So he ignored Xavier's initial hostility and set out to "win him for God"—knowing that in Francis there were the makings of a wonderful "trumpeter of Christ." Thanks to the collections of the faithful Ines Pasqual and the alms sent regularly from friends in Flanders, he was able to tide Xavier over recurring financial crises. As Francis had a warm and generous heart and was really incapable of sustaining enmity against anyone, by degrees he was drawn into the conversation—made, for the time being, less spiritual for his sake.

Inigo could hold the other's interest; he had stayed with his relative, Don Diego of Alcala. He had travelled a great deal and had met people Xavier would have liked to know: the Emperor, the Doge of Venice, Vives, various cardinals, the pope, the Inquisitors, the French officers who had fought with Xavier's brothers at Pamplona, the pirate Doria, Saracens, and infidels of all sorts; he could tell of England and Flanders, of Rome and Jerusalem, of strange journeyings by land and by sea. At some stage in the talks—probably when Peter Favre went home to Savoy to bid farewell to his family before returning to Paris for his ordination, after which he was to join with Inigo in whatever enterprise the latter decided upon—Francis lowered his guard far enough to let the older man know of his ambitions: that benefice, the canonry in Pamplona Cathedral, which his brothers were trying to secure for him; the chair of philosophy in the Beauvais College.

The latter appointment had its hazards, as the fate of every new master was decided by the students. If they approved of him, all was well; they advertised him and fetched their friends to his classes and popularized him in every way; if that happened he was a made man. But it was not unknown for a master to be hooted and pelted off his rostrum, and there was worse still—sometimes students simply withdrew in silence, taking their unpaid fees with them, and the professor found himself speaking to the winter straw or summer grasses that carpeted his empty hall. No master remained once the scholars forsook him; if Francis went to the Beauvais, he would have to face the risk all new masters ran. . . . .

At this point Inigo intervened, telling him not to worry; when he got his Licentiate and began to teach, the pilgrim would see that he had students. He kept his word. When, soon afterwards, Xavier began to expound Aristotle in the Beauvais, Inigo was indefatigable in finding good students and fetching them along, until "soon he was in a strong position as a teacher of a numerous and intelligent class." The winning of Xavier took time and patience and prayer. Father Polanco writes: "I have heard out great moulder of men, Ignatius, say that the toughest dough—*la pasta mas ruda*—he ever handled was young Francis Xavier, in his first dealings with him."

"There is a story," says Fr. Brodrick, "repeated in all the biographies of Francis, from the first printed to the very latest, that Ignatius broke down his resistance by constantly dinning into his ear the text: *What shall it profit a man if he gain the whole world and lose his own soul?* Such a frontal method of attack is quite uncharacteristic of the great spiritual strategist to whom it is attributed, and not a shred of real evidence exists that he employed it at all. . . . . For seven months during the year 1533, Francis and Ignatius had the room at Ste. Barbe to themselves owing to the absence of Favre in Savoy, and it must have been then that the Basque fortress [of Xavier] hauled down its tattered flag and capitulated to the Basque besieger [of Loyola]."[22]

Between 1533 and 1534, Inigo had the happiness of seeing his little band of three double its numbers. Two young Spanish students came on to Paris from Alcala, not only to complete their studies but to get in touch with Inigo of Loyola whose fame had lingered in Alcala long after he had left that town's schools and prisons. One, Diego Lainez, was the son of a merchant of Jewish descent and had distinguished himself by taking his Master's degree with honors in Alcala at the age of twenty. His companion, Alfonso Salmeron, "who excelled at Greek and Hebrew," was the son of poor parents and came from that jewel among Spanish cities, Toledo. "They had hardly dismounted from their horses after the long ride to Paris when Inigo chanced to meet them." In the spring of 1534 both did the Exercises with the fervor native to the temperaments of old and new Castile, fasting completely for the first three days and continuing for two weeks on nothing but bread and water.[23]

Another volunteer who soon afterwards joined the ranks was Nicholas of Bobadilla. He was a poor but brilliant scholar of Valladolid and Alcala, and had been a master in the latter college; but he held the post only long enough to provide him with sufficient funds to proceed to Paris where he intended doing further study of languages. Besides being poor in worldly goods, he was also poor in health, which perhaps accounts for his slightly eccentric, outspoken manner. These disabilities, however, seem to have rather enhanced him in Inigo's eyes.

The fourth fruit of that vintage year was Simon Rodriguez, a young Portuguese student who had qualified for one of the fifty burses with which King John III of Portugal had endowed the Ste. Barbe. His strong character had some very human weaknesses which stood out in marked relief. He was something of a snob, one of those who "dearly love a lord"; his natural ability and charm of manner were offset by a certain irresponsibility and lack of discretion, coupled with a mulish streak of obstinacy; in later years he was to give Ignatius plenty of opportunity for storing up merit in heaven—through the exercise of patience, forbearance, and resignation in the "situations" Rodriguez seemed to have had a genius for creating.

In contrast to the previous Companions of Alcala and Salamanca, Inigo's Paris followers did not wear sackcloth, or go about begging. To all outward seeming, they were the same as the other students, except that they were not seen in the taverns or on the other pleasure jaunts. Favre did the Spiritual Exercises first, early in 1534; then the others, at different periods, Xavier being the last and most fervent of all. "He not only fasted severely but trussed his limbs up tightly, mindful of the pride he took in his former vaulting on the Ile de Paris; so tightly did he tie himself with ropes that he was unable to move and made the meditations thus trussed."[24]

During 1534 the seven held many discussions as to the future and how they might best "help souls." The six disciples had all emerged from the long retreat not only reformed and renewed, but aflame with zeal and resolved to unite with Inigo in whatever spiritual enterprise he might decide upon. But he did not decide alone; all seven voted on the matter and unanimously agreed to make vows of chastity and poverty, with a third vow—"to go to Jerusalem and labor there for the conversion of the infidels, unless some unforeseen impediment prevented them from doing so." If within a year this project proved unfeasible, they would go to Rome and offer themselves to the pope for the service of the Church, "to be sent anywhere the supreme pontiff wished, including lands subject to the Turks or other tyrants who hated the very sound of the word *Christian.*" In these phrases there is an echo of Inigo's own experiences in Palestine. The "unforeseen impediment" recalls the refusal of the Franciscan Superiors to allow the pilgrim of 1523 to remain in the Holy Places; the phrase "Turks and other tyrants" brings memories of the harsh treatment the pilgrims received from the gangsters who robbed and did violence to those who had paid them for protection.

Having determined the end—and the means—Inigo and his six companions made their way, at dawn on the feast of the Assumption, 1534, to Montmartre; there they crystallized their resolves by a solemn and formal, if private, dedication of themselves and their lives to God. Peter Favre had been ordained priest on May 4; when they reached the ancient chapel of St. Denis, about six hundred paces from the summit of the hill, they opened the door with the key given them by the Benedictine nuns of the abbey further down the hill and prepared the altar for Mass. Before receiving Holy Communion, each in turn pronounced his vows "in a loud voice," the celebrant making his vows last of the seven.

Although a tablet was afterwards erected claiming Montmartre as the birthplace of the Society of Jesus, the claim is not quite correct. No Order comes into being until it has received formal approval from the Holy See; in 1535 the companions had not yet asked or obtained ecclesiastical sanction. In September, 1539, Pope Paul III gave verbal approval and, a year later, formal canonical approbation for the new order. But certainly the idea conceived in the mind of Inigo stirred into life that morning at Montmartre; his Company was as yet in the womb of time, but it had form and being. The seven who came down the hill after the morning oblation were happy men. Sitting by a fountain on the hillside they enjoyed a frugal *agape*, bread spread with spiritual joy, water flushed with the wine of charity. There they spent the day, speaking of holy things, as

153

the heat haze of the August day lay on the great plain of St. Denis spread beneath and beyond them. They did not descend to the city and the student quarter until evening. "Then they returned, rejoicing as the apostles coming down from Olivet on the evening of Ascension Day."[25] Seven trumpets had been sounded for Christ.

... In Paris, Inigo suffered from gastric trouble which, by this time
[the winter of 1534-35], had become chronic. Every fifteen days he had an
attack that lasted for at least an hour and brought on a fever; once the attack lasted for sixteen or seventeen hours. He had now completed his
Arts Course, spent some years studying theology, and had also gained the
Companions. His malady went from bad to worse, none of the several remedies he tried doing him any good. Finally, the doctors told him that the
only course left to him, if he wished to be cured, was a sojourn in his native
air. The Companions too advised this, urging him strongly to go. . . . But
just as he was about to leave Paris, he heard that accusations concerning
him had been made to the Inquisitor of Paris; as no summons came, Inigo
went looking for the Inquisitor . . . and asked to be brought to trial.
                                        (Autobiography of St. Ignatius.)

    . . . He wished to stay in Azpeitia to satisfy in some measure for the
ignorance of his youth. . . .
            (Father Araoz—relative and contemporary of St. Ignatius.)

    . . . He went to his native place that he might give some edification
there where he had formerly given scandal to so many. . . .
            (Chronicon of Father Polanco, Secretary to St. Ignatius.)

    . . . And he told his brother, who was insisting that he should leave
the hospital and go stay in the Casa-Torre, that he had not come there to
be invited to the Casa, nor to reside in palatial houses, but to sow the word
of God and to give the people some understanding of the enormity of
mortal sin. . . .
    (Evidence of Andres de Oraa of Azpeitia at the Canonization Enquiry,
    August, 1595.)

I NIGO'S continuous and rigorous penance, and the demands made
   on his energies by his studies—commenced, as they were, so late in
life—undermined his once strong constitution. He visited doctors, tried
many remedies, but all in vain. He grew steadily worse until, finally, the
verdict was pronounced that unless a sojourn in his native air cured him
nothing could do so. The alarmed Companions begged him to follow the

physicians' advice; besides, they added, when in Spain, after having rested and recruited his strength, he could go on to visit the families of Xavier, Lainez and Bobadilla to "arrange their affairs." All that would take some time, but they would meet him again in Venice, to which city they would proceed when the last of the band completed his finals in 1538. Inigo could go on to Venice when he had fully recovered and had discharged the business in regard to his Spanish followers' family affairs. When the others reached the city on the Adriatic, their leader would probably have all in order for the projected pilgrimage to Palestine.[1]

Putting their funds together, they bought him a *quartago*—a pony or a medium-sized nag. Inigo, though of a build that tended to grow stocky with the years, had not yet recovered from the loss of weight which resulted from the seven years' severe fasting that followed his conversion; his subsequent seven years as a poor student in the Montaigu and the Ste. Barbe had not made him any heavier, so the chestnut pony was adequate to the burden and stouthearted enough for the 550-mile journey that lay ahead. This nag will be heard of again in 1552, enjoying a pampered retirement. But before he went clattering away with his new master down the Street of the Dogs, there was an unwelcome delay.[2]

Someone had been busy laying information with the Inquisitor; rumors said that a trial was in the offing. Clearly, to leave Paris during the Lent of 1535, as had been Inigo's intent, would be to give the impression that he was a guilty man fleeing from justice. Having waited a few days for a summons that never came, the pilgrim went in search of the Inquisitor of Paris, the Dominican Father Lieven. He told Father Lieven of the rumors going the rounds, explained his reasons for the proposed journey to Guipuzcoa, and asked that the trial, if there had to be one, be expedited; he was a sick man, anxious to try the last hope offered him by the doctors, and he had Companions in Paris whom he did not wish to leave under suspicion because of their association with him. The Dominican made light of the accusation, but asked to see the *Exercises*; having read them, he professed himself pleased and edified. Deciding that this was an opportune moment to get official guarantees of his orthodoxy, the pilgrim fetched a public notary and "two or three masters for witnesses" to the Dominican convent in the Rue Saint Jacques and obtained a sworn statement attesting to his faith and morals. Polanco adds:

"On this occasion the Inquisitor praised the *Exercises* (about which controversy had arisen) and asked Inigo if he might have a copy of them for the profit of his own soul."[3]

Easter fell on March 28 and Inigo, cleared with the Inquisitor, set off alone for home some day during Easter week. "While on the journey his health began to improve." It is possible, from various documents, to get a fair idea of the outward appearance and bearing of this man of forty-four, riding south from Paris on his "little chestnut nag."

Not very tall; white skinned, with a high color in his cheeks. He was genial looking, if somewhat serious. He had beautiful blond hair but was going bald on the temples and forehead. . . .

A little bit of a Spaniard, slightly lame, with joyful, lively eyes.

He was of medium height; perhaps it would be more correct to describe him as on the small side and short-legged though all his brothers had been tall, well-built men. His face was that of one bearing authority and responsibility. His forehead was broad and smooth, though bearing the traces of wrinkles; his eyes were sunken and their eyelids shrunken and wrinkled because of the tears he so often shed. He had medium sized ears, and his nose was high and curved; his color was inclined to be high; in his later years his baldness gave him a venerable aspect. His expression was joyfully grave and gravely joyful, so that his serenity rejoiced those who beheld him while his gravity calmed them. He limped a little on one leg but was not deformed, and he walked in so careful a manner that it was hardly noticeable. His two feet were all calloused, severely so, having gone for such a long time barefoot and walked so many journeys.

He allowed his beard to grow fairly long; later in life, when he went to live in Rome, he trimmed it shorter; his portraits show how he kept it.

In contrast to his lack of inches he was inclined to bulkiness of chest and torso. He must have possessed a wonderful constitution and enjoyed great health and strength when young, for the fact remains that, in his mature years, though weakened by fasting and suffering from chronic stomach and liver ailments, he nevertheless put on weight easily. . . . His face was not long, as some painters have portrayed him, but short and round; his chin was the shape of a shield.[4]

This was Inigo, jogging through France in April, 1535. Thirteen years had passed since he left the *Casa-Torre* for Montserrat and Jerusalem. His brother Martin Garcia and Dona Madalena were both alive and well, their family of four sons and five daughters now grown to manhood and womanhood. Pero Lopez, the priest of the family, had died at Barcelona in 1529 as he was returning from a journey to Rome. Since the letter brought by Martin Saez from Alcala in 1526, little was known of Inigo in Loyola until a letter was received from Paris six years later. In this letter, still preserved, the writer referred first of all to family matters; he congratulated a niece—probably on her marriage; he advised Martin Garcia to send the son who was to receive higher education to Paris rather than to Salamanca—a student would gain more by four years in Paris than in six years or longer elsewhere. "In all Christendom there are not such educational facilities and helps as are to be found in Paris." Fifty ducats a year should cover the boy's expenses, but Don Martin should not be stingy. The letter continues:

> If he is coming here, you would be wise to send him about eight days before the term opens on October 1. I will do all I can to help him apply himself to his studies and to keep him from wasting his time and his virtue. . . .
> . . . You say that you are surprised at my long silence and glad that you have at last heard from me. There is nothing to marvel at. A great wound requires different treatment and dressings when raw and bleeding, when beginning to heal, and again when nearly healed. In the same way, at the beginning of my road, I needed one remedy; later, different ones; any of them might have been harmful if applied at the wrong time.[5]

Giving reasons for his silence, he cites, firstly, his studies and "many conversations, though not on worldly matters"; secondly, his newly acquired habit of judging all actions by their capacity for adding to the greater glory of God and "procuring the good of souls," which habit led him to decide that letters to his family would neither increase God's glory nor contribute much to the conversion of the Loyolas. He has something to say on the subject of divine and human love:

> . . . In this life I no longer find myself able to love anyone, only in so far as it helps to make God better served and praised; for he who

loves anything for its sake or his own sake does not love God with all his heart. . . .

In this life men lose sleep, are anxious and worried about amassing this or that; they want bigger houses, larger incomes, higher social status; they wish to make a great name for themselves in their countries and localities so that people will speak of them after they are dead. It is not for me to condemn such, but neither do I commend. For, according to St. Paul, a man should use the things of this world as though he used them not; possess them as though he owned them not; and even, having a wife, be as though without one. . . . For the manner of this world lasts, for oh, so short a time. . . . I beg you, for the love of God Our Lord, work with might and main to gain treasure in heaven; win a great name there and strive to live in the memory of Him who must one day judge us.

For he has given you full and plenty in this world, that through these worldly goods you may gain eternal riches. Give good example to your children, servants, and relatives—a pious word to one, a just rebuke to another (but without violence or anger); giving this one favor in the home, the other one money and farms; do much good to poor orphans and all in need. Don't be close-fisted with what the Lord has given you in so openhanded a manner. Our rest and happiness in the next life depends on how much of good we do in this. In the Iraurgi you have plenty of opportunity for doing good, so for the love of Our Lord Jesus Christ bestir yourself, not only to think in this wise but to desire and to do. To those who desire, nothing is difficult, above all in what they undertake for love of Our lord.

Remember me to the lady of the *Casa* and to all the family, and to all who you think would like me to send them a remembrance; tell them to commend me to the Lord who has to judge us. . . . So I remain, praying that His great and infinite goodness may give us the grace to know His most holy will and to accomplish it in full.

The Year 1532.   Poor in goodness—Inigo.[6]

In the third week of April, 1535, exciting news was brought to the *Casa-Torre* of Loyola by Juan of Eguibar, a son of Errazti the smith and Maria Garin. Juan was a sutler, doing good business selling victuals and other merchandise to the armies on both sides of the Franco-Spanish border. He had been to a fair in Bayonne, about thirty miles northwest of Loyola. On his return journey, rather than cross the lonely pass of

Behobia after dark, he decided to stay overnight at an inn halfway up the pass, a house six miles from any human habitation. He had often stayed there and was made welcome; on this occasion the innkeeper and his wife had surprising news for him. He would have company for the night; not only that, but his companion was from the Iraurgi; they did not think that anyone from Juan's locality except the dealer himself had ever stayed at their inn before; but just an hour before, an Iraurgi man had ridden in from France. The smith's son was frankly incredulous. Who on earth could be coming from France to the Iraurgi?

So wishing to see who the traveler was, he went with the inn-keeper's wife and put his eye to a slit in the door of the room where the stranger was. And there he saw Inigo of Loyola on his knees praying. He recognized him at once and rode posthaste to Azpeitia and gave the news to all Inigo's family and relatives.[7]

In the morning Inigo set off alone to cross the Pyrenees—not knowing that his foster brother had spied on him, recognized him, and was gone posting to Loyola with the news of his coming. On a lonely stretch of road, a place much frequented by robbers, he saw two armed men riding toward him. The riders, Inigo on his tired nag, the others on fast horses, met and passed; before long the pilgrim heard the others wheel their mounts and ride along at his heels. He "felt a little afraid," but, never lacking in courage, drew rein, turned in the saddle, halted the men and demanded their business. They replied that they were serving-men of Don Martin Garcia of the *Casa-Torre* of Loyola and had been given orders to scour the mountains between the Iraurgi and the pass of Behobia until they found their master's brother; having found him they were to give him safe escort to the *Casa-Torre*.

Inigo declined the escort. He must have sent the men back to Loyola, for the next to meet him was a priest, Don Baltasar. He also had been sent by Martin Garcia "to see if the traveler were really Inigo and, if so, to accompany him the rest of the way." But the traveler was strangely uncooperative and asked Don Baltasar to ride on ahead. When the priest demurred, Inigo flatly declared that if he were not allowed to complete his journey alone, he would return the road he had come; to this Don Baltasar replied that, if Inigo did so, he himself would ride with him to France. Eventually a compromise was reached, Don Baltasar agreeing to ride a certain distance ahead while the brother of the lord of Loyola

160

followed on the chestnut pony. But at some point on the way Don Baltasar, looking back, saw that Inigo was no longer riding behind. The good man got flustered and put spurs to his mount, either riding back towards Behobia or on towards Loyola. Meanwhile the *quartago* was trotting steadily down a side road little better than a bridle path, bearing Inigo to his destination—which was not the *Casa-Torre*, for he had decided to stay in the hospital for the poor at Azpeitia.[8]

The first biographers of St. Ignatius translated the words "aforesaid priest" (meaning Don Baltasar) wrongly, rendering it as "many priests"; later writers exaggerated the error, and painters and stained glass artists helped to perpetuate it, until today, even in the *Santa Casa* of Loyola, the homecoming of Inigo is depicted as something it was not. There is absolutely no foundation for the story that a great gathering went out to meet him: his family, nobles on horseback, priests walking in processional order, and every man, woman and child in Azpeitia bringing up the rear. According to the evidence of the witnesses for the canonization, his arrival was almost unnoticed. The Loyolas did not know about it till next day, when Catalina of Eguibar rushed to the *Casa-Torre* to tell of how she went to give alms to a beggar at her door and recognized him as Inigo, "who had been reared in her mother's home." There is plenty of evidence that his family were at first both angry and humiliated to find him in the beggars' hospital and to hear that he was begging in the streets of Azpeitia. Local tradition singles out a farm in a shady mountain defile at which he called, having lost his way on the mule tracks that crisscrossed the slopes. He was put on the track for Azpeitia, a few miles further on. He certainly did the last stretch of the journey alone.

He came one Friday, about five in the evening, to the hospital of the Magdalen in Azpeitia and stayed there, lodging with the poor, and neither his relatives nor other noble persons of these parts could persuade him to go to the *Casa* or to an inn or any lodging but the hospital.[9]

The town had two hospitals, St. Martin's and the Magdalen. If the former attracted the soldier, the latter attracted the penitent come to "give some good example where formerly he had given scandal to so many." Both were outside the walls of Azpeitia, but the Magdalen was the older and poorer of the two; it was also the farthest from the *Casa-*

Torre, being three hundred paces to the northeast of the town. It was administered by one Don Pedro and his wife, "leading citizens who, not being in any need themselves, undertook for the love of God the care of the Magdalen hospital, which was always thronged by many poor people both from the district and other areas."

> And there Inigo lodged, although his brother Martin Garcia of Loyola and others . . . remonstrated with him; nor would he change to an inn even when they begged him to do so, telling him how badly it looked for a Loyola, a son of the Casa-Torre family, to lodge in the beggars' hospital, and how undecorous it was for him to go about begging—he who came of the family who should give the alms, not ask them. And he stayed in the hospital for three months, treating himself with great severity and begging from door to door, but not for himself; whatever he got by begging or by gift—for many devout persons sent him abundant alms—he divided among the beggars in the hospital, sitting with them at their table, eating with them, and dividing his food with them; he gave in all things a great example of humility, poverty and patience, being a man truly spiritual and holy.[10]

He began begging the very morning after his arrival and, as has been seen, Catalina of Eguibar was not long about letting the family in the Casa know that Inigo had come and was living as a beggar, sleeping and eating in the Magdalen and begging from door to door. "And this was a thing felt keenly by his relatives, especially his brother." The news spread like wildfire through the valley, from farm to farm and from smithy to smithy. The Captain, Inigo de Loyola, who had been injured at Pamplona, and whose conversion of life had been a nine days' wonder some thirteen years before, was now back; and not in his home but in the Magdalen hospital.

All in Azpeitia, the witnesses say, "were full of admiration for that gallant lad and vain" of other days, now returned to them in so different a guise. A poor brown robe replaced the bright clothes of the courtier; he no longer carried arms but went about begging and explaining "the infinite malice of a mortal sin"; he who had hitherto ridden on a fine horse or mule, caparisoned with the colors of Castile or Najera, now went "barelegged with rope-soled sandals," to the amazement and edification of all. But Don Martin was extremely annoyed; having failed in his attempts to get Inigo to change his lodgings, he sent him a present of a bed.

Several witnesses relate that the recipient of this gift never slept in it. If "by reason of the many attacks of illness he suffered while in Azpeitia," he agreed to leave off sleeping on the floor for a night or two, he would sleep in a bed no different from the beds of the other beggars.

In a letter written in 1595, a niece of St. Ignatius related the following incident:

> One day he [Inigo] asked our father [Martin Garcia] to send him a little wine. I, then a little girl, was sent to take it to him. When I came to the room where he lodged in the hospital, he asked me to do him the favor of bathing his shoulders with it. They were in a pitiable and swollen state from much scourging, in fact they seemed to me to be gangrenous. But I saw them only on that occasion for he did not wish me to come again.[11]

Besides his example of poverty, humility, patience, and mortification—atonement for the example he had formerly set the little town—he began gathering first the children, then their elders, for religious lessons. Don Martin took umbrage at this and came again, trying to dissuade him, telling him that "no one would come at his call." Whereat Inigo replied that if only one child came he would be well employed. The instructions became so popular that every child in Azpeitia was to be found that summer sitting in the Magdalen hospital listening to this unusual teacher. Soon the grownups began to come too, until it was necessary for the catechist and his huge class to go into the open air, as the hospital could not hold all who came. And sometimes, at the edge of the crowd, could be seen the tall figure of the lord of the *Casa-Torre*, listening to the simple but profitable instructions.

Some of those same children testified with pride at the 1595 Enquiry: "I learned what I know of my religion from Padre Ignacio." One said, "He used to teach the prayers and the commandments and he often examined me, to see if I knew them." The catechism sessions sometimes had their distractions:

> One day he was teaching Christian doctrine and was examining a crowd of children and young people in a church in this town, when two sons of Margie Gabiria were being examined; they had a bit of a stammer or impediment and used to pronounce their words incorrectly; and Marina Saez from Arana laughed too much at this and

Ignacio stopped the lesson, turned to her, and told her that if she laughed at those boys again he would put her up instead of them and ask her every question, to see how much she knew.

Another day he was examining an overgrown fellow and the lad made a mistake when answering and all the crowd laughed at him; whereat Ignacio reproved them much and said that he would put them up and give them the hardest questions he had and soon it would be seen how much *they* knew. And though I was often present, never after that day did I see similar conduct; instead, all were quiet and attentive, and never laughed or caused disorder in the class; and everyone tried to commit to memory all Ignacio taught.

I was there [says another witness] one day when he examined a young lad, an iron-worker, and some laughed as the boy was rather ugly, being squint-eyed. Ignacio stopped the lesson and took the lad's part and scolded them. And the boy [son of Errazti, who worked in his father's smithy], persuaded by Ignacio and his teaching, got the wish to become a priest; and the said Martin became a good Mass priest, very exemplary and a great confessor in after days.[12]

The man who was supposed to be in his native air to recuperate and build up his health was teaching daily in the Magdalen, often speaking for three hours at a stretch; every Sunday and holiday the local priests invited him to give catechism lessons in the church where he had been baptized. As his fame spread the crowds increased, coming in great numbers not only from the valleys of Guipuzcoa, but from Navarre and Viscaya and provinces even more distant. People climbed walls and trees, and at the hospital windows groups gathered to look out on the crowds and on the man who had drawn them. It was remarked that although he looked poorly and had ordinarily a thin, delicate voice, when giving the homilies every word he said could be heard "far away down the road."

You could hear every word he said, even at three hudnred paces away. . . . The crowds were so dense that the fields by the Magdalen were filled and the grass and briars withered from being trampled on. . . . To be out of the crowds I stayed in the hospital corridor and a wonderful thing it was to hear this man, who every other day had a fever, speaking daily from noon to three without ceasing . . . From Ascension to Pentecost he took a commandment for each of the ten days and gave us an instruction on it. He said such things and spoke in such a manner that many in the crowds who came made great reforms in their lives.[13]

The witnesses from Azpeitia at the 1595 Canonization Enquiry who had been actually living in the town in the summer of 1535, and who had seen and heard Inigo, gave evidence regarding cures. In every case, if asked to bless a sick or otherwise afflicted person, Inigo would always say, "I am not a Mass priest," but would make the sign of the cross on the forehead of the sufferer. Two cases of possession were recorded: one an epileptic among the hospital beggars, another a woman from Viscaya who had been possessed for four years and who was brought all the way by four men of her province. In each case there was an immediate cure.

A fishwife from Zumaya, wasting away of a *tisica*, heard of the wonders being worked in Azpeitia and came and listened to his sermons for two days before deciding to approach to ask Inigo to pray God to cure her. When she made her request, she was told that he was no priest; but he prayed for her and signed her forehead with a cross, and she went home. In less than three weeks she was back, completely cured, and bringing "fresh fish and oranges and gifts in a basket." One can imagine the swirl with which she swung the fish basket from her head to the ground, her arms as strong now as any of the Zumayan fishwives, delighted to show her gratitude in a practical way. Inigo did not want to take the gifts but neither would he hurt her feelings, so he told her to go around to the plaza and sell all she had brought and give the money to the poor. But she had already given alms in thanksgiving, and told him so, "imploring him to accept the presents she had brought him." So he took all, and there was a fine supper in the hospital that evening.

Though the witnesses did not attest to very many or very remarkable cures, they all remembered other healings, no less wonderful, particularly the reconciliations Inigo effected among the estranged. He seems to have had a special gift for patching up quarrels between married couples and between fathers and sons. Most of the rows between the husbands and wives were because of some local girls of the town, three in particular, who were the scandal of the Iraurgi. The trio came to listen to the sermons and were suddenly converted, "quitting the occasions which had made them what they were." Not only were they converted, but they decided to go on pilgrimage to Rome and Jerusalem as an act of penance. One died on the pilgrimage; the witnesses in 1595 could not remember what became of the second; but the third, fittingly named Madalena, had "the joy and good fortune of seeing and speaking with Padre Ignacio in Rome" on her way back from Jerusalem. In early 1539 she returned to Azpeitia, the proud bearer of a letter for the *Casa-Torre*. Madalena ever afterwards led a good life "though she had before that been the cause of contention between many of the couples reconciled by Inigo."

One day a visitor came to the hospital to see the pilgrim. It was his sister-in-law, Dona Madalena from the *Casa-Torre*, come to beg him to visit his home. Excusing himself on the plea of tiredness, he said he would go another day. She seemed particularly anxious that he should go that day; it was her nameday, the feast of the Magdalen, July 22. She asked him again "for the sake of the souls of his parents and forefathers" to return with her; but he replied as before.

> And then going on her knees, Dona Madalena prayed him for the sake of the Passion of Our Lord Jesus Christ to go to the *Casa* of Loyola. To this he replied, saying "How well you know how to ask me! For love of Our Lord's Passion I will go to Loyola; aye, and even to Vergara and all [the relations]." So that night he went to the *Casa-Torre*; but he returned to the hospital at a very early hour the following morning; and it was common property that although a bed had been made ready for him in his home, he did not sleep in it.[14]

There was more in Dona Madalena's insistence that Inigo should come to Loyola than the natural desire to receive her brother-in-law once again in the house of his birth. All was not well in the *Casa-Torre*; either Martin Garcia or one of his four grown sons needed admonition just as much as the sinners who came to hear the sermons in Azpeitia. The will of the head of the household, made in 1539, in which he acknowledged three natural children, has made Martin Garcia the suspect in Polanco's reference:

> Each night a certain man in that house was visited by his paramour; on the occasion of Inigo's visit to the *Casa*, he (Inigo) waited for and admitted her and drew that woman from her sinful ways.[15]

166

A Father Tablares relates that the saint had once mentioned this incident to him.

> He told me that when he went back to his country, being in the house of his family, he knew that one there was cohabiting with a woman not his wife, admitting this woman secretly each night to the house. He (Ignatius) waited and, intercepting her, asked "What brings you here?" And she told him all that went on. He took her to the apartment made ready for himself and putting her in there remained on guard so that she might not go sinning.[16]

At the first glimmer of dawn he set the prisoner free. This incident occurred on July 22. Before sunrise next morning the lord of Loyola's brother was back in the hospital and the *Casa-Torre* knew Inigo no more. He was nearing the end of his stay in Azpeitia, and he was leaving behind him a changed town. Even the Franciscans, the parochial clergy, and the Isabelitas had patched up their long-standing differences; Inigo got them to sign a little concordat, to which he was one of the signatories. The Town Council drew up a list of rules concerning the administration of the local charities; in the clear-cut phrasing and methodical divisions there are traces of the mind that planned and drafted the *Exercises*. An interesting point is that a means test featured in the regulations; the alms given—in many cases by people who worked from dawn to dark to earn an honest livelihood—were not to be squandered on the work-shy or on plausible strangers who made a good living by exploiting the charitably-minded and—cuckoo-like—lived on Azpeitia while the local orphans and sick poor went in need. Such vagrants were to get short shrift.[17]

Before he left Azpeitia, Inigo signed a document renouncing his claim to the Loyola estates; he made over his share of the patrimony to Don Martin to defray the cost of erecting a bell and endowing a fund to pay bell ringers. It was to be rung at noon each day, to remind all who heard it to kneel and say a *Pater* and *Ave* to obtain the grace of repentance for all who were in the state of mortal sin, and another *Pater* and *Ave* to ask the grace of perseverance for all who had repented of past sin. The bell was to be hung in St. Sebastian's church and, when it rang out daily at noon, the *frailas* in charge of the various hermitages in the valleys and mountains were to ring their small bells. This daily tolling came to be known as "the sinners' bell." Martin Garcia, in his will, left an annuity to pay the various bell ringers. "I had the intention," he wrote, "of leaving another memorial of my brother, Inigo, but this seems best to me."

The pilgrim not only helped that unprepossessing candidate for orders, Martin Eguibar, on his way to the priesthood; he obtained a very much desired grace for another of his foster brothers, Juan of Eguibar, the man last heard of posting from Behobia to be first to Loyola with the news of Inigo's homecoming. Juan and his wife had no heir, all their children having been stillborn; though—thanks to Juan's profitable business with the French and Spanish armies—they were comparatively well off, they grieved very much over their childlessness. When Inigo appealed for alms for the poor of the hospital and the district, this couple was among his most generous helpers: "They were the very first to come to his aid, being obliged, as it were, to make the poor their adopted children." And early the following year, "they had their reward for their alms given to Inigo for the poor; that which they lacked, they got, *Laus Deo!*"[18] Thus the town scrivener, Aquemendi, one of a family traditionally at enmity with the Loyolas. In connection with this anecdote it is noteworthy that even today childless couples, not merely from nearby localities but from the farthest ends of Spain, come to Loyola to ask St. Ignatius to intercede for them with God that they may be blessed with children; and it is not unusual to see a father and mother with an infant back at the shrine on a pilgrimage of thanksgiving.

Azpeitia was indeed a changed place. Swearing had ceased; the dishonest had given their ill-gotten goods to the rightful owners; the gamblers had been so completely converted that the Urola was strewn with packs of cards and every millrace cluttered with playing cards, dice, and all the other paraphernalia of the local games of chance. The girls who went about "wearing yellow veils and red caps, just like decently married women, and who were so lost to shame that they did not mind saying that they had covered their heads for so-and-so—though all knew their real relations with the said men, some of whom were married and some even clerics—mended their ways after hearing Inigo's sermon on the subject." Everyone remembered that occasion, for the preacher was perched in a cherry-tree.

During his stay in the Iraurgi, Inigo spent much time with the local clergy. Though his brother Pero Lopez was dead, another Loyola, Andres, was among the priests of Azpeitia. "And he (Inigo) counselled those priests who had allowed themselves to be diverted from the obligations of their office, so that there was a wonderful change in the clergy of that town."

He certainly had made generous returns to his native parish for the bad example he had given there in other days. Besides winning souls he won all hearts.

People used to try and touch his clothes, for they held him in much devotion and esteemed him as a saint. . . . The love and esteem in which he was held and the veneration for his holiness and virtues increased daily. . . . He had such a gracious way with all, that each one thought, "Here is a man who understands me"; and so holy was he that all obeyed him and would do willingly as he asked them, so that at that time all in Azpeitia was ordered for the service of God and the peace of the people. . . . He was thought as perfect and holy as though he had come from heaven; and it was as if an Apostle should come among the people, they respected and honored him so, following him about to hear him teaching and giving homilies. . . .

. . . Always in Azpeitia his name will be held in love and devotion and good will. . . . Everyone loved him.[19]

The kindly nature of Inigo is nowhere more clearly delineated than in that one little phrase, "Everyone loved him." Hence, when he announced that he was leaving, there was general consternation. No more crowds; no more talks; no more cures; no more conversions! Above all, no more meetings with Inigo, whom everyone loved. The fathers of the town council were sent to ask him to remain; they did so, pointing out the wonderful results of his three months' stay among them. What could Azpeitia and Guipuzcoa not expect if he would consent to stay indefinitely? But he said that "in Azpeitia he was in the world, and he could not serve God as he ought while in the world, and as he could do elsewhere." One valley, one parish, one town, one province, even one nation, could not satisfy the zeal of a heart dedicated to the greater glory of God; the world was too small for the man who wished to establish the kingdom of Christ in every place and in every heart. He had sounded a trumpet in one green valley; he had to cross the crest of the Pyrenees and let all Christendom hear the reveille.

He decided to go away on foot as a poor man. Don Martin took this decision badly and as an affront to himself; he insisted so strongly that Inigo, always willing to yield to another in things of no great importance, consented to go by horse to the frontier of Guipuzcoa, not very far from Loyola. Before he left, wishing to please Don Pedro and his wife, the administrators of the hospital, for their charity to him, he left them the little chestnut nag on which he had ridden from Paris. And "for years afterwards the same nag was for all there a constant reminder of its owner."

In 1552, Father (later Saint) Francis Borgia and Father Ochoa, who were on a visit to Azpeitia, wrote to St. Ignatius in Rome.

> ... And from Loyola we went to the hospital of the Magdalen where Your Paternity had lodging when you came to Azpeitia; and indeed we have enjoyed ourselves in the Lord, lodging in the same house, and especially Padre Francisco (Borgia) who ate at your little table and in the same room where you used to sleep.... And we found too the same chestnut nag which Your Paternity left at the hospital over sixteen years ago. He is very fat and very well, and to this day is of much service to the hospital fold. He is the most privileged being in Azpeitia, and can wander at will, even among the wheat fields, without anyone pretending to notice him. And Padre Francisco says of him: *Respexit Dominus ad Abel at munera eius.* ("God had respect to Abel and his offerings.")[20]

Even the saints' nags find their rewards!

The date of departure is not recorded, but it was about the end of July or early August. Before leaving Spain he had errands to do.

> Recovering from a grave illness, he wished to despatch the business entrusted to him by the Companions, so he determined to set off without money. But his brother was much opposed to this, saying that it was a shame for him to want to go on foot; and at last the pilgrim consented to the extent of going on horseback as far as the border of the province, his brother and relatives accompanying him.[21]

Then he set off walking, retracing the road to Pamplona, the same road over which the French litter-bearers had jolted him when carrying him home wounded in 1521. He had left Loyola for good; behind to the west was the old stone keep, the home of his fathers, wherein he had fought—more bravely than in the wars—his first fierce encounters with the world, the flesh and the devil; the Iraurgi saw his most notable spiritual victories; there he force-marched his soul on its first rapid advances in the way of holiness; and his last visit to that pleasant valley of his childhood had seen him exercise a brief but intensive apostolate, the fruits of which were abundant, valuable, and lasting.

In Obano, fourteen miles from the capital of Navarre, lived one of Xavier's brothers, Juan. As Inigo neared the walls of Pamplona he could have noted the spot where the cannon ball struck him in 1521. He could have gone through the very street down which he had once chased with drawn sword the men who had inadvertently jostled him when passing by. But he says not a word of his visit: simply, "He went to Pamplona." The captain he went to visit, Xavier's brother, had fought against him during the wars in which he was lamed; this Navarrese captain had married an heiress. There is no mention of Inigo's having gone on to interview the head of the family, the older brother Miguel, in the little castle of Xavier, thirty miles further north; nor is there any indication whether the missive he brought from Francis was addressed to Miguel or to Juan.

In the letter Xavier tells his brother of how badly off he is; of how deeply indebted he is to Inigo, "who has often helped me with money and friends and often preserved me from bad company"; and he endeavors to reassure his family that the reports they heard of Francis from "some vicious and mean fellows" are not true. If Francis had those talebearers, he would give them what they deserved; he had been associating with some heretics, but, "now that these people have been brought to light in Paris, I would not for the world have anything to do with them." He thanks Inigo for all the good that has befallen him and, again mentioning his dire fianacial straits, implores his brother to send him something by his friend. There is no record of how Inigo was received by Xavier's brothers.[22]

From Pamplona he went to Almazaran to visit the parents of Lainez; this meeting also goes unrecorded. When Peter Favre visited the same family six years later, he wrote telling Lainez that they could not have done more for him had they been his own parents, and he in turn loved them as though he had been their son. From Almazaran Inigo continued south, finally reaching Toledo, where he visited Salmeron's parents, "very poor but good and virtuous people." In Toledo was a friend of his early days in Paris, one of the first three whose conversion had been so complete as to cause a great tumult "especially among the Spaniards." He was a canon in the Cathedral. The meeting with him reminded Inigo to inquire about the former companions of Alcala and Salamanca; but "none of them was disposed to follow him." It would not have been Inigo's first time in Toledo; Velazquez and his household had often been there;

171

one wonders if during his visit in the autumn of 1535 he ever noticed a spirited youngster of eight playing in the streets of that city—young Pedro Ribadeneira, the future Jesuit and the founder's first biographer, was then a boy in Toledo.

There are documents which indicate that Inigo went on to Madrid. There he was fortunate in meeting again a noble lady, Leonor de Mascarenas, who had formerly befriended him in Alcala and who was now in charge of the Emperor's heir, Prince Philip. The future Philip II was then nine; on various occasions in later life he remarked, "I saw Ignatius; I knew him when he went dressed in a brown robe." Inigo did not delay in Madrid; he had gone there to find Arteaga, then with the court, but finding that the one-time companion had now no intention of becoming a "trumpeter of Christ," he wasted no further time but went on towards Valencia, hoping to get a passage there for Genoa. Near Valencia he detoured somewhat to visit the Carthusian monastery of the *Val de Cristo;* another of the three first Paris converts was there, the Bachelor of the Sorbonne, Juan de Castro. Inigo remained eight days with the sons of St. Bruno; years later, letters of friendship and brotherliness passed more than once between these Carthusians and the founder of the new company.[23]

> And his friends in Valencia wished to dissuade him from embarking for Genoa, saying that Barbarossa was on the sea with a great fleet of galleys. . . . But although they told him enough to strike fear into his heart, they did not make him change his plans.[24]

This reference to Barbarossa's great fleet of galleys suggests that the pilgrim reached Valencia earlier than October-November, 1535, the date generally accepted for his arrival at that seaport. By the autumn of 1535 the "great fleet" of almost four hundred fast galleys had been reduced to a mere fourteen small ships, and Barbarossa spent most of the time between mid-August (the date of his crushing defeat by the combined forces of the Emperor, the pope, the Portuguese, and Andrea Doria at Tunis) and the following spring in Algiers. There the old sea-wolf licked his wounds, for though his body escaped the thousands of steel blades ready to run him through at Tunis, his power and pride and prestige had received blows all but mortal. As Barbarossa was the all-engrossing topic of conversation for the peoples who lived along the Mediterranean coasts, from the Golden Horn right round to Gilbraltar, and as the septuagenarian sea-rover was only in the prime of his fighting life in 1535, St. Ignatius of Loyola will not take it amiss if at this point—where the histories of the Captain of Suleiman and Captain of God cross in time—a few minutes are devoted to the contemplation of Barbarossa and his career.

It is not quite correct to speak of Barbarossa as a pirate or corsair, as these terms were then nonexistent; besides, the sea-rover whose red beard gave him his nickname was far more than a Drake or a Bligh or a Blood. This Albanian who wrote his name in letters of blood and fire on the thirties and early forties of the sixteenth century—when everything had to be done on the grand scale or else not attempted at all—was the youngest of four brothers and had followed the sea from an early age. Heavily built, hook-nosed, fearless and cruel, he was a superb mariner and as a sea fighter and master strategist was unsurpassed in his time. The age-old enmity between the peoples on the northern and southern coasts of the Mediterranean became intensified after Granada, when Spain, under the regency and the direction of Ximenes, succeeded in establishing various strongholds on African soil. To all intents and purposes two-thirds of the Mediterranean was a Spanish sea, and one-third Venetian, since Genoa—as though exhausted after having, the previous century, presented Columbus to her lord, the sea—was in a state of decline. The smoldering resentment of the peoples of north Africa towards the Latins who had become sole masters of the Middle Sea finally expressed itself in bands of sea-looters, ruthless, cunning, and patient enough to master not only the mariner's and shipbuilder's craft but to study the Mediterranean, its coasts, its islands, its every mood. Of these sea raiders, Barbarossa was the most famous and most feared.

His crews said that he could smell a storm coming up; he could steer a ship through narrows and shallows where no mariner living could follow. He could hide and camouflage his galleys just as he could change the silhouette of a landscape or a town or a stretch of coastline overnight by leveling whole villages, or a mosque, with its domes and minarets, or a line of forts, to delude ships' masters far out to sea; when the latter, straining their eyes into the glare of the African sun for some well known landmark, found it missing, they usually altered course, ending up by sailing into Barbaross's trap. His enemies sought the sea-rover here, there, and everywhere but never found him, though he had a disconcerting knack of turning up when and where he was least expected. He seized the papal galleys and forced their crews to row to the tune his whips whistled as they fell unmercifully on the bare backs bent to the oars. With his underlings, Sinan and Beat-the Devil and the Fat Arab, he harried all western Mediterranean shipping and swooped on the coastal towns of Italy, France, and Spain, sacking and burning and massacring, carrying off the inhabitants wholesale. The women and children he sent to the slave marts and harems of Algiers and Barbary; the men were chained to the oars of the galleys where they were beaten to work and worked to death. The Genoese Admiral, Doria, under Imperial orders to bring in Barbarossa alive or dead, was a worried man, for though his galleys coursed the Mediterranean like greyhounds after a doubling hare, the elusive rover always managed to escape them.[25]

These were the tales the Valencians told Inigo of Loyola in the latter months of 1535. Barbarossa continued to be the scourge of the south for another decade. In 1546, after a brief retirement, he died full of years and crimes. On his grave above the mouth of the Bosporus his seamen raised a grey granite stone bearing an inscription in Arabic: *Dead is the Captain of the Sea;* and for many a year no ship rounded the Golden Horn without firing a salute to the memory of Redbeard.

But notwithstanding Barbarossa, Inigo embarked for Genoa sometime in the end of November, 1535. A tempest in which the rudder was broken all but wrecked his ship, and men who seldom prayed, prayed for a miracle. Inigo "examined his conscience and prepared himself for death, having neither fear because of his past sins nor dread of the condemnation they deserved, but being filled with great sorrow and confusion for not having employed well the graces and gifts God had given him."[26] The ship made Genoa safely, and he continued on foot to Bologna. He never saw Spain again.

PART III
Precious Metal

*. . . The nine Companions arrived in Venice at the beginning of
1537 . . . after two or three months they all set out for Rome to receive the
blessing of the Pope before going on to Jerusalem. . . .*

(Autobiography of St. Ignatius.)

*. . . Those who were not priests were ordained at Venice. . . . The
pilgrim resolved to wait a year before saying Mass, to prepare himself
and to ask Our Lady to get him a place with her Son. . . .   (Ibid.)*

INIGO walked from Genoa to Bologna; at one stage of his journey he
found himself on a high path running by the side of a deep river, probably the Reno. The path kept getting narrower until finally he found himself on a narrow ledge high above the water, unable either to advance or
retreat.

>He began creeping like a cat, being seized with a great fear be-
cause at every move he made he thought he was about to fall into the
river. This was the most exhausting and terrifying experience he
ever had. At last he got clear. But just as he was coming into Bologna,
he fell off a wooden footbridge; and when he dragged himself out, all
dripping and muddy, many passers-by laughed at him. Entering the
town he began to beg, but although he traversed Bologna from one
end to the other, he did not get as much as a farthing.[1]

Polanco says that "as it was winter and Lombardy a country of
much clay, he walked knee-deep in mud to Bologna . . . he stayed at the
Spanish College where he was made welcome and given clothes to wear
while he washed his own." This university town seemed the ideal place
to resume his theological studies. After a few days, a substantial sum of
money arrived from Isabel Roser of Barcelona; so as there was no further
need for him to beg, he prepared to attend the lectures, the term being not
too far advanced. But the climate tried him; the snows fell early, and from
the 10th to the 17th of December he was in bed with the old gastric trouble and bouts of ague. Early in 1536 he moved on to Venice, a town where
he had friends since the year of his Jerusalem pilgrimage. Isabel Roser—

now evidently recovered from the former financial setback to which Inigo referred in a letter to Ines Pasqual in 1533— follwed up the donation of twelve escudos sent to Bologna with a promise of future alms. A letter from Inigo to a Barcelona friend states: "She (Isabel Roser) also promises to send me in April sufficient to enable me to finish my studies . . . which I hope to complete in a year from this Lent."[2]

Venice had no university, but there was no dearth of learned men there, some of them theologians. To study the pilgrim added that work peculiarly his own, "giving the Exercises and engaging in spiritual conversations."Among those who did the Exercises was an Andalusian named Diego Hoces, who had known Inigo in Alcala.

And although he (Hoces) had a slight wish to do the Exercises, yet he did not do them straightaway. Having finally resolved to do them fully, he began them; but after three or four days he told the pilgrim that he had come to his retreat armed with many books to be able to refer to them, in case he found himself entangled in any deceits—for certain persons had put him on his guard against the Exercises, and he feared to find some taint of heresy in them. Hoces profited more than most from them, eventually becoming a Companion of the pilgrim. He was also the first (of the Company) to die.[3]

In fact, the Company of Jesus had not yet received official papal approval when Hoces' happy death took place in Padua in 1538. Although "swarthy and rather ugly looking," in death he looked so different a person that his companion "could hardly tear himself away from the entrancing sight of the dead man's countenance, and wondered that he felt no grief, only immense joy." That same day Ignatius was assisting at Mass in the Benedictine monastery of Monte Cassino and, at the words "and all the saints" in the Confiteor, "he saw Hoces all glorious among the blessed, a sight which gave him such consolation that he wept for very joy."[4]

A few letters written by Inigo from Venice during 1536 are of interest. The letter already mentioned, in which he refers to Isabel Roser's alms, was written to a James or Jaeger Cassador, a priest of German descent who was then Archdeacon of Barcelona and later became bishop of that diocese. He had on several occasions sent money to the pilgrim in Paris. Ignatius replies, in typical methodical fashion, to each of six points referred to in a letter of Cassador's. One point concerns an old friend, a rich merchant of Barcelona, gravely ill; the writer advises Cassador to help the sick man put himself in the proper spiritual dispositions and to settle his affairs, since he may not have long to live; "and there is no one from whom he will take such exhortation better than from yourself."

As he has no sons nor other near relatives for whom he is obliged in justice to provide, the best and wisest thing he could do would be to give to Him from whom he received all. . . . To leave legacies to friends for the upkeep of horses, dogs, hunting-packs, or for fine funerals and worldly pomp and show, is conduct with which I cannot agree. St. Gregory laid down two degrees of perfection: one, when a man leaves all that is his to family and relatives and follows Christ Our Lord; the other, which is better, when a man, leaving all, distributes what is his among the poor. You know the text: *If thou wilt be perfect, go and sell all thou hast and give to the poor.* I understand this to mean that it is better to give to the poor, when one has no poor relatives whose need is not as dire as that of the poor not related to one. But if one has relations as poor as the poorest, more should be done for them than others not related to one.[5]

Two letters which he wrote in June and September of the same year were to Sister Teresa Rejadell of a relaxed Benedictine convent. The first letter gives instructions for discerning the source of the various inspirations that motivate conduct. It also tells her how she may recognize scruples and is, in fact, a short commentary on and application of the rules laid down in the *Exercises* in connection with these matters. He counsels her to avoid false humility and excessive fear, to be on her guard against illusions, carefully sifting the thoughts and interior movements of the soul; he ends by giving rules to overcome the stratagems and wiles of the enemy.[6]

This letter is the first to be signed other than Inigo. Although the pilgrim was enrolled in Paris University as Ignatius, he was known in that city as Inigo de Loyola. Years later, in a letter to Francis Borgia, he refers to "the very special devotion and reverence I have or wish to have for that glorious saint, Ignatius of Antioch,"[7] whose feast he seems to have kept as his name-day or, as the Catholics of Spain still so charmingly put it, *el dia de mi Santo,* "my Saint's day." The devotion to this second patron, for whose name he relinquished the name he received in baptism, probably dated from the days of this convalescence at Loyola, when he read in the Golden Legend of St. Peter's second successor in the see of Antioch; the letter of the aged bishop, written to his flock while on his way to martyrdom in Rome, with its expression of the noble, generous, and holy spirit that animated the first Ignatius, would have touched similar chords in the heart of the later Ignatius, the converted captain of the house of Loyola. The words of the great martyr-bishop penned in the early years of the second century, have heartened and spurred many in the course of almost twenty centuries, but few found such an inspiration in them as did Inigo de Loyola:

> I would rather die [wrote Ignatius of Antioch] for Jesus Christ than rule the last reaches of the earth. My search is for Him who died for us. My love is for Him who rose for our salvation. You can do me no greater service than to suffer me to be sacrificed to God while the altar is still prepared and the victim ready. Thus forming yourselves into a chorus of love, you may sing to the Father in Jesus Christ that God gave the Bishop of Syria the grace of being transferred from the setting to the rising sun. . . . It is good to set, leaving the world for God, and so to rise in Him. . . . Suffer me then, please, suffer me to be thrown to the beasts; through them I can reach God. I am the wheat of Christ; let me be ground by the teeth of the wild beasts that I may become pure bread. . . . As I write to you, though I am still in the land of the living, my longing is for death. Desire has been crucified within me and no longing for anything material flames in my heart; instead, the unfailing fountains of living water spring up with each heart-beat and speak to my soul, saying: *Come to the Father! Come to the Father!* . . . Beg for me that, through the Holy Spirit, I may not fail. . . .[9]

It is little wonder that Ignatius took for his patron this saint whom God had called to meet the deadly danger of Gnosticism; he also adopted his motto: "My love is crucified." "Although," comments Father Rahner, "time and space separate them and although, speaking historically, they are far removed from one another, the same mystical insight inspires them; their fundamental ideas are identical and these latter are expressed in principles singularly parallel."[9]

In September, 1536, Ignatius writes to Sister Teresa again; he refers to her letter telling him that, although she sought spiritual advice from various persons, she had not been greatly helped. Ignatius agrees that the advice she had got was too general. "When an adviser is not specific, he understands little and helps less." He treats of mental prayer; if meditations in which the understanding is active leave one physically tired, he recommends as tranquillizing even for the body "those prayers which are regulated and restful, where the understanding rests instead of laboring, and all is done without effort either interior or otherwise." When one has determined to devote one's life, one's being, and all one's energies to God, the balanced mind in the healthy body are great helps to the promotion of God's greater glory. "The body in health can do much, but the ailing body—as well I know—cannot do very much."[10]

A life of a saint without references to his—or her—teaching on prayer would be as much of an anomaly as a life of a great painter containing no mention of his masterpieces. As this seems the most appropriate stage to refer to Ignatius' teaching on prayer, the following compendium, summarized from the writings of three authorities on the subject, outlines the main features of what Ignatius taught regarding prayer.[11]

The pith and core of his instruction on this all-important theme is that prayer—before all else—must permeate a man's entire life. Always and in all things God must be kept in mind, since "man was created to praise, reverence, and serve God Our Lord." To ensure that the will, in the decisions preceding the sequence of actions that make up each individual life, may always choose "that which most leads me to the end for which I was created," the whole being must be constantly orientated to God.

St. Ignatius has been accused of placing obstacles to the natural spontaneity of the soul in prayer; his methods have been described as too rigid for some and too complex for others; these criticisms almost always start from the premise that the saint's teaching on prayer is mainly embodied in the Exercises. It is true that in the Exercises at least five methods of prayer are listed and subjects for meditation are given; but as has been elsewhere stressed, the book of Exercises was never intended by its author to be a treatise on prayer or a book of meditations; it is a manual for the use of directors of retreats. Nevertheless, the final chapter, "The Contemplation for Obtaining Love of God"—which is in the nature of a climax and an epilogue to the thirty days' retreat—illustrates the fundamental Ignatian principle that the soul should strive above all to know and love God; this achieved, all other good will follow. The well known prayer from this Contemplation—

Take, O Lord, and receive all my liberty: my memory, my understanding, and all my will; all I have and possess. Thou hast given it all to me; to Thee, O Lord, I restore it: all is Thine; dispose of it according to Thy will. Give me Thy love and Thy grace, for this is enough for me—

echoes, says an Irish Jesuit commentator, "the *I live now not I but Christ liveth in me*" which in St. Paul represents the consummation of all his striving and suffering. It has its counterpart in the *Love and do what thou wilt* of St. Augustine, in the *to love and suffer* of St. Teresa, and kindred mottoes of St. Bernard, St. John of the Cross, and others.

In the case of any saint who founded or reformed an order, the practice and traditions of the order show more clearly than anything else that particular saint's teaching on prayer. So in the Jesuit *Constitutions* one finds the authentic Ignatian prayer.

He desires "to see all members of the Society animated with such a spirit that they do not find less devotion in works of charity and obedience than in prayer and meditation, since they ought to do everything for the love and service of God our Lord. . . . During their works and studies they can lift their hearts to God; and if they direct everything to the divine service, everything is prayer." He was not forming Carthusians, or Benedictines, or Dominicans, or Franciscans, but men who were to serve the Apostolic See "in a special way, under the standard of the Cross." His order was such a novel departure from accepted sixteenth century ideas of the religious life that the more traditionally minded, and even some very holy people, were greatly scandalized when the pope approved of an order that had no office in choir and showed other deviations from the rules and practice of the older orders. There is a parallel between the lightly armed, extremely mobile forces with which, on the military plane, *el Gran Capitan* made the Spanish army the envy of every monarch in Europe and the adaptable, untrammeled, spiritual militia which Inigo first visualized as "trumpeters of Christ," that force which was to hold itself in readiness for the reigning pontiff's every order and to undertake the most varied activities. For the life his followers were to lead, Ignatius was inspired to give a training in prayer which would give them the best possible preparation. He laid down the minimum time a Jesuit could allow for daily prayer, adding that this minimum could be added to by superiors "for souls do not all advance at the same pace"; in regard to the additional time permitted to prayer, account must be taken of devotion and of the varied circumstances of persons, times, and places.

Writing to the scholastics in Coimbra, he said: "Though study does not give you time for very long prayers, yet you can meet this desire by making of your work one long, continuous prayer, undertaking all for no other reason save the service of God." In a letter to Father Nadal he is more explicit still:

> Considering the studies they (the scholastics) have, except for daily Mass, one hour for prayer and examination of conscience, and weekly confession and Communion, they cannot have long meditations. Let them rather exercise themselves in seeking the presence of God Our Lord in all things and at all times, whether conversing, walking, looking, tasting, listening, thinking, in everything they do. For it is true that the divine Majesty is in all things by His presence, power, and essence. And this kind of meditation, which finds God in all things, is easier than that which raises us to more abstract divine things. . . . And if we dispose ourselves, this good practice will eventually bring us great visitations of Our Lord, though our prayers may have to be brief. . . . Let them often offer themselves and their studies and labors to God Our Lord, reflecting that we accept them for His sake and sacrifice our tastes in order to serve His Majesty by helping those for whom He died.[12]

Fusion of work and prayer was the main point stressed. Though no stranger to mysticism himself, he was reserved on the subject whenever he wrote concerning prayer. "He said little," writes Suarez, "concerning union with God and simple contemplation; he stopped at the frontiers of the contemplative and unitive life, for beyond that lie regions where the Holy Spirit should teach, not man." Only when he wrote to the recipients of spiritual graces akin to those he himself had received did he lift the veil of reserve with which he habitually veiled his own intense life of prayer. One of the most frequently stressed points in these letters is that prayer should be directed "not towards the obtaining of consolation for oneself but rather for light to know what God's will is in one's regard and for the strength to fulfill it." There is little of either rigidity or complexity in advice such as the following:

> Where your soul finds something to its liking, stop and taste and enjoy the food God has given you. Do not be anxious to proceed, though your whole time of prayer be taken up with that one

thought. . . . It is not words and ideas—however abundant—that satisfy the soul, but understanding and tasting interiorly those things meditated.[13]

Bonaventure, writing three centuries before, had told his Franciscan novices the same: "Once you have found Christ, cease your praying; rejoice with him whom you have been seeking." Earlier still Gertrude and Bernard, and after Ignatius, Teresa and later Francis de Sales, were to express similar advice in words slightly different. Teresa wrote "If you would make progress in prayer, remember that it is more important to love much than to think much; and love consists not in the extent of our happiness but in the firmness of our determination to try to please God."

It is true that most of St. Ignatius' advice regarding the higher states of prayer was given not as *general* instruction but in individual letters. This is understandable if it be remembered that he was contemporary with the *Illuminati* and had, in fact, at Alcala and elsewhere fallen under suspicion of being tainted with some of the errors of that sect. Side by side with the splendid generation of mystics that graced the Spain of his time and among whom he himself gets a high place, there sprang up several pseudo-mystics, the most notorious of whom was Madalena de la Cruz, a nun of Cordoba, the fame of whose sanctity drew crowds from all over the peninsula. When before her death in 1544 this *beata* confessed herself to be an imposter, her holiness a sham, the wonders which she had worked for almost four decades the effect of demoniac possession, there was no small reaction against mystics and teachers of mystical prayer. "There have been cases recently" writes St. Teresa to her Carmelites, "in which women have been subjected by the devil to serious illusions and deceptions." And when she herself went to found a Carmel in Medina del Campo, calumniators said, "Here's another Magdalena de la Cruz." It is correct to say that Ignatius was circumspect both as to whom and what he advised in the matter of mystical prayer; but it is clear from his writings, particularly his letters to souls of prayer, that he was not—as has been sometimes stated—a director opposed to infused contemplation, who advocated the ordinary ways to all and sundry.[14]

As regards his own personal prayer, the fragment of his spiritual diary which escaped the flames to which he consigned that journal and which covers the year between February, 1544, and February, 1545, affords ample proof, if proof were needed, that he had received the gift of infused contemplation similar in manner, if not in degree, to that granted St.

Francis of Assisi and St. John of the Cross. The triple attraction in the interior life of Ignatius was for the most Holy Trinity, for the Eucharistic sacrifice, and for "a loving service of God and souls"—his own generous nature, acted on by grace, spurring him to spend to the end the gifts and graces which he had so humbly received and so gratefully acknowledged.

Perhaps one of the longest passages written by St. Ignatius on prayer and on the gifts of mystical prayer occurs in a letter written to Francis Borgia in September, 1548. This letter, too long to quote in full here, shows the reverence of the writer for the working of the Holy Spirit in souls, and in it Ignatius—far from insisting that his is the only method of prayer—stresses the point that the paths by which souls go to God are many:

God sees and knows what is best for us; and being omniscient, He indicates the way we should follow. But even though we have the help of His grace, we often experience difficulty in finding the right road and may have to go some distance on several before we find the one that is really our road and begin to make some progress.[15]

Towards the end of 1536 the Companions, now nine in number, left Paris. Favre, in charge of the little group since Inigo's departure for Spain, had enrolled three further volunteers, all French—le Jay, Broet, and Codure, the two former being, like Favre, already ordained priests. All the nine had taken the Master's degree but had not completed the further courses which they were studying. Francis I and the Emperor being at war, feeling in Paris ran high against Spaniards. The Companions, knowing how wars tend to worsen as they lengthen, feared that the roads might be blocked and all frontiers closed if they waited longer. Despite the opposition of some friends in Paris and the persuasions of others, they made ready to leave for Venice. Inigo, who knew more about the hazards of war than any of them, had written from the Venetian capital to the Dominican, Fray Guzman, asking him to do all he could to obtain a safe conduct for the travelers; but there is no evidence that his letter arrived before the Companions left Paris in November.

The five Spanish and four French scholars took a circuitous route through Lorraine, Southern Germany, and Switzerland to avoid, as far as possible, the various armies. It was arranged that, if they met French troops, the Frenchmen were to answer for all; if they met Imperial soldiery, the Spaniards were to act as spokesmen. They were dressed alike in costumes that were neither religious habits, nor scholars' gowns, nor pilgrim garb, yet having features of each. They wore broad-brimmed hats and carried staves, and they had rosaries around their necks and knapsacks—containing their Bibles, passports, university parchments, and other papers—on their shoulders.

It was an exceptionally cold, wet winter. At the start, Rodriguez fell ill of a fever; a few days later two Portuguese, one a brother of Rodriguez, overtook the party and begged them "to return to Paris and sanity." But to all the arguments, based on common sense and ordinary reasonableness, Simon Rodriguez just said, "No—but you two should come along with us." Finally the two horsemen had no option but to turn and ride back the way they had come. The next upset was caused by Master Francis Xavier, whom last we met expounding Aristotle in the Beauvais College to large and intelligent classes. Xavier wished to punish his limbs for their share in his former vanities and, in his eagerness to mortify the legs that had won him such renown at the student sports, bound cords so tightly around his thighs and calves that by the time his Companions discovered the cause of his limping and lagging behind, his bonds had vanished in swollen folds of protesting muscle; a bad night was spent by all doctoring Francis and praying for his recovery. This untimely attempt at penance caused a delay and must have given the leader—kindly, gentle Peter Favre—a scare; he would not wish to arrive in Venice without the roommate so dear to Inigo and himself.[16]

It rained all the way to the German frontier; and from then on to Venice, the nine travelers suffered much from frost and snow. Country folk near Metz, seeing the group all dressed alike passing by, concluded that they were reformers "off to reform some country." When the Companions left France for Upper Germany, they made their first contacts with convinced and practicing Lutherans; turning south, they went through country where the Anabaptists and Calvinists had become well entrenched. At Basle they visited the tomb of Erasmus who had died a few months previously. On by Lake Constance and the Zwinglian strongholds they went, "half dead with the cold and the hardship of trudging through the snows." The journey was probably in the nature of an eye-opener for most of the Companions, to whom the Reform was an abstract matter debated hotly in the schools but meaning little in real life. Accustomed to think of the Turks as the only real danger to Christendom, in this close-up view of the schisms and sub-schisms they began to realize the disrupting forces at work from within, steadily disintegrating the fabric of the faith—the Seamless Robe that had, for more than a millenium, warmed and clothed Europe. Already a man's religion was becoming a matter of locality and nationality. The word *foreigner* was in the process of acquiring a newer, more alien meaning that winter when Favre and his eight Companions journeyed from Paris to Venice. A bare half century before, the foreigner was a man separated from one by a line of hills, a sea, a broad river, sentineled marches, a man who spoke a strange tongue, who gave his allegiance to another prince, who lived in, served—perhaps fought for—other realms, other causes. Now he was the man from the far side of a spiritual frontier; most formidable, if intangible, barriers had sprung up within a generation, and these frontiers were closed as they were erected. The new era of international suspicion and hatred had begun.

On January 8, 1537, Inigo was at the Hospital of the Incurables in Venice, attending to the poor patients, when he was told that nine strangers awaited him in the courtyard. Hastening down, he found them—his old roommates, Favre and Xavier, and the seven others. He embraced each in turn, weeping as he noted their sodden, mud-caked gowns, their worn appearance, their light luggage. The administrator of the hospital, a benefactor and friend of the pilgrim, already informed by the hospital servants of the new arrivals, put a room at their disposal and provided water and towels and dry clothing and a good meal. The ten who sat down to supper in the Incurables that night were happy men. Inigo had to hear about the fifty-four days' journey through winter snows, through embattled armies, through "heretic country." Favre gave an account of his stewardship, presenting the three new Companions; Inigo introduced the eleventh "trumpeter for Christ," Diego Hoces. Also in Venice were Xavier's relatives, the de Eguia brothers with whom Inigo had lodged in Alcala and both of whom would eventually join the ranks, Don Diego becoming the confessor of Ignatius himself.[17]

Some of the Companions stayed at the Incurables, some went to St. Paul's hospital; no ships would leave for Jerusalem until early summer, so the pilgrimage could not be undertaken for another few months. Rodriguez tells how they spent their time in the hospitals:

We made the beds, scrubbed the floors, emptied and cleaned the pots, and kept the wards clean; we carried the dead with reverence to the graves we had dug for them and waited on the sick hand and foot, both by day and night, and with so much happiness and joy that all who lived in the hospital were amazed at us, and some notabilities of the city who heard of this came to see, and thought such service a thing to be marveled at.[18]

Of all the ten, Francis Xavier excelled in the exercise of heroic charity. Ignatius, remembering the earlier resistance of Xavier—"the toughest dough he had ever handled"—must have smiled to himself; Xavier had not been half-baked by the Exercises; the tough dough made the best bread.

After two months as wardsmen in the Venice hospitals, the Companions set off for Rome to get the blessing of the pope, Paul III, for their projected pilgrimage. Inigo remained in Venice; he feared that his presence might wreck their hopes, for there were two persons at the pontifical court in whose good graces he did not think he stood. One was a Doctor Ortiz, a Toledan. Ambassador of the Emperor, he had been very hostile to the pilgrim in Paris, when Inigo was a poor student there and Ortiz a famous lecturer; the other was Cardinal Carafa, whose displeasure Inigo had incurred at Venice by writing him an honest if impolitic letter on the newly formed Theatine Order—the apple of the Cardinal's eye. Carafa was an exemplary churchman, but he had a hasty temper and was particularly touchy on anything concerning the Theatines, an order in which he was deeply interested. But if Inigo did not go to Rome, he drew up some instructions to the pope, explaining the plan for the pilgrimage to the Holy Land and mentioning their wish to devote their lives to apostolic work in Palestine. They were also to ask permission to receive Holy Orders.

They traveled by Loreto and reached Rome on Palm Sunday, which in 1537 fell on March 25. It had been a hard journey, with bad weather all the way and little alms; they were once reduced to eating pine cones and on another occasion had to pawn a breviary to pay the captain who allowed them on his ship from Ravenna to Ancona. It took a good deal of begging in Ancona markets, where the stall-women gave "one a radish, another an apple or some other fruit," to make enough money to redeem the breviary and buy some food.[19] But the news the returning Companions brought back to Inigo more than made up for all their misery on the way to Rome. To their surprise Dr. Ortiz, from whom nothing but opposition was expected, became their protector, introducing them to the pope as specially distinguished scholars of Paris. Paul III, a humanist scholar, invited the ten to the Vatican on Easter Tuesday to hold a theological debate while he dined. The Companions gave such a good account of themselves that the Pontiff not only gave the pilgrimage his blessing—though he told them that he doubted very much the possibilities of getting to Palestine that year—but sent them away the richer by thirty-three golden crowns, which item was entered in the papal account as "33 golden crowns to eleven scholars of Paris who are going to the Holy Sepulchre"; the date of this bounty was April 29, 1537. The pope also gave those not yet priests permission to be ordained by any bishop living outside a forty-mile radius of Rome; and he gave them faculties, signed and sealed by the Cardinal Penitentiary, to absolve, when ordained, not only in ordinary but reserved cases.

Following the pope's lead, several other ecclesiastics gave them liberal donations for their Palestine journey; this money they sent on to Venice, so that Inigo could arrange with the ships' masters for their passage to the Holy Land. Ignatius tells of their return:

> The Companions returned to Venice as they had gone to Rome— namely, on foot and begging, and they went in three groups each containing men of different nationalities. . . . They brought from Rome bills of exchange for two or three hundred golden crowns which had been given to them as an alms to pay the expenses of their voyage to Jerusalem; they did not wish to take the money except in the form of bills of exchange, and afterwards, not being able to go to Jerusalem, they returned the same bills to those who had given them.[20]

Rodriguez states that the pope would not take back the thirty-three golden crowns he had bestowed on them, but that he admired the evangelical motive that inspired them to return the money. In Venice they resumed their work in the hospitals. Eight of the band, Ignatius among them, received the dignity and power of the priesthood on June 24, 1537, at the hands of the Bishop of Arbe. Documents recording the ordination describe Ignatius as "Master of the Liberal Arts, and also a cleric of Pamplona Diocese"; this brings echoes from the past, when the Corregidor of Azpeitia was, in 1515, thundering against the Bishop of Pamplona, demanding the surrender of Inigo Loyola, then in the episcopal prisons—"no tonsured youth, but a layman . . . not having been tonsured nor having kept the rules for the tonsured!" A short time before the ordination day, the papal legate in Venice presided when the Companions renewed their vow of perpetual poverty previously taken at Montmartre. The nuncio also authorized the new priests to preach and explain the

Scriptures throughout the Venetian Republic. Ignatius wrote to Verolay, a friend of his in Spain, just a month after the ordination. Having related all that had happened to himself and the Companions in the previous year, up to their ordinations, he continues:

This year, great though our hopes were of getting to Jerusalem, there is no ship and no hopes of a sailing, since the Turk is on the sea with an armada. So we decided that the bills of exchange for 260 ducats given us in Rome should be returned to the donors, for we do not wish to use the money when we cannot make the voyage, and we should not like anyone to think that we have a hunger or thirst for the things for which the worldly die. We are leaving here, two by two . . . traveling about Italy for another year, to see if there be any hopes of going to Jerusalem; and if it be not to the service of God Our Lord that we should go there, we will wait no longer but go ahead with the work we have commenced. . . . We would like to get other Companions, not lacking in education. But we must refuse rather than receive to avoid taking those not likely to persevere. Praying God Our Lord, by His infinitely great goodness, to give us the wish to cooperate with His grace, so that we may know his most holy will and in all things fulfill it.

From Venice, 24th July 1537.   Poor in goodness—Inigo.[21]

Barbarossa, now back on the seas again in command of Suleiman's fleets, was stronger than ever. He held the mouth of the Adriatic, hailing Venetian craft with gibes about the yearly bridal between Venice and the sea. "Your bride, the sea, is mine," he would roar, "the Adriatic is mine—and Suleiman's." As 1537 wore on and on, the hopes of the Companions for a sailing to Palestine grew thinner and thinner; Barbarossa not only hemmed in the merchant fleets of Venice, but raided, burned, and plundered at will up and down the east coast of Italy and entrenched himself strongly on the islands in the Adriatic.

It was a sorry year for Venice. Commerce was at a standstill; the rich became poor while the poor became destitute. Europe was in such a turmoil that calls for help went in vain. Central and northern Germany and Scandinavia were embroiled in religious wars and disputes; the English King was mourning his third wife, Jane Seymour, who had died in childbirth; Martin Luther was writing of Henry VIII in supercilious

190

terms, "Squire Harry wishes to be God and do whatever he pleases." Italy was weakened by the continual dissensions between rival city-states; the temporal power of the papacy was but a shadow of what it had been. No one knew when or where the Turk would make his next attack—by land or by sea. Vienna, defenseless since the defeat of the Hapsburgs' army, was asking for aid. Pope Paul III stated that only another Crusade could save Christendom. Venice, worst off of all, saw no aid forthcoming; the port faced east, the point from which danger always had threatened Europe. The Senate of the Most Serene Republic was forced to levy a 50 per cent tax on the goods and capital of the merchant princes; and the citizens, infected by the general atmosphere of desperation, ate, drank, and made merry, expecting death every morrow. Among this populace, many of whom had thrown faith, hope, and charity overboard, the Companions of Jesus exercised a compassionate and zealous apostolate in that year of fear.

It is a notable thing that although for many years before 1537 and for thirty-three years afterwards there never was a year, save that year, without one or more pilgrim ships sailing from Venice for the Holy Land.[22]

Thus Ribadeneira notes how Providence deflected the Companions from a good enterprise to direct them to a better.

Those who were ordained in June were to say their first Masses in September. But Inigo decided to wait a year and more, as he wished to make a more rigorous preparation; it is possible that he still had hopes of getting to Jerusalem and offering his first Mass in that hallowed city. In late July the Companions dispersed, Inigo, Favre, and Lainez going to Vicenza, Xavier and Salmeron to a town halfway between Venice and Padua; two others went to Bassano, two to Treviso, and two to Verona—all of which towns were about a day's journey apart. The three at Vicenza found a shell of a house which had been sacked in the wars and uninhabited for some years; it had neither doors nor windows; there they lodged, sleepng on some straw which they themselves gathered. Each week a different Companion was Superior; each day the other two went to beg in the town nearby, but probably because of the bad times common to all Venetian towns that year, the alms they received were meagre. The one whose turn it was to be Superior had a special task while his community of two went begging—he had to bake. The turning out of an edible farl of coarse bread for the brethren returning weary and dispirited after a fruitless day's questing was, no doubt, regarded by these Masters of the Liberal Arts as a great feat, somewhat on a par with "taking the rock" in the old days at Paris University!

Thus they spent forty days, "attending to nothing but prayer." This six weeks "in the desert" seems to have been for Ignatius a second Manresa, shorter than the former, but no less abounding in interior consolations and spiritual visions. Various adventures befell the Companions in their respective solitudes, Rodriguez being smitten with fever while le Jay was tempted to leave the Company altogether and become a hermit; in each case Ignatius came to the rescue, somehow knowing of his sons' afflictions without being told and although a day's journey away.

When this long retreat ended, all met at Vicenza and the first Masses were celebrated sometime early in September. Afterwards a discussion took place on future plans; it was decided that, if by November no vessel left for the Holy Land, Ignatius, Favre, and Lainez should go to Rome to ask the pope how they might best serve him and the Church of Christ. During their absence the others were to continue the apostolate begun earlier that year in Venice; but they would move further afield to the university cities of northern Italy: Ferrara, Siena, Padua, and Bologna. In the towns they were to preach short sermons, live on alms, lodge in hospitals, and attend the sick; in all things the greater glory of God and the salvation of souls was to be their aim. In these cities, with their large numbers of students, it was to be hoped that the more generous hearted of the scholars and the younger Masters would volunteer to join the ranks. The major schisms had for core men of intellect and university education; those who would work to restore "all things in Christ" should not be any less learned.[23]

It should be noted, [writes an American educationalist] to correct a general historical error, that in Ignatius' mind there is no conception of Counter Reformation, there is no malice to fight Protestantism; there is simply his own spiritual conversion and the following of the light then given him, and the desire to bring that light to men in whatever way God saw fit to send His willing servant. . . .[24]

Before the Companions dispersed, there was one last matter to be decided. What should they reply when asked who and what they were?

All at once betook themselves to prayer and considered this matter, and seeing that no one among them was head, only Jesus Christ who was the only one they wished to serve, it seemed to them most fitting that they should take their Captain's name, calling themselves the Company of Jesus.[25]

Polanco, who tells this, implies that the title was suggested by Ignatius, who did not like hearing the "followers of Inigo" dubbed *Iniguistas;* but never a man to act on merely negative and exterior reasons, he had other, higher motives for electing that he and his sons should serve under the name that is above all names. Polanco adds:

Father Ignatius had such revelations regarding this matter [of deciding what name the Company should take] and received such signs of approbation and confirmation of the same that I have heard him say he would think it a sin against God to doubt its suitability.[26]

Devotion to the name of Jesus was, one might say, in his blood. His grandmother, who had lived in the times and heard the sermons of St. Vincent Ferrer, the great Dominican preacher of the holy name, put the letters IHUS at the beginning of her will. In the hermitage of San Martin, near Loyola, as in other shrines of the Iraurgi, a Gothic IHS was carved. At Arevalo and Najera, the Franciscan poet-friars had sung of their recently canonized brother, Bernadine of Siena, so devoted to the name of Jesus that "he and his fellow preachers were eventually nicknamed Jesuits, a name invented out of hatred but full of honor." All Inigo's letters began with the heading IHS; he chose the emblem as the seal and blazon of his Company and desired that houses of his order should display it in a conspicuous place. His own constant ejaculation in later years was "Ay, Jesus!" "Alas, Jesus!" In the diary of his soul, he wrote a resolution: "When vesting for Mass I will make the intention of imprinting on myself the name of Jesus."

Most commentators agree that his early military life gave Ignatius the title of *Company* for his spiritual militia. One authority on the saint points out that the word *compagnia,* in the Italian of the time, signified not only a military group under a captain but also an association or congregation devoted to some special work. When official documents came to be prepared in Latin (as the new order took form), Ignatius did not translate *Compagnia* by using a Latin word with military significance

193

such as COHORS, LEGIO or MILITIA, but used *Societas,* although, in the first Formula of the Institute, he uses the phrase "to *fight* under the Standard of the Cross."[27] The name "Company of Jesus" was to be the occasion of dispute both during the lifetime of Ignatius and after his death. When told in 1554 of certain opposition that had arisen to the name of the Society, its founder wrote, "The name has a deeper root than the world knows of and cannot be changed."

But in the last months of 1537 all that was in the future, and the Companions, going joyfully to the areas and work assigned them, replied "priests of the Company of Jesus" when inquiries were made as to who they were. Their methods of preaching the Gospel in the towns of northern Italy were simple; the one whose turn it was to be Superior would prepare the sermon, his subject borrowing an *escano,* or bench with a back to it, from some neighboring shop; the preacher then mounted the improvised pulpit while both "called to all with voice and with bonnet" to come and hear the word of God. Those who availed themselves of the invitation and waited for the sermon were not asked for alms; confessions were heard if requested; the children were rounded up for Christian doctrine lessons, likewise the uneducated. As might be expected, the Companions caused no small sensation, particularly as they usually preached in the market square where they had to compete with the vendors of fish, fruit, flowers, and other merchandise in the matter of shouting. Most of them spoke deplorable Italian and, no doubt, raised many a hearty laugh.[28]

But before the Companions went on this mission and before Ignatius left for Rome, there was yet another trial by the Inquisition. The servant brought from Navarre by Xavier, Michael Landivar, and a Toledan named Arias had come from Paris and joined the Company in the summer of 1537. Out of step with the others from the beginning, in a very short time they dropped out of the ranks or else were told to go. Soon serious calumnies about Ignatius began to circulate in Venice. An effigy of him had been burned in Paris, it was told; he had been a suspect of the Inquisition there; before that he was all but expelled from Paris University; he had been imprisoned in Salamanca and also in Alcala. All that was not for nothing, rumor added; no smoke without a fire. In view of the spiritual projects now being undertaken, Ignatius could not afford to have his orthodoxy or morals impugned at the start, so he went to the papal nuncio and asked for a trial; a public edict was circulated, bidding all who had any accusations to make against the accused to do so by a given date. The outcome was that all the rumors were denounced as base, false, frivolous, and vain, and Ignatius left the court with a cleared character—"a priest whose life is religious and good, whose teaching is holy, whose state of life and reputation are excellent, and who has, by both his preaching and example, greatly edified Venice."

In the journey to Rome he [Ignatius] was visited by God in an unusual manner. Within a few miles of that city towards which they traveled, he entered a church and was praying there when he experienced great movement within his soul and clearly beheld God the Father placing him with His Son.[29]

At this point, the amanuensis, Polanco, adds: "And I, the writer, interrupted him saying that I understood that Lainez had given further details of that occasion. He replied that Lainez' account would have been correct, but that he himself might not have remembered all the particulars."

Lainez in a sermon given at Rome three years after the death of Ignatius said:

It seems to me that our father always regarded this [vision] as confirmation of the name Company of Jesus. We journeyed to Rome by the road from Siena, and all along the way the father was engrossed in spiritual thoughts, especially dwelling on the thought of the Blessed Eucharist. Master Favre and I, Lainez, used to say Mass each day; he (Ignatius) did not, but he used to receive Holy Communion. Then one day he said to me that it seemed to him that God the Father had imprinted on his heart these words: *I will be favorable to you in Rome.* And our father, not knowing what these words signified, used to say to me, "I do not know what is in store for us; perhaps we may be crucified in Rome." After another while he told me that it seemed to him that Christ stood by him with the cross on His shoulders, and the Eternal Father by His side, and the Father said to His Son: *Wilt thou take this man for servitor?* And Jesus took him [Ignatius] saying: *I want you to serve Us.* And on this account his devotion to the name of Jesus became exceedingly great, and he wished that the congregation should be called the Company of Jesus.[30]

La Storta is about ten miles to the north of Rome, at the junction of the old Roman roads, the Via Claudia and the Via Cassia. It was the name of a parish, and the little church now there was renovated in 1700 by the Jesuit General of that year. In Ignatius' time an inn stood there, and stables where the great changed their carriage horses. It was similar to many little churches that studded the old pilgrim routes to Rome. It is certain that the saint himself regarded the La Storta vision as "approbation and confirmation" that he was now enrolled and commissioned under the banner of Christ. In his diary for February 23, 1544, he wrote:

> While I was preparing for Mass, at the thought of Jesus coming to me, I felt moved to follow Him, He being represented to me interiorly as head or *caudillo* of the Company, which is greater argument for embracing poverty than any human reasoning. . . . Moved to devotion and tears . . . and, while vesting, these increased and multiplied . . . and this "thinking with" or "experiencing with" Jesus seemed to me to be the work of the Blessed Trinity, and I suddenly remembered the day when the Father placed me with the Son. And when I had finished vesting for Mass, I found within me so intense a longing that the Name of Jesus might be imprinted upon my soul, that the force of my desire brought on tears and consolations. Thus I began Mass, aided by much grace and devotion, weeping quietly and for a long time, even until the time of unvesting afterwards.

Such were the fervor and tears to which the memory of the La Storta vision, recalled seven years later, could move him.

Continuing onwards from the little chapel standing at the fork in the great road to the north, the Companions covered the last three leagues of their journey, entering Rome by the Flaminian Way, the ancient pilgrim road which today passes in beneath the Porta del Popolo and continues along the Corso. The first church they saw—and probably visited—was that of Santa Maria del Popolo, facing them as they came in by the gateway spanning the Via Flaminia. The church is on a slope which was covered in ancient times by poplar and walnut trees and was said to be haunted by Nero's ghost. In the Augustinian convent close by, Friar Martin Luther of Erfurt, later of Wittenberg, stayed for a month in 1510. Ignatius would have seen many changes in Rome since his previous visit, fifteen years before. There were then about 55,000 inhabitants; after 1527 and the sacking of the city by the Imperial troops, the population sank as low as 25,000; by 1538 it had again risen to 50,000, but a high proportion of that number was homeless and destitute. Recurring wars, with the famines and plagues which followed, left vast areas of Italy desolate, and the ruined peasants from provinces near Rome moved into the capital to beg. The numbers of women on the streets for the decades subsequent to 1527 are usually adduced as proof of the low tide of morals in the city at the time; they could just as well be quoted as evidence of the extreme and widespread poverty.

In vain one searches writings of Ignatius and the first Companions for details of the pulsing life of Rome when they first settled there. The only recorded remark on the subject is Ignatius' comment to Lainez and Favre, as they entered the city: "He said that the windows were all closed, which meant that they were likely to meet with many contradictions."[31] More likely the closed windows indicated cold weather, for the winter had begun. But if the Companions supply little background for the apostolate they so soon were to undertake in the Eternal City, other visitors have left accounts of what Rome looked like in the middle decades of the sixteenth century. One such was Benvenuto Cellini, the Florentine. When the three Companions arrived in Rome toward the end of 1537, Cellini—up to a short time previously the pope's goldsmith, silversmith, and jewel-setter—was cooling his heels in the Castle Sant' Angelo prison and calculating the best opportunity for an attempt to escape from a jailer "who suffered from the humors, one day imagining himself to be an oil jar, the next a frog, the next a bat." St. Peter's was being rebuilt; lumbering oxen from the Campagna drew huge blocks of dressed stone and marble into the city for the churches and palaces in course of erection on the ruins of those sacked in 1527. Michelangelo was painting the *Last Judgment* in the Sistine Chapel. The city was packed with princes of Church and realm, with ambassadors and high dignitaries of all sorts, most of whom supported retinues and had personal bodyguards and many officials, servants, and hangers-on.

Cellini, moping in his high keep above the Tiber, could look through squintholes at the river below and wonder would it come up again, as it had done in 1530 "at twenty-two of the clock, bursting its banks and flooding Rome without warning." That was the day when the Genoese robber was hanged in the Campo di Fiore, much to the great metalworker's satisfaction, the fellow having robbed him. An accomplice had been hanged a few days previously, while a third was sent to the galleys. And the thought of the galleys would have reminded the prisoner of his own escape the previous summer when, going out to the seaside to spend a few pleasant hours away from the city heat, he had had to fly for his life when a Moorish ship, flying a pennant with the crescent, came bearing down on the little cove where peaceful and honest Romans were enjoying the sea breezes.

In the nights the sounds of fifes and cornets floated up, as itinerant musicians did the rounds of the taverns, while sometimes the baying and growling of the fierce mastiffs that guarded the gates and doors of the great could be heard, and in the mornings the clatter of hooves as the young bloods and their followers rode out to the hunting and falconing. When the midday Angelus rang, the whirr of many wings and a shadow falling across the shafts of light on the cell wall told the captive that the great flocks of pigeons in the ruins had been startled and had taken flight. In the afternoons he heard the water carrier, driving his donkeys laden with brimming pitchers before him, as he cried his wares; the shouts of a Lombardy peasant, passing with yoked oxen to plough up some vineyard or garden before the pulverizing frosts set in, reminded him of how the antique dealers, mostly Jews from the Ghetto, would soon be plodding along at the ploughman's heels, ready to pounce on the turned sods for old coins and precious stones, for a portion of an urn or pillar or statue—there were plenty of rich customers in Rome always ready to look through such treasure trove.

This was the Rome into which Ignatius, Favre and Lainez trudged, weary after their three weeks' walk from Venice. Lainez recorded how "Our Father received Communion each morning during the journey at either Favre's or my Mass." Ignatius was an ardent advocate of frequent Communion. Writing to "the people of Azpeitia" he reminds them of their good resolutions of 1535 and exhorts them to the frequent reception of the Blessed Eucharist as the greatest help to living holily and well. In 1542 he writes to Spain's leading Grandee, Francis Borgia, duke of Gandia, in the same strain. And he advises his own sister:

> Go often to Holy Communion, that your soul may be united with Our Lord in true hope and thus grow in lively faith and that greatest of our needs—without which we cannot be saved—charity.[32]

When Sister Teresa Rejadell's sister died, Ignatius wrote to console her; he urged her to communicate daily:

> As regards daily Communion, you know that in the primitive Church all Christians received every day; and our holy Mother the

Church has never, either by canon or letter, forbidden this custom. Neither did any of her theologians hold that a person moved by devotion to receive daily might not do so . . . . St. Augustine . . . once exhorted all to receive every Sunday; elsewhere, speaking of the most holy Body of Christ Our Lord, he says: "This Bread is *daily* bread; so live then, that each day you may be able to partake of it."[33]

Meanwhile, the three Companions enter Rome, while Ignatius utters a warning: "We must needs proceed with great prudence, and we had better not speak to any women, except the most illustrious." Francis Xavier had had an unfortunate experience in this regard, incurring suspicion when a certain lady lapsed from virtue; he was fortunate that the real culprit was discovered before the rumor gained currency. Father Codure found himself in an almost similar predicament. The women in Rome were best avoided, so for the first months there was no hospital work. Besides, there was not the same need for service of the sick as there had been in other cities. Foreign visitors and pilgrims were lost in admiration of the vast, well equipped, efficiently run institute, *Santo Spiritu*, the doors of which were open to the sick poor of all nations. Within its walls, patients not only received free treatment and care during illnesses but new clothes and a gift of money when being discharged; in the adjoining orphanage, boys were taught a trade and apprenticed to the same, while the girls got marriage dowries.

Lainez took off his shoes outside the city walls and entered Rome barefoot. Ignatius, his mind still on the vision of a few hours before, noted the closed windows and wondered what trials awaited them. When they first set out from Vicenza for Rome, he had walked like a man with winged feet, setting such a pace that his two Companions, though they were many years younger, had to beg him to go slower.[34] Now that they had reached their goal there was no further need for haste. Ignatius Loyola would not leave Rome again during the less than two decades of life remaining to him, save only for a few necessary journeys to places at no great distance from the city. For Rome was to be his Jerusalem. The pilgrim had put the long roads of Europe behind him forever.

XII

. . . While they were living at the vineyard, he set himself to work, helping souls and giving the Spiritual Exercises to several persons . . .
(Autobiography of St. Ignatius)

. . . . I remember often hearing our Father say that he wanted none in the Society just to save their souls if, beyond that, they did not all make ready to save the souls of others. . . .
(Memorial of Father Goncalves)

. . . . There was not a mother who had so much care for her sons, especially those who were delicate or infirm, as had our blessed Father Ignatius. . . . *(Ribadeneira's Life of Ignatius)*

THE PROMISE Ignatius had received from God at La Storta, "In Rome I will be propitious to you," was speedily fulfilled. Soon after their arrival a nobleman offered them a small house in a vineyard which covered the site of the present Piazza di Espagna and all the slope up from the Spanish Steps to the Trinita dei Monti. Then, as now, the twin towers of the Trinita soared above the cypresses; but the church, today the property of the Sacred Heart order, was in 1537 the church of French friars—the Minims—and was comparatively new, having been built at the turn of the century. That portion of the city was still fields and gardens and vineyards; the hut of the three Companions, on the slope of the hill and facing the Trinita, was a wretched dwelling affording little shelter, for there were cracks and splits through which passers-by could observe those within. A son of their benefactor's, who gave evidence at the beatification process of St. Ignatius, testified that his father, owner of the vineyard, told his vine-dresser Antonio to note well the sort of life these foreign priests led. Antonio reported "great things": although he gave them bread, he never saw them eat it; they gave it away for the love of God; although he had given them beds, when he peeped in on moonlit nights the three were sleeping on the ground; they led holy lives, Father Ignatius in particular, who was to be seen going along the streets preaching and "teaching catechism to the street wenches, and engaged in many other good and holy works."[1]

Lainez tells that "two of ours," meaning Favre and himself, went to the Sapienza College, where they lectured on Scripture and other sacred subjects by order of the pope, Paul III. They continued at this for a year and a half; at first Lainez did not please either himself or his hearers, but he was young enough and humble enough to correct and amplify his course of lectures, which dealt with the canon of the Mass. "All were then quite pleased."[2] The Ambassador-extraordinary of the Emperor to the Holy See, Dr. Ortiz, who had proved such a good friend to the Companions when they visited Rome the previous Easter, again became their advocate with the pope; and it was possibly on his recommendation that Lainez and Favre got the lectureships at the Sapienza.

"Meanwhile," says Ribadeneira, "Father Ignatius' principal charge was to move men's hearts towards virtue and enkindle within them the fire of the love of God." As in former cities and towns, he was busy "helping souls and giving the Exercises."[3] One of his first conquests in Rome was the Ambassador, Dr. Ortiz. Ortiz was a native of the la Mancha country southeast of Madrid, that portion of Toledo province later immortalized by Cervantes and the knight-errant, Don Quixote, whom he sent riding full tilt against its windmills. He had studied in Alcala and Paris, occupied the Chair of Scripture at Salamanca for some years, and during his second sojourn in Paris won distinction as a theologian. In his earlier contacts with Ignatius at Paris and Venice, Ortiz had regarded with some suspicion the man who had run into trouble with the Inquisition at all the universities where he himself had been. The Ambassador inclined to the opinion that Ignatius, if not a heretic, was at least lacking in orthodoxy.

Once the two met, however, the Ambassador not only realized how unfounded his suspicions had been, but seems to have succumbed at once to that extraordinary power of attraction Ignatius possessed. He volunteered to do the Exercises, fully and well; and to secure solitude and complete isolation from worldly affairs, he went to Monte Cassino, the cradle of the Benedictine order and the most famous of all the abbeys of the sons of St. Benedict, and spent the whole of Lent, 1538, in retreat. The Exercises of the first week, with prolonged and concentrated considerations on the Four Last Things, were a bit too much for the poor diplomat, and he told Ignatius that he was beginning to feel the strain; "whereupon to cheer him up and rouse him from his stupor, Father Ignatius danced one of the Basque dances, reviving his retreatant's drooping spirits to such an extent that he was then able to resume his meditations with renewed enthusiasm and to carry them through to the end."[4]

Ortiz emerged from his retreat a new man; he told others that in the past he had schooled his understanding, but that in Monte Cassino his will had been to school and learned how to conform itself to the loving will of God. Polanco adds that the Ambassador, his retreat ended, begged to be allowed to join the Companions, but that Ignatius dissuaded him; he was too advanced in years, too portly in figure, too delicate in constitution to undertake their laborious life. Besides, God had already placed him in a position where he could do much for His glory and the spiritual good of his neighbor. Ortiz returned to Rome after Easter, so grateful to Ignatius that he remained his staunch friend and champion until his death ten years later.

Others made the Exercises about the same time. Cardinal Contarini was one; he was so taken with them that during his retreat he copied out the entire contents of Ignatius' now famous little book. The Cardinal, unlike some of his brethren in the Sacred College, was in no need of reform; he was a man of integrity and nobility of character, indefatigable in his efforts to promote reform within the Church. Love of riches and moral laxity were so prevalent among the Roman clergy that contempt for the men who held high posts within the Church—a very different thing from contempt for their office—was widespread. The papacy had become almost a political preserve, the cause of interminable feuds between the Farnese and the Sforzas, the Medici and the Colonnas; besides, the temporal possessions of the Holy See were being constantly threatened by the presence in Italy of now French, now Spanish armies, with the result that the various popes of the first half of the century, to maintain liberty and safety, adopted the diplomatic methods in general use at the time among the powers of Europe. As respect for the men who ruled the Church declined, so the influence of the Church dwindled, and Europe beheld a new phenomenon—the rise of the prince who wielded absolute power. Henry VIII was a typical example of such a monarch, claiming the spiritual as well as the temporal allegiance of his subjects. Truly could Luther write: "Squire Harry thinks he is God."

One cannot think of Ignatius of Loyola, limping a little at times on the long trek from Rome to Monte Cassino to give the Exercises to Dr. Ortiz, and back again to see how Cardinal Contarini is faring in his contemplations, without recalling a veritable litany of great names—the men who were his contemporaries: More and Erasmus and Vives and Machiavelli; da Gama and Cortes; Magellan and Pizarro; Botticelli and Michelangelo; Titian and Raphael; da Vinci and Durer; Luther and Melanchthon and

Calvin; Rabelais; Copernicus; the Medici and the Farnese; the Borgias and the Hapsburgs; the Valois and the Tudors; and the meteors of the Mediterranean, Suleiman and Barbarossa; such names still echo in the halls of time.

One day when Ignatius was returning from a visit to Ortiz in Monte Cassino, he met a young Spaniard—a Castilian, Francis Estrada. They fell into conversation and the nineteen-year-old Francis told of how he had come from Spain some years before, Dr. Ortiz having got him a post as a page in the household of Cardinal Carafa in Venice—the hot-tempered Theatine Cardinal to whom the mention of Ignatius Loyola was anathema. In February, the prelate's volcanic temper erupted and he dismissed on the spot every Spaniard in his employment. Francis Estrada was penniless and decided to go south to join the Emperor's garrisons at Naples.

And our Father asked him (says Polanco) where he was off to and what he meant to do with himself. And having heard his story, he proposed to him a better squadron and a better Commander than he sought (at Naples). Having detained him, he ordered him to do the Exercises and, while doing them, Estrada determined to give himself wholly to Christ and to the service of souls.[5]

At the end of Lent Ignatius wrote to the Companions working in pairs in the various university cities of Northern Italy, summoning them to Rome:

.... We have not been able to fulfill our vow of going to the Holy Land; but behold, here in this land of Italy, the centre of Christendom—as we have seen with our eyes and experienced for ourselves—the great God has opened a vast field for our evangelical labors, calling us to reap an abundant harvest in souls, ripe for conversion and reformation. We see too, further away, the immense fruit to be gathered elsewhere, among the faithful as among infidels.

So it seems, my very dear brothers, that it is to this great enterprise God invites us; we can with His great help continue the mission and apostolate, rooting up and planting, fighting vice and heresy and spreading the faith of Jesus Christ to the ends of the earth.

But the most certain means to secure this end is to link ourselves together, forming one lasting chain, fastened and firm, under one head, adding to our vows of poverty and chastity that of obedience. To erect on our Company a religious order capable of multiplying itself in all countries on earth and of subsisting to the end of time, is to give those bonds of charity that unite us an eternal quality not limited by our lives.

This voluntary bond, this cementing union, far from changing anything, would rather fortify us and lend nobility to the designs we already have had in mind. And indeed, is it not through visible things that God lets us know this—by the great harvest we have already reaped, as by the new Companions, so capable, which He daily adds to our ranks? But what guarantee have they for the future—these new brothers united to us in loving friendship and tender charity—if we do not do as I propose? Moreover, I do not ask you (and the extreme importance of the matter forbids me to do so) to give me a decisive answer immediately. Take time for reflection; meditate much and recommend the whole affair to God. Let us in one fervent prayer beg Him to make known to us His most holy will, so that our final determination may result in His greater glory, which is now and must be always the rule and goal of our desires. . . .[6]

On receipt of this letter the Companions started out for Rome—all save Hoces who, his labors already done, had gone to his reward, Ignatius having been given a vision of his soul's entry into heaven. The travellers arrived in pairs at the hut in the vineyard on the slopes of the Trinita dei Monti "between the two Paschs," that is, between Easter and Pentecost. It was the early and delightful Roman summer, so if all did not fit into the shack, one or more could sleep in the open; if anyone slept out of doors, surely that one was Ignatius, so fond of watching the stars in their courses. Fortunately they did not have to remain in such cramped quarters for long, being soon lodged "close by the Sixto Bridge and near to where Dr. Ortiz lived." By the following autumn, however, they had moved again to a house near the Melangolo Tower in the present Via Delfini.[7]

After some delay, caused by detrimental rumors which soon were in circulation concerning them, the Companions got permission to preach in various Roman churches. Ignatius in the church of Our Lady of Montserrat gave his sermons in Spanish; all the others preached in Italian of

205

sorts. Lainez rather mournfully relates that he preached "at least for my own mortification."[8] At this juncture Francis Xavier is not mentioned; he had arrived in Rome so ill and wasted that the general opinion among the brethren was that Xavier, in covering the two hundred odd miles between Bologna and Rome, had made his last journey. Neither the runner of Paris nor his Companions had as yet any idea of the marathon Francis was to run from west to east, bearing the flame of faith to strange peoples "over the bent world" before laying him down exhausted to die at the gates of China. Soon after his arrival, however, Francis recovered and went to preach in the church of St. Louis of France, possibly because his French, after eleven years in Paris, was fluent enough to permit the French colony in Rome to understand him.[9]

It was rather unfortunate for the Companions that the pope, who had shown himself so favorable to them, should have to leave Rome and Italy just when a new storm of persecution, the worst yet experienced, burst upon them. Paul III set off for Nice to ask those lifelong rivals, Francis I and the Emperor, to forget their rivalries and antagonisms and make common cause against the Turk. The primary cause of the new persecution suffered by Ignatius and the Companions during the pope's absence from Rome was a series of sermons then being given by a popular preacher of Rome, one Fray Augustin. The friar had already been in trouble in his own diocese, where he had been obliged to retract publicly some previous pulpit utterances concerning the doctrines of grace and private judgment. The Companions—having met with no response when they asked the friar in a private interview to cease preaching heresy—began to give sermons refuting those preached by Fray Augustin. The other factor in the persecution was Michael Landivar, or Miguel the Navarrese, previously met with in the role of calumniator of Inigo in Venice and earlier in Paris, in which city he made an attempt to murder the man who had won the heart of his master, Xavier. Having also failed in his attempt to join the Companions at Venice, Landivar now retaliated with an intense campaign of defamation against the pilgrim and his followers. Fray Augustin also denounced them from his pulpit, his worst diatribes being reserved for Ignatius:

... Inigo of Loyola, a wolf going about Rome in the guise of a shepherd; a jailbird, a fellow who had cheated the Inquisition at Alcala, Paris, and Venice. Loyola and his Exercises raised a storm in

Paris which is still remembered in university circles there. . . . And all this can be borne out by a man of incorruptible faith who, attracted at first by Inigo of Loyola, has—in common with other Spaniards—now left him, renouncing him and his works with horror.[10]

The incorruptible was none other than Landivar, whose one object in life seemed to be the spreading of calumnies and detraction about the Companions throughout Rome from the Easter of 1538 to the following November.

Ignatius could not afford to allow such accusations to go unchallenged at the very time when the foundation of the Order was being considered, and in Rome of all places where it was essential that his character and that of the Company should be blameless. The infamous rumors circulated so rapidly that already people were beginning to look askance at the Companions; a Cardinal voiced suspicions of Ignatius; two schoolmasters withdrew their children from the Companions' catechism classes. "Many thought," wrote Ignatius to a friend, "that we were doomed—either to the stake or the galleys."[11] It was the eighth time he had faced allegations of heresy; but the Roman campaign against him was most dangerous in that it menaced the very existence of the Company and all their plans for the future.

Without delay he acted, seemingly on the sound and tried military principles that attack is the best form of defense and that an enemy is best attacked at his weakest point. The weak link in the conspiracy against him was Miguel the Navarrese. Ignatius went to the governor of Rome demanding a trial to vindicate his character; Landivar appeared as a witness swearing that the man previously known as Inigo of Loyola had been condemned as a heretic at Alcala, Paris, and Venice. But when shown a letter he himself had written to a friend some years previously, telling a very different story of Ignatius, he broke down under examination and was not only convicted of calumny by the governor but banished from Rome. The other calumniators had not yet appeared to give evidence; all Rome knew of the matter by this time and Cardinal Carafa gave orders that the trial was to be dropped. This did not suit Ignatius at all, as he did not wish the Order to be born under the shadow of a hushed-up trial and its founder to continue with no definite pronouncement on his orthodoxy. So he kept pressing for judgment, despite the fact that his accusers hastened to retract their false statements and that some of his friends thought he was being rather dogged and uncharitable in the matter. He writes to a friend in Venice:

> If they say we are unlearned, rude, lacking in eloquence—even if they say we are depraved, deceivers, unstable—we will suffer them to say so and bear it in silence, by the grace of God. But what afflicts us is when they say that our teaching is erroneous and when they indict our manner of life as blameworthy. For our teaching and our lives are not ours—they belong to Christ and His Church.[12]

At this moment, by one of those coincidences which the world calls chance and heaven calls the will of God, the three people best able to prove the innocence of Ignatius all arrived in Rome about the same time, each on private business—the former Inquisitors of Alcala, Rome, and Venice. Ignatius called upon them to testify what they knew of him; this evidence was overwhelmingly in his favor. At the same time the bishops and other authorities in Ferrara, Siena, and Bologna sent affidavits testifying to the teaching and the conduct of the Companions. The judgment, which names Ignatius and eight of the Companions, declares that "far from meriting any infamous judgment, their life and teaching is praiseworthy; and the same holds for the Spiritual Exercises which they give others."

This persecution and trial lasted almost eight months. The sentence was given in November, 1538; and on December 25 of that year Ignatius was to celebrate his first Mass, for which he had spent eighteen months "preparing, and asking Our Lady to place him with her Son." Fittingly he offered this Mass in the Church of St. Mary Major, in the Crypt or Grotto of Bethlehem Chapel in which are preserved relics of the Manger. It was not the Holy Land, but a little portion of it, brought long years before to the old, old church of Our Lady of the Snows. The celebrant was in his forty-eighth year; several stages of his spiritual journey already lay behind him—the converted soldier, the hermit given to mortification and prayer, the Jerusalem pilgrim, the scholar, first among the schoolboys, later among the students of the principal universities of Europe, the apostle to the people—and now Ignatius of Loyola was truly the priest of the Most High.

The winter of 1538-1539 was a terrible one in Rome and indeed throughout most of Europe. From Christmas Eve until May 25 a continuous frost gripped Italy. There were storms of hail and thunder and recurring blizzards. To add to the general misery famine spread. A contemporary chronicler writes:

> Prices soared; grain, wine, olives and oil, milk, meat (of even the worst quality) were dear, and to this was added an unbearably intense cold, frequent snows, and torrential rains, which from Christmas Eve, 1538, fell almost without interrruption until May 25, 1539.[13]

Simon Rodriguez also recorded that winter:

> Everywhere in the streets and squares numbers of people, weak with hunger, overcome with the cold, lay down at night on the ground to sleep. Many a one of these desolate, wandering beggars never rose next morning, but their attenuated corpses, stretched here and there all over the city, spelled plague.[14]

In their house near the Melangolo Tower, beside the monastery of St. Catherine of the Ropemakers, the Companions could not sleep while misery cried in the streets outside; they were appalled, not only by the sufferings of the poor, but by the passivity of the city authorities and wealthier classes.

> No eminent person seemed worried over the situation. No one took the trouble to visit the hospitals, indeed no one bothered to inquire into the calamitous misery or gave any show of compassion. . . . To remedy, in as much as in them lay, such great necessity, they [the Companions] begged and collected money and bread in all quarters; they made some herb stews and searched for the poor in the streets and piazzas and fetched them to the house; there, having washed their feet, they fed them, doctored their ills and sores, and taught them some catechism. . . . Sometimes they put the sick in their own beds, they themselves sleeping on the floors; and they begged hay and fuel and food from their friends, carrying such alms home on their backs through the city. At times as many as two or three hundred were crowded into their house, all being fed and comforted. The Companions also visited almost two thousand people shivering in the wretched houses of Rome's poorest streets, helping them with the money which had been given as alms to the Company by friends.[15]

Some rich Romans, hearing of the charity of the Fathers, came to the house packed with frostbitten, starving poor and saw for themselves. Ashamed of their own inactivity in the face of such distress many offered to help, and Ignatius' gifts of organization and direction got a chance to extend themselves. One helper, a Roman parish priest, was so impressed by the life and charity of the Companions that he took it upon himself to act as a foster father to them from then on, paying their rent and eventually placing his church, Our Lady of the Wayside, at their disposal. Later on this Canon, Pietro Codazzo, became a Jesuit.[16]

Ignatius, who in Spain never lacked helpers and followers among "the devout female sex," seems to have had to ask for such help in Rome. He called on various noble matrons, mostly Spanish ladies of title married into Roman families, inviting them to alleviate, both by personal effort and money contributions, the general misery. Among these ladies was Marguerite of Austria, natural daughter of the Emperor; the widow of a Medici, she had come from Florence the previous November to wed the pope's nephew, the Duke of Parma. During the spring of 1539, the Duchess, with other noble ladies, organized emergency hospitals and subscribed and collected for the relief schemes organized by the Companions. It is significant that Ignatius should have been the Companion to recruit the help of these ladies; of all the band he had had most training in the formal etiquette of the class in which Marguerite moved. As a matter of fact, he could have given the noblest Romans lessons in courtly manners and ritual, for in Arevalo and Valladolid, in Madrigalejo of the High Towers, in Toledo and Segovia, he had known the ceremonious ways and courtly speech so beloved of the Castilians. His training by Isabella's Major-Domo, Velazquez, was not wasted, though he little thought, a quarter of a century before, when sighing over *Amadis* and the knights and ladies of romance, that "the witty remarks and fine speeches he would make" to impress some real or imaginary lady would be uttered—in a vastly different context—to impress upon the great ladies of Rome the needs of their city's poor.

In the midst of all the coming and going in their house, Ignatius found time to welcome one visitor in particular; it was Madalena, Azpeitia's erstwhile bad girl, one of his first converts during the visit to his native valley a few years previously. She was returning from her pilgrimage to Jerusalem. It must have been rather galling for the poor Companions to meet one who had managed to achieve what they had failed—so far—to accomplish. But Madalena would seem to have taken two or three years to do the pilgrimage, as she left Azpeitia for Jerusalem towards the end of 1535. No doubt Ignatius asked her many questions as to how she had traveled and about conditions in Palestine. When she left for Spain, he gave here a letter for Loyola; a little while afterwards, some other travelers left for the homeland and to them also he entrusted a letter, addressed to "Don Martin and Don Beltran, lords of Loyola," as though he knew that his nephew had succeeded to the seignioralty.

> IHS. . . .
> Some days ago I wrote you a letter, giving it to Madalena de Sendo and Rozas, so this one will be short; for that party left here by a very circuitous route and will probably be a long time before they arrive home, so this is likely to arrive sooner. I enclose a copy of the judgment passed in our favour—you might like to have it. . . .
> The Bachelor Araoz (a nephew of Dona Madalena of the *Casa-Torre*) is now with us here; and I think God is going to make him very well off in this world and the next. Last Christmas Day, in the Church of St. Mary Major, in the chapel where the crib in which the Infant Jesus was placed after his birth is preserved, with His aid and grace, I said my first Mass. I beg and wish by the love and reverence of His DivineMajesty that we may continually remember one another in our devotions, each of us mindful that when his hour comes he must give an entire and strict account of his life.
> Poor in goodness,   Inigo[17]

Don Martin Garcia's hour had come, and he had rendered his "entire and strict account" ten weeks before Ignatius' letter was penned.

About this time—possibly owing to the fact that Madalena de Sendo, a woman with neither money nor influence, had succeeded in making her way to Jerusalem and back—the hope of doing the pilgrimage seems to have revived somewhat. One day when four of the Companions were conducting a theological debate before the pope as he dined, Paul III inquired: "Why are you so anxious to go to Jerusalem? If you wish to engage in fruitful work in God's Church, you will find a true Jerusalem here in Italy." Bobadilla, who was present when the pope made this remark, adds, "and when these words were reported to all the Companions, they began thinking of a new Order."[18] About the middle of the cold and hungry Lent of 1539, when they were so busy attending to the needs of the poor and sick, they met for deliberations late one night, at a time when the meeting would not interfere with their charitable work; it was decided that they form themselves "into one body, in which each was thoughtful and careful for the others, for the greater good of souls." The decision was made subject to the confirmation and approval of the Holy See. At further meetings other questions were discussed, a whole month —with prayer and discussions—being devoted to deciding whether, to the vows of poverty and chastity which already bound them, they should add that of obedience, seeing its "unparalleled efficacy in defeating pride and arrogance." In the discussions, each Father's vote had equal value; Ignatius did not claim any priority, and the youngest of the ten had as much say as any of the others. All voted unanimously for the vow of obedience.

Meanwhile, the long protracted winter dragged itself out. Ignatius found that he had to devote many hours to letter writing. All sorts of people were writing to him at the very time when he and the Companions were debating and praying about the vow of obedience. Among his correspondence was a letter from thirteen-year-old Catharina de Badajoz, one of the maids-of-honor brought by Juana of Aragon from Spain when she came to Italy to marry the Duke of Colonna. Catharina was "holy and learned"; she knew several languages and composed Latin verses; she was to die in 1553 at the age of twenty-seven. On March 23, 1539, she sent Ignatius a note from Naples:

> After greeting Your Reverence I want to let you know that I have been here in Naples for the past seventeen months and always hoping to hear news of you and all the senores—servants of Jesus Christ —to whose prayers I commend myself, not being so daring as to commend myself to yours. Were it not that I feared to annoy you, I would keep walking after Your Reverence as the Canaanite followed Christ my Lord.
>
> I have not forgotten anything of all which, on another occasion, you told me to do; for indeed your words are not the sort a person readily forgets. But I find myself always dissatisfied with this world and have the thought of death continually before me. I beseech Your Reverence to deign to write and tell me what I ought to do. As for other news, this Father [Bobadilla] can tell you all.
>
> Marc Antonio salutes you. I have read this letter to his father and he also sends you greeting.
>
> About Dona Isabel [Roser], I do not know whether she is alive or

dead. I send greetings to Senor Maestre Favre and Senor Don Diego and Senor Esteban de Eguia, and ask them to be my good advocates with you; for I, although a sinner, wish always to serve you and them, and in my unworthy prayers I never cease to ask Our Lord to conserve you all in His holy service. I remain—praying God that your noble and reverend self may continue to advance in His holy service for the consolation and salvation of many.

From Naples, 23rd March, 1539.
She who confides in God and in your holy virtue and teaching,
Your Reverence's humble servant,
Catharina de Badajoz.[19]

The Marc Antonio mentioned was the Colonna heir; his father "who also sends greetings," Ascanio Colonna. Poor Catharina must have found life trying as one of the youngest of the ladies Colonna's wife had brought with her to Italy. Bobadilla had been sent by the pope to the Isle of Ischia to try to reconcile the Duke and Duchess who were perpetually quarrelling. Why Bobadilla should have been chosen rather than any of the others is not stated; he seems to have been a rather difficult man, courageous and energetic, but with eccentricities which must have amused—if sometimes they riled—his brethren; he liked to be the one called upon when assignations somewhat out of the ordinary and which appealed to him turned up. The achieving of even a temporary truce in the bickerings of Ascanio Colonna and Juana of Aragon was no small feather in Bobadilla's cap; and he was just the sort to wear it at an angle on his return, in case the other Companions might underestimate him and his work.

The minutes of the various discussions held by the Fathers to decide their future have been preserved; regarding the vow of obedience to the pope, it was considered of such importance that all mention of it outside meetings was vetoed, leaving each individual perfectly free to think and pray about it and come to his own independent decision. On May 3rd it was decided that the vow should be made through the head of the new Society; that the members should be ready to travel wherever the pope thought fit to send them; that they should teach the people the commandments of God and Christian doctrine, spending forty days teaching catechism to children; and that the superior of the Society should decide the employment of each member. This was the blueprint of the future

Society of Jesus. Fifty years later, Bobadilla, in a letter to Father Acquaviva, wrote:

> Divine Providence, *quae est abyssus multa*, changed the vows of Montmartre into others, better and more fruitful, substituting the religious life for our pilgrimage to Jerusalem.[20]

Further meetings during May saw regulations drafted concerning the acceptance and probation of novices; the tenure of office of the superior of the Society; the acceptance of houses or churches; the dismissal of candidates who had proved unsuitable. Finally it was decided that Ignatius should summarize in brief the nature and characteristics of the new order; this *Formula Instituti,* which reduced all the essential elements to five heads, was then sent to the pope through Cardinal Contarini, the churchman who the previous year had copied out the text of the *Exercises* with his own hand during his long retreat. In September the Companions were gladdened by a letter from the Cardinal telling them that the pope, having read the *Formula,* had blessed and approved it, and that the Bull of Approbation was being drawn up. It took a full year, however, before official papal ratification of this verbal approval was obtained, for the authorities to whom the pope submitted the *Formula* made various objections. Ignatius and his Companions proposed omitting office sung in choir and certain mortifications common to the cloister; these innovations were opposed by some and others queried the vow of obedience to the pope as being superfluous. One venerable Cardinal was totally opposed to the founding of yet another religious order—the Church, in his opinion "had too many orders, brawling among themselves and with seculars, causing the laity to turn anticlerical. If half the existing orders were suppressed, or amalgamated with the Benedictines, Cistercians, Franciscans, and Dominicans, the Church would be saved much scandal and dissension."[21]

Ignatius "prayed as though all depended upon God, and worked as though all depended upon human effort." He began by making a powerful assault on the seemingly adamant heart of old Cardinal Guidiccioni, promising three thousand Masses if that good prelate withdrew his opposition. This was somewhat in the nature of a heavy spiritual mortgage upon the unborn Society, seeing that there were as yet but ten priests to say the Masses; in 1541 Francis Xavier records having 250 of his portion of the holy debt paid off. Powerful friends in Rome and throughout Italy were approached and their intercession and aid invoked. Within a year the

214

heart of the aged cardinal had capitulated, and the Bull *Regimini Militantis Ecclesiae*, canonically establishing the Society of Jesus, was signed on September 27, 1540.

During these two years of trials and discussions and prayers and apostolic labors, the steps of future brethren were already being turned towards the Society. Two in particular came by strange ways, one forsaking a great name, the other a promising future, to follow Ignatius "for the greater glory of God and the good of souls."

In May, 1539, Spain was plunged into mourning when the Empress, after a brief illness, died. Few royal couples of that or any other age were as happy in their marriage as Charles and his beautiful wife, Isabella of Portugal. Her death at Toledo was the climax in a series of mounting trials. He could not bear even to attend her funeral but retired to a monastery near Toledo, where he shut himself up with his grief for seven weeks, entrusting the funeral arrangements to the care of Francis Borgia, Marquis of Lombay, heir to the Duke of Gandia. Borgia and his wife not only held high positions in the Imperial household but were intimate friends of the Emperor and Empress. As he reined in his charger at Alcantara Bridge, high above the bend of the Tagus, waiting to take over the funeral cortege and convey it on its long journey to Granada, the Marquis, one of the first nobles of the Imperial Court, may have reflected that his sun had set; for it was already being rumored that the Emperor would never remain in Spain after Isabella's death. Borgia and his wife deeply grieved for the gracious and lovely lady, beloved by all Spaniards. The funeral set out. On May 16th the rose colored towers of the Alhambra could be seen—they were nearing Granada. Next day, after solemn Requiem Mass and Office, the coffin enclosed in its outer casing of lead lay in the Chapel of the Kings all day, while the Marquis of Lombay kept guard. Since May 2 he had not left the royal casket out of his sight; at the interment on the evening of the 17th, his task would be completed when, having identified the corpse as that of Isabella and sworn to the same, the dead lady would be buried beside the *Reyes Catolicos*.

Art has been enriched and matter for thousands of sermons provided by the famous incident in the crypt beneath the royal chapel when the Marquis, stepping forward to verify the remains and gaze once more on Isabella's lovely, Madonna-like face, turned aside while the coffin was hastily uncovered and—in shocked realization that the corruption to which all humanity is heir spares neither rank nor beauty nor goodness—resolved to renounce the court and the world. He could not recognize Isabella's features in the sight that met his gaze, but he swore that he had guarded the remains every inch of the road from the bridge at Toledo; he had slept on the church pavements at each halting place on the way; the corpse could not be any but that of the Empress. His duty done, he stood back until the coffin lay in its last resting place, turned away without speaking even to his dearly loved wife, strode to his lodging, and locked himself in for the evening.[22]

Eleven years later, his wife dead, the future of his eight children arranged for, Francis Borgia, then Duke of Grandia, rode out of his city and province, renouncing his title, his wealth, the happy home life that had been his, to journey to Rome to join the Society of Jesus and meet the Ignatius with whom he had been corresponding for several years.

> His departure for Rome caused great edification [wrote the rector of the Jesuit College in Gandia to Ignatius] as did the sight of my Lord Duke's obvious delight in leaving the land of Egypt, and his farewells to his children, his people, and his possessions. We feel quite ashamed when we compare our renunciation and his, our cowardice and his courage, our meanness and his generosity.[23]

When the news of the Empress's death reached Rome in 1539, the pope dispatched his relative, Cardinal Farnese, to Toledo as papal nuncio on a special visit of sympathy to Charles. In a house opposite to that in which the Cardinal was lodged lived a widow with her four girls and two boys. One of the boys, Pedro, waited on the Cardinal at table, making such an impression on the great man that when leaving for Rome he asked Dona Ribadeneira, the widow, if he might bring Pedro with him as a page. Young Ribadeneira was then thirteen. "The Cardinal," he writes in his Confessions, "promised to make a great man of me, and my mother, who was very keen on my becoming a priest, agreed; that was how I came to be sent away so young and with unknown strangers and at a time when not many left Spain for Rome. . . . We traveled at our ease and in great style, arriving at Rome and being lodged in the Cardinal's palace which was then a much finer palace than the pope's."[24]

Although Spaniards were more inclined to travel to the Indies than anywhere else in those times, there was a considerable colony of Spaniards in Rome. Among these was a relative of young Pedro's dead father, the diplomat already encountered in these pages—Dr. Ortiz. Ortiz did his best to keep an eye on the Toledan page, who indeed needed someone to admonish him, for not only was he a thoroughly spoiled boy before ever he left Toledo but he seemed possessed of an imp of mischief, being seldom out of trouble. He could boast to his fellow pages that he had been injured at seven when he tried to stop a runaway mule; that he had a leg broken when playing; that he had traveled from Toledo to Rome. Having to live up to the name he gave himself for bravado, one night, when the pope gave a banquet for his Farnese relatives, Pedro flung his lighted torch at another page who had made a face at him and threw the whole place into an uproar. At Candlemas in 1540, as the Cardinals and their households filed past the pope and kissed his slipper, young Ribadeneira, impudent and vain, reached up and kissed the pope's hand. Paul III asked who the young page was, but the boy was not reproved, either by the pope or by his own master, Cardinal Farnese.

When Dr. Ortiz had to go to a conference in Germany, he felt uneasy at leaving this wilful, temperamental young relative behind. If he tried his tricks in the ambassador's absence and found no one to plead for him, what would befall him? Calling Pedro, he told him that, if he was in trouble and did not know to whom to turn, he was to go to the house by the Melangolo Tower and ask for Father Ignatius. Ribadeneira soon kicked over the traces again. One day, when it was his turn to wait on his master, he was missing; the Cardinal spent the day in the Campagna; returning to Rome in the evening, he enquired for Pedro, but the page, not content with playing truant from his duties, had failed to come home. No one knew where he was. That same night Ignatius and the Fathers, answering a knock at their door, found the boy imploring shelter for the night and begging Father Ignatius to go to the Farnese palace next day to be his intercessor with the Cardinal.[25]

In the morning Ignatius set off to plead for Pedro; he had probably heard all about the audacity and quick wit and quicker temper of the page from his friend Ortiz. Cardinal Farnese was well acquainted with Ignatius. When he heard of Ribadeneira's latest prank, he laughed, promised immediate forgiveness, and told Ignatius to send him back. But the lad announced that he wished to remain and become a Companion. Ignatius, however, sent him back to the palace, telling him that he could not take such a step on the whim of a moment and advising him to consult some of his friends in the palace and elsewhere. But within a short time, the boy was back again—and a less promising subject for the vow of obedience could hardly be imagined; the new postulant had not even made his first Communion; he seemed in no hurry to undertake the Exercises. The best thing about him was his age—he was between fourteen and fifteen when accepted in 1540, and so had plenty of time to reform. At first he was allowed to go about in his page boy's livery and given time to think of starting the Exercises; he not only kept on putting them off, but began to tire of his new life and pine for the palace; Ignatius waited and prayed and finally Pedro capitulated, saying "I'll do them, Father; I'll do the Exercises."

He did them and made his first Communion at Christmas (1540). It would be edifying to relate that Ribadeneira, like all the others who did the Exercises, was completely and immediately transformed. But such was not the case. He went to bed in his clothes to save time in the mornings, the early rising bell being the bane of his young life; he broke the rules of the refectory and carried his breakfast to his cell, bolting it there to save further precious minutes. He made faces at another novice behind the Minister's back—the Farnese page boys seemingly being adept at making grimaces. He banged doors, raced along corridors, came downstairs like a thundering avalanche and, when sent to sweep, raised such dust that what the floors lost the tables, chairs, and walls gained. The Novice Master complained of him to Ignatius; the boy was hopeless; he disturbed the whole house and nothing could be done with him. Ignatius pointed out that, because of his youth and former mode of life, Pedro had more to subdue than the others; he was not really doing too badly; he would yet make a fine Jesuit. So the Fathers were soon treated to the spectacle of the novice going about with things tied to his legs, to remind him not to rush downstairs; and he tried to do a bit better in the kitchen, where he was sent to do some cooking. He still had his bad days; once when Ignatius had a very special guest, Pedro, who by then had ideas about his culinary prowess, produced an egg pasty that looked delicious and fetched it to the table, certain that it would earn him a compliment. Alas, the promising looking crust concealed nothing but burned-up egg, and Ignatius, noticing that the cook waited for praise, spoke sharply to him. "How dare you stand there," he asked, "after handing such a dish to a guest?"

With all his faults Ribadeneira was a special favorite of the Jesuit founder. On one occasion he was asked by Ignatius if he knew what it meant to be a secretary. "To keep secrets faithfully," answered the young novice. Soon afterwards he was summoned from the kitchen and trained for a while as Ignatius' secretary. His handwriting and spelling were bad, and Ignatius, who wrote a good hand himself, was kept busy correcting the letters and other documents which Pedro penned. "This

218

fellow will never come to any good," said the founder one day, when the amanuensis handed up some papers, worse written, worse spelt than usual; and he threw the documents away. But Pedro "beat his cheeks and wept" and was forgiven. Ribadeneira was the prototype of the problem child and Ignatius seems to have had the knack of knowing just how such adolescents should be handled—when to be lenient and when to be firm, the right moment for a rebuke, or a word of praise or encouragement.

Pedro was not yet sixteen when he was sent away, with Araoz and Estrada and other young Jesuit students, to study in Paris. They traveled on foot, wearing such garments as they could find—the Society not having yet decided upon a habit—the only thing common to all being their threadbare clothes. They begged their way and slept in various charitable institutions and hospitals in the towns on their itinerary. Father Ignatius had given orders that the weakest member of the group was to take the lead each day and set the pace for the others.*[26]

Ribadeneira remembered seeing Ignatius teaching catechism in the Church of Our Lady of the Wayside; he himself was as yet only a novice, but "I did not hesitate to speak to our father, then a holy man of fifty, afterwards. I told him that his speech was very inaccurate; that he had made many mistakes because he spoke Italian as though it were Spanish. 'Good,' he said when I admonished him, 'You note down the mistakes I most commonly make and advise me about them.' So I began to observe him diligently from that day out, when he read and spoke, and noted the foreign words he used and his inept pronunciations and the like. But his errors were so many and his speech so sprinkled with them that it was hard work jotting them down and I despaired of his amendment, and told him that I might as well give up the task. He said meekly and quietly, 'Very well, Pedro, I must only continue to serve God with what He gave me' (meaning his faulty Italian). I was then only a lad of fourteen." There is no doubt but that Ignatius had a really soft spot in his heart for Ribadeneira; perhaps it was because Pedro was the living proof that the Exercises and the ascetical teaching they embodied were as effective to form a refractory, vain, capricious boy of fourteen to Ignatian standards as they had been in the winning and formation of more mature men for the primitive

---

*When they were leaving Rome, the yong Jesuits proposed to Ignatius that Ribadeneira, being only a lad, and not strong, should ride while they walked. "Pedro may do as he likes," replied the Saint, "but if he be a son of mine, he will walk like the others."

Company. Polanco, who became the saint's secretary some time after Ribadeneira's departure for Paris, writes to Lainez in 1547:

> As for Pedro, I know and see that, apart from the charity Father Master Ignatius has for all, and particularly for those of the Company, he loves him more than any; and he wishes him to have all possible advantages that may profit him for the future, not only in his studies, but in every way.[27]

And a year later the secretary writes to Pedro:

> I write because Father Master Ignatius, on account of his affection for you, does not wish to determine your affairs himself, but has committed them to Father Lainez and myself.[28]

All the letters of Ignatius referring to his Benjamin breathe a fatherly care and tenderness, and certainly refute—as Father Rey, S.J., points out—the legend of Ignatius the iron-hearted, the stranger to sensibility, the man who knew not how to love. Yet his affection for this young Companion did not allow him to hold Pedro in Rome. He sent him far away to study at a very immature age and with the minimum of money. When, a few years later, Pedro became melancholy and faced a possible breakdown, he was sent back to Rome "to revive his sorrowful spirit near the warm heart of Saint Ignatius. And one happy day, broken-up, famished, the sad imprint of his unfathomable nostalgia upon him—having crossed central Europe by the German route, on foot, and hungry, and in face of dreadful dangers—he arrived in the Eternal City at the very moment when Saint Ignatius was making his preparation for Mass. . . . How the strong, unchanging spirit of Ignatius mellows and becomes gentle as he throws open his arms to his beloved, disfigured Pedro!"

Even before the Companions obtained official canonical approbation, their services were already in demand. The pope, as though the fourth vow were actually in force, had begun to send them in different directions. Broet and Rodriguez went to Siena. The archbishop of that city could write to Ignatius:

> . . . He is so holy, your—or rather, our—Broet, and with so charming a manner that he pleases and is accepted by all. He exhorts by word, aids by example, attracts by humility, and by his charity in-

flames to holy living. . . . People throng to hear his sermons and to go to confession to him. The best of our university students are doing the Exercises; and a priest who had won a certain notoriety for his authorship of lewd comedies has been converted, making public apology from the pulpit and deciding to spend the rest of his life as a Franciscan.[29]

Lainez and Favre were assigned to brigand-infested Parma, where a monk was preaching Lutheranism and where the general state of morals was deplorable. Lainez tackled the heretic, while Favre gave the Exercises, founding a Confraternity of the Holy Name which has lasted down to the present day. Bobadilla was trying to reconcile the Colonna couple; it was no small triumph to return to Rome with the news that he had achieved even a short term truce. Ignatius himself was yet to have trouble trying to make peace between the same pair. Francis Xavier was in Rome, acting as secretary for Ignatius. The Portuguese ambassador, whose king was anxious to evangelize his possessions in India and the East, had been told by the pope to go to Ignatius for six missionaries. "Senor Ambassador," writes Ignatius, "there are only ten of us Companions. If you take six for India and the East, only four remain for the rest of the world."

Favre had hardly finished his work in Parma when he was dispatched to Worms in the capacity of official theologian to Dr. Ortiz, papal legate to the Diet. The conference between Catholics and Protestants fell through; Favre wrote telling Ignatius of the affection he felt for the Germans he met there and of how much he would have liked to converse with them, "especially with their chief speaker, Philip Melanchthon."[30] Le Jay was elsewhere in Italy, while the four in Rome, Xavier, Codure, Salmeron, and Ignatius, continued their apostolate in the Eternal City.

Early in march, 1541, Ignatius called all who could be spared from their missions to deliberations concerning the Constitutions. He himself, with Codure, had already drafted forty-nine points for discussion, the most important of which were the rules for admission into the Society, the causes for which a member might be dismissed, the exact meaning and scope of the vow of poverty, the examination and formation of novices, the attributes essential in the General, the teaching of catechism to children, the habit or clothes to be worn, and regulations concerning the recitation of the divine office, the celebration of Mass, and similar matters.

The *Constitution and Rules of the Society of Jesus,* like those of other orders, may be found in any large library; it is not proposed to recapitulate them here; but it is noteworthy that the *Spiritual Exercises* and the *Constitutions* are not only mutually complementary but are the two greatest documents left by their author to posterity. The *Spiritual Exercises* were the Saint's legacy to all men; the *Constitutions* are the special inheritance of his own sons. "The *Exercises,*" writes one commentator, "are to the *Constitutions* what the soul is to the body." And another says, "The *Constitutions* translate that spirit with which God our Lord wrote in the hearts of our first fathers, and which the same Lord communicates by means of the *Exercises.*"

Although Paul III had approved the outline of the Society's aims in 1540, Ignatius seems to have taken his time about drafting the *Constitutions* in final, definite form; indeed, they were not completed until shortly before his death in 1556 and did not come into force until after that date. In his *Summary of the Constitutions,* the Saint is emphatic in stating that, for the promoting of the service of God, written Constitutions are secondary to the "interior law of charity and love which the Holy Spirit engraves upon the heart." One reason why he delayed so long about drawing up the rules for his Society may have been that he wished to see them in action before finally fixing them in the written code.

It is generally conceded that in the pages of the *Constitutions* where Ignatius described the qualities needful for the Jesuit General, he unwittingly depicted himself. The head of the order, elected for life, must be a man of holy life, fervent in prayer, closely united with God; he must be an example for all the brethren, excelling in humility and charity "which should shine forth in him, particularly for the Company," and delight both God and men. He is to be completely master of himself, unperturbed interiorly, composed in his exterior, especially circumspect in his conversation. He must know when to be kind and when to be firm, when to be meek and when to uphold the right; not to be deflected from doing that which he judges to be most pleasing to God, nor yet incapable of compassion for his sons; in correction, charitable, recognizing that the right to reprehend others comes from God. . . . He must not be small-minded or chicken-hearted, but capable of undertaking and suffering great things in the service of God; he must be a man who perseveres in doing good, who does not lose heart when opposed—even by the great and powerful of this world; neither pleadings nor menaces are to move him from what he deems the right course of action. Prosperity is not to puff him up nor adversity to dishearten him; he must be ready to die, if necessary, for the good of the Company in the service of God Our Lord. As regards qualities of mind, judgment and intelligence are essentials . . . . a flair for dealing with various sorts of men, prudence, the ability to discern the spirits that move men to action, to be a counselor to whom those in spiritual need may turn, to be discreet in conversation and dealings with all—both those of the Company and outsiders. The Father General should be a man careful and far sighted when embarking on some new enterprise, strenuous to forward projects already undertaken and thorough in perfecting them. His health, age, etc., must be in accordance with what befits authority; his strength must at least be adequate to the requirements of his post so that he may be able by his office to forward the glory of God. The brethren should not elect a General so old that he is incompetent, nor one so young that he lacks experience and is unaccustomed to authority. "And though one or more of the qualities specified be wanting, at least let the General not be lacking in virtue, in love of the order, in good judgment, and in learning."

Once the Jesuit Order was approved, the election of the permanent superior became imperative. Though it must have been a foregone conclusion that Ignatius would and should be General, the election was held when as many of the first Companions as possible could be spared from their respective missions to come to Rome. Those who were unable to come—Favre, who was in Germany, and Xavier and Rodriguez, who were then in Portugal waiting for a ship to the East—gave their votes in writing. There were three days of prayer for guidance. All voted for Ignatius except the founder himself, whose vote was cast in favor of whatever father the majority might choose. When the result was known, Ignatius asked them to consider the matter a second time; so after further days of prayer, all voted again; the result was the same. Still pleading his "wish to be governed rather than to govern," his unfitness, his "evil habits, past and present," Ignatius again asked them to choose another. At this point Lainez demurred, saying that if Ignatius did not yield, he himself would leave the Society. Finally, the founder offered to take counsel with his confessor, a Franciscan of San Pietro in Montorio. He spent three days in the Franciscan convent on the Janiculum hill and made a general confession; but if he hoped that the confessor, on hearing of his early vanities and sins, would agree that Ignatius was no fit man to be the superior of an infant order, he was mistaken. The Friar's decision was that he ought to accept the authority to which he had been elected.[31]

So on the Friday of Easter Week, April 22, 1541, the founder and first General of the Society of Jesus, with the Companions, visited the Seven Churches of Rome—St. Peter's, St. Mary Major's, St. John Lateran, the Holy Cross of Jerusalem, and the three outside the walls, St. Lorenzo's, St. Sebastian's, and St. Paul's, finishing at the latter, where they went to confession, assisted at the Mass offered by Father Ignatius, and pronounced their vows according to the formula agreed upon. Except for a few minor changes of wording, these vows and those still made by all professed Fathers of the Society of Jesus are identical. The phrase that gives the professed Jesuit's vow its distinctive quality is "I promise special obedience to the supreme pontiff with regard to the missions mentioned . . . and likewise to be diligent to see that children are taught the rudiments of the faith." The intention of the vow Ignatius had specified in the *Constitutions*: "that we repair to whatever part of the world the supreme vicar of Christ shall determine to send us for the greater glory of God and the aiding of souls, whether among the faithful or infidels."

Jesuit obedience has come in for much criticism, mainly because of the comparisons Ignatius made in paragraph 547 of the *Constitutions*: "Obedience to superiors, in all matters where there is no question of sin involved, should be to leave oneself at the behest of divine Providence, in the person of the Superior, as though one were a dead body, to be moved here or there or treated in any manner, or as a stick in an old man's hand, that is placed where he wills and aids him who holds it in the manner he wishes . . . so he (a subject) may employ himself in joy, being certain that he is conforming himself to the divine will, far more than if he succeeded in doing other things following his own will and judgment." But this was no new invention: St. Basil, St. Benedict, St. Francis had all said the same thing in different ways; the vow and practice of obedience is common to all religious Orders. But in the older Orders, fixed obligations, particularly that of attending at set hours for choir, ensured constant practice in obedience; in the Order Ignatius had founded there were no such obligations and, even in the early years, the Society was finding its members called to the most varied activities in all parts of the world; if practicies of mortification and attendance at choir were to be non-obligatory, they had to be replaced by something to ensure that "the greater glory of God and the good of souls," the order's *raison d'etre*, would be effectively promoted at all times and in all circumstances.

The best comment on the Ignatian concept of obedience is in the letter he wrote two years before his death to the Jesuits of Portugal, who, following the example of their superior, the rather unstable and unpredictable Rodriguez, had shown a lamentable lack of comprehension and a failure in the practice of obedience. Ignatius begins by citing examples of obedience in both the Old and the New Testament, particularly "of Christ, who redeemed a world lost for lack of this virtue—*becoming obedient unto death, even to the death of the Cross.*" He goes on to state that he does not mind if other orders should outshine his in fasts, vigils, and such mortifications; but he wishes his to lead all in observing perfect obedience, in the abnegation of self-will and self-opinion, for a Jesuit must regard his obedience to his superior as obedience to Christ in the person of the superior. All the virtues of the religious state being dependent on obedience, he who fails in the latter fails in the vital bond of religious life. He gives grades of obedience: obedience in executing orders, obedience of the will, obedience of the intellect—proving that the latter is, in its perfect practice, the most pleasing holocaust a man can make of himself to God. He gives the means by which obedience may be won and safeguarded: humility and meekness, the strong faith that sees God in the superior, accepting orders with docility, without query. But he allows that representations may be made, "in regard to a command given, if anything occurs to you different from the superior's opinion and which, after having prayed about the matter, you think you ought to declare and propose to him." Finally, he counsels superiors to be careful about obedience, since on it depends the well-being of religious families, and begs all to bear in mind the example of Christ in the matter of obedience and to obey "for love of Christ our Lord."[32]

In his "Rules for Thinking with the Church," the epilogue to the *Exercises,* their author crystallizes for the exercitant, Jesuit and non-Jesuit, lay and clerical, the norms of filial obedience which should inspire "the true Christian, who sees in our Holy Mother, the hierarchical Church, the true Spouse of Christ Our Lord . . . in which only one Spirit holds sway, governing and ruling for the salvation of souls." The Jesuit *Constitutions,* the maxims on obedience written by the Saint before his death and bequeathed to the Society, the formula of the vow for professed Jesuits, and the duty imposed on the General of placing himself and the entire Society at the disposal of every newly elected pope—all point to the immense solicitude of Ignatius for the Church. Realizing that, to command obedience, authority must not only be centralized and strong but upheld and respected by the majority, he set himself to restore the credit of the papacy, to reinforce the central spiritual authority by every means in his power, to uphold it with all his strength and with all his powers as General of that Society he had first named "Trumpeters for Christ."

XIII

. . . . Man assigns the office but God gives the discretion. I want you. . . . to act without any scruple, as you judge from the circumstances what ought to be done, notwithstanding rules and ordinances. . . .
(Letter of St. Ignatius to Father Olivare Manare)

. . . . The hospitals ought to be visited at the hour best suited to health and you should shrive and comfort the poor patients and also bring them something whenever you can . . . .
(Letter of St. Ignatius to Frs. Lainez and Salmeron in Trent for the Council.)

. . . . Our rest and happiness in the next life depends on how much good we do in this. . . .
(Letter of St. Ignatius to his brother, Don Beltran of Loyola.)

IT has already been mentioned how Ignatius replied to the Portuguese Ambassador who asked in the name of his king, John III, for missionaries for India and the East, telling him that if six of the Companions were allocated for the needs of these rich colonies of Portugal, "only four would be left for the rest of the world." King John had first been put in touch with Ignatius by de Gouvea, the former Rector of the Ste. Barbe in Paris—the same who had intended to make an example of Inigo on his first appearance in that college and who had ended up by becoming his champion and his friend. As early as autumn, 1538, de Gouvea wrote to Ignatius and the Companions concerning the matter. He got the following reply from Favre, writing in place of Ignatius:

> We well know your zeal which makes you thirst for the salvation of those souls in the Portuguese Indies, where the harvest is already white. Would that we were able to help you and your king and the souls whose plight arouses such zeal. But there are some obstacles which prevent us from acceding not only to your desires but to those of many others. We Companions—all of us—have offered ourselves to the supreme pontiff, the Lord of all Christ's harvest fields, signifying to him by our oblation that for whatever he in Christ may dispose, we are ready; so that if he sends us to those lands to which you sum-

mon us, we shall joyfully go thither. Our reason for thus resolving to subject ourselves to the judgment and will of His Holiness is because he knows best what is fitting and needful for the universal Church.

For some time past, several persons have been bringing pressure to bear in certain quarters here to get us sent to those other Indies which the Spaniards daily conquer for the Emperor. . . . But the will of His Holiness seems to be that we remain where we are, and indeed there is an abundant harvest to be reaped in Rome. Distance, however, does not scare us, nor the drudgery of learning new languages; we only wish that whatever is most pleasing to Christ may be done . . . *not that we are sufficient to think anything of ourselves, as of ourselves,* but we hope in His abundance and riches. . . . We have come through great tribulations since we came to Rome, but have reached the end, emerging unscathed. Rome does not lack those who hate the Church's light of truth and life. Be you vigilant and promote the building up of the Christian people with the example of a virtuous life, as you have up to now been active in defending the faith and doctrine of the Church. How can we think that the infinitely good God will conserve the truths of holy faith in us if we fly from the good life? It is to be feared that the principal cause of the errors of doctrine is rooted in erring conduct; and if the latter be not corrected, the former evil will never be completely eradicated.

Yours in the Lord,

Peter Favre, etc., his assistant, and the brothers.[1]

After repeated appeals from Portugal both to His Holiness and to Ignatius, the latter finally agreed to part with two for the East—Rodriguez, just back from Siena, being sent on to Lisbon in the beginning of March, 1540, and Bobadilla summoned from Naples to Rome to follow Rodriguez to Portugal and thence to the mission fields. Bobadilla arrived back in Rome ill, however, and "lame in one leg." Ignatius himself was also ailing that week and in bed; the Portuguese Ambassador, waiting so that the Jesuit chosen might travel in his entourage on the long overland route from Rome to Lisbon, could not delay any longer. The youngest in the house, Ribadeneira, was a witness of the swift turn events took on March 14, 1540; in later years he told the story:

Our Father called Master Francisco Xavier saying: "Master Francis, you know that His Holiness has ordered that two of ours must go to India, and that Bobadilla was the one chosen by us; now, because of this illness, he cannot go and the Ambassador cannot wait until he recovers. The work is yours." To which the blessed Father joyfully and instantly replied: "Pues, sus! Heme aqui!" [Good! Here I am, willing and ready!"]

And he spent that day and the next mending some old pants and such a soutane—quite indescribable!—and went away looking a sight; truly it could be seen that God was calling him to what we have since witnessed. . . . And Master Lainez told me that once, when he and Xavier were on a mission together in Italy, and being lodged in a hospital and sleeping in the same bed, Father Francis used to wake up sometimes, saying: "Lord Jesus, how fatigued I feel! Do you know what I was dreaming? That I was carrying an Indian on my shoulders, and his weight was such that I could not bring him along."[2]

Xavier's last day in Rome was spent in waiting on the pope for documents testifying to his mission as papal legate to the East, in darning and mending his poor clothes, and in writing out and sealing three papers. One of these stated that he agreed with and gave his consent in advance to every decision the brethren might make in the years ahead regarding their manner of life; another document contained his vows, which he charged Lainez to pronounce in his name—for he was leaving Rome six months before the Society received canonical approbation; the third paper was his vote for Ignatius as General. Some of his biographers relate that when he went to bid farewell to the founder, then ill in bed, the sick man noticed the thinness of the soutane in which Xavier was setting out to cross not only the Alps but the seas and ocean that lay between him and the East. Ignatius took off a warm vest he himself was wearing and made the other put it on. The words, "Go—enkindle and inflame the whole earth," may or may not have been the older man's farewell to his fellow Basque. If the command were not actually spoken, it was because there was no need for Ignatius to express, to a soul as close-knit with his as was Xavier's, his apostolic desires which embraced the whole world; and Francis needed neither to be told the mind of Ignatius nor to be urged to the faraway harvest fields. His ardent spirit was already racing eastwards, though his heart, as his later letters tell, kept constantly straining back to the west, to the brethren—dearer than Juan and Miguel, his blood-brothers in Navarre—and to his beloved father Ignatius, in that Rome to which he would return no more.

Within a year of his election as General, Ignatius found his correspondence becoming daily more and more burdensome and voluminous, as his sons dispersed "to various posts in Portugal or the Indies, in Spain, in Paris, in Ireland, in Naples, in Parma, in Placenza, in Brescia, and the March of Ancona." Favre, le Jay, and Bobadilla are in Germany; Xavier gone to India, whence he is to sail to Ceylon, Malaya, and all the islands of the eastern ocean—not excepting Japan; Rodriguez, whom King John held in Lisbon, is preaching in Portugal; a band of young Jesuits has left for Paris and the lecture halls; Araoz is to go to Spain. Later Favre and Lainez and Salmeron, later still Canisius, will make history in Trent at the great Council of reform. To follow their journeyings and other itineraries undertaken by the first generation of the Society of Jesus would be not only to embark on the grand tour of Europe but to take a trip around the world. As such travels would keep the reader too far and too long away from Ignatius, with whom this book is primarily concerned and who, throughout the diaspora of the Companions, remained in Rome, only one of these missions will be here recounted—the one that was, to all appearances, a failure—the mission to Ireland.

To Rome in the weeks preceding September, 1541, came the Irish bishop, Redmond Gallagher—later to die a martyr's death during the Elizabethan persecutions. This Bishop of Killala had been sent to the pope by the Ulster chieftain, Conn O'Neill, to beg for priests and to report to Paul III concerning the wave of persecution then threatening to submerge the Church in Ireland. His Holiness was not unaware of the attempts being made by Henry VIII to drag Ireland into the schism which already separated England from Rome. The Irish clergy, bracing themselves and their flocks to meet the first, fierce onslaughts on the faith, had the unhappy experience of witnessing the open apostasy of Dr. Browne, occupant of the primatial see of Armagh. Browne, "whose mind had been happily freed from the thralldom of popery," was promptly rewarded by Henry with the Archbishopric of Dublin. This first of the "King's Bishops" thus intruded into the See of St. Laurence O'Toole was consecrated by Cranmer, having received neither canonical election nor papal sanction.*

---

* Note: A letter from Henry VIII to Dr. Browne has a sting in its tail, when the King reminds the archbishop that he made him "and could just as easily remove you again and put another man of more virtue and honesty in your place."
State Papers of Henry VIII, Vol. II. Letter of July 7, 1537.

The pope meanwhile nominated a Scot then in Rome, Dr. Wauchope, to the vacant archdiocese of Armagh. When Conn O'Neill's emissary, Dr. Gallagher, arrived in Rome, Dr. Wauchope asked the pope to send some of the Companions to Ireland; he knew Favre, who had been to Worms and Ratisbon, and he probably had met Ignatius and the others. Salmeron and Broet were nominated for this difficult and dangerous mission to a country which was, to those in Rome, says Father Brodrick, "a misty island indeed, a terra incognita, blacked out by the great bulk of schismatic England."[3] The mission of the two Jesuits whom Paul III sent as his nuncios, though in the nature of a diplomatic embassy and rather tentative and exploratory in character, was also intended as "a gesture of sympathy . . . to a people, faithful but beleagured."

Dr. Gallagher could have given Fathers Salmeron and Broet some idea of what to expect when they reached their destination. The dearth of priests had become acute: some were exiled, some in hiding, some in irons; already the King had made martyrs and gave orders that religious houses were to be leveled. "If their nests are allowed to remain, those birds [the religious] will soon come back to roost there." But before the houses were leveled, any valuables found within them were confiscated. Mass and the sacraments were proscribed; death to the priest, death to the lay Catholic who was caught defying the king's edict.

Apart altogether from the religious question, the country was in a state of great unrest. Through the adroit system known as "Surrender and Regrant," the minor Gaelic chiefs were being wiped out. Heads of clans would be offered protection against more powerful neighbors who compelled them to pay levies; the English armies would fight their battles if only they surrendered their lands; they would get back their estates on a new basis, live under a new legal code, and get a fine English title to boot. Petty chieftains who compromised, and they were not few, were eventually obliterated; for their own people disowned them, making them pay heavily in raids and burnings and killings for their betrayal of the old Gaelic civilization, while their new masters despised, bullied, and chivvied them. They were the first to go down before the colonists and middlemen hovering on the rearguard of the king's armies, eager and ready to grab the lands of any chief who had not fulfilled his agreement according to the new code, and who was wavering between the old regime and the new. Because of these small local wars being waged for several portions of Irish territory, and the major offensive just begun to bring the soul of Ireland into subjection, there was general chaos and upheaval.

This was the Ireland to which the two Jesuits were dispatched. Father Salmeron was a second choice; Codure was to have come with Broet, but he died and the rather hasty-tempered Spaniard was sent in his stead. Ignatius, knowing that he had teamed two men of opposite temperaments and anxious to give them what help he could on a mission truly perilous, drew up sets of instructions for them. He tells them when and to whom they are to produce the papal bulls; he warns them to beware of revealing their mission to chance acquaintances met on the way; in Paris they are not to go to the university but to lodge quietly in the town; they are, however, to make a secret visit to the young Jesuits studying there and, before leaving Paris, "let all meet in your lodging and have supper together and recommend yourselves to their prayers." They are to be especially careful when they reach the French port of embarkation, also when they are on board ship and on landing in Scotland, "for the king's spies are everywhere."

They are to dress alike, in dark clothing. On arrival in Scotland they are to go to the King, James V, and get a letter of recommendation to the "*Hybernici.*"[4] They are advised to beg their way; this they did not have to do as a young nobleman, Francis Zapata, who had been a notary in one of the papal chancelleries, offered to accompany them and to pay all expenses of the journey. Zapata was anxious to become a Jesuit, but Ignatius seemed in no hurry to accept him; possibly the offer to share the hardships, labor, and dangers of the two Fathers bound for Ireland was undertaken by the young man as an earnest of his sincerity and goodwill.

A separate letter contained further instructions "On how to conduct business and converse in the Lord." It is set out in Ignatius' typical, methodical fashion:

> In dealing with persons, especially those of your own or lesser social class, according to their dignity and authority, speak little, and after the others; listen long and with pleasure; afterwards answer to the various points, and when finished take your leave. If they reply, answer as briefly as possible; let your farewells be brief and gracious.
>
> When conversing with persons of note, see—in order to win them for the greater service of God Our Lord—of what temperament they are and adapt yourselves to them. For instance, if a man is of an

emotional nature, speaking rapidly and gaily, let you too adopt a like style; speak of good and holy things, but do not put on grave, phlegmatic, or melancholy airs. With those who are in bearing very correct, slow-spoken, liking to discourse of grave and weighty matters, you ought to speak in similar manner; thus you will please them—*and have made yourselves all things to all men.*

Note well that when two quick-tempered persons converse, if they be not both of the same mind on their subject, there is grave danger of disagreement. So one who knows he is hasty-tempered should beware and go into such conversations well armed by his self-examinations and with resolves to suffer anything rather than have a quarrel, especially if he knows that the person he is dealing with is lacking in self-control.* In conversations with the serious, there is less danger of precipitate words causing the other to become annoyed.

In all conversations with those whom we wish to win and to take in the net of the greater service of God Our Lord, let us follow the same plan adopted by the enemy when he wishes to draw a good soul into evil—only our strategy is meant to draw souls toward good. For the enemy goes in the same door as the soul, but he comes out by his own; he approves of its conduct and forbears to contradict it until he becomes familiar with that soul, drawing it even to good and holy thoughts, lulling it into peace. And then by degrees he procures his own ends, attracting the soul under pretext of good into some difficulty of error or illusion, always luring it to evil. Let us, to draw souls toward good, agree with and praise others concerning any matters good in themselves, tolerate other things which are bad in themselves until, gaining their love, we can win them to better things; thus though we go in their door, they come out ours.

If we meet with persons tempted or sad, we should speak kindly to them and at some length, showing ourselves joyful exteriorly and interiorly, going contrary to their dispositions the better to edify and console them.

In all conversations, especially those which involve reconciliations and those in which spiritual advice is given, be on your guard, remembering that all one says may or will be made public.

---

* This was obviously meant for Salmeron!

In business affairs do not waste time; I mean, if you promise something for tomorrow, let it be done if possible today.

If you have any charge given you, better let Master Francisco [Zapata] see to it. . . . None of you should touch any money. . . . I repeat, take care that each one of you three may be able to say that he has not touched a penny of the money belonging to this mission.[5]

This last injunction suggests that the pope or others in Rome had given the travelers some money to take to distressed persons in Ireland. There is a third document reminding the Fathers that their principal duty in Ireland will be "to assist that country in its spiritual needs and to assuage, as far as is in their power, the conscience of the supreme pontiff and also the Illustrious and Very Reverend Protector of that province."

What to do on arrival in Ireland:

Firstly: Visit the Catholic leaders, especially the four principal men of that land, praising in the name of His Holiness their constancy and zeal for the Catholic religion and encouraging them to persevere.

Visit also the Catholic bishops, doing the same; if giving bad example or not living in their cathedrals nor visiting their flocks, not having the divine office said nor looking after their priests, or showing other defects visible to all, exhort and admonish them to better conduct becoming those in good odor with the Holy See.

Here Ignatius plainly shows how little those in Rome realized the true situation in Ireland. He continues, telling them to note how the word of God is preached, how the sacraments, particularly confession and Holy Communion, are administered, "helping with all your power the ministers of the Catholic religion." They themselves are also to teach (although they know no Irish!); if they come across apostate preachers or parish priests, they are to try to deprive such men of the occasion of doing harm to the faith of others.

The nuncios are to travel poor, "in board and lodging aiming at the simplest, making do with a half or a third of what the ordinary expenses would come to." They are not to have horses or mules; if given money in alms, they are to give it over to some honest, good people of the place where they received it, so that it may find its way back again to the poor, or be spent for some pious purpose. They are to visit the sick and strengthen them in the faith; if they can start grammar schools and staff them with efficient Catholic masters, it would be good, and also if they could establish hospitals and shelters for the poor and orphanages ... "without accepting any money, as laid down by our Institute, or without accepting any alms in return for your labors." Finally, if necessary for the glory of God and the common good, they must not refuse to risk their lives, but without doing anything rash or tempting God; generally speaking, though, they are to proceed with all possible dexterity and prudence, taking counsel of the Catholic lords of Ireland, so as not to be taken prisoner "by the English governing that country."[6]

Despite his zeal and desire to further the mission of Broet and Salmeron, Ignatius' ignorance of conditions in Ireland in 1541 rendered his instructions practically useless. "He thought," writes Father Brodrick, "that Ireland was another Guipuzcoa, which needed only exhorting to be well. But the wounds of the country, half inflicted from without and half received in the house of her friends, went far too deep for mere spiritual G.P.'s such as Broet and Salmeron to heal."[7]

War had broken out again as the papal embassy to Ireland set out in September, 1541. At Lyons they met Cardinal Beaton, the Primate of Edinburgh, a prelate whose private life was no great example to his people. He told them that they were undertaking the impossible: "For all the cities, towns, fortresses, and castles of Hibernia are in the English King's hands and his soldiers hold all the harbors. And besides, of all mankind," added the Cardinal, "the Irish are the wildest people, being barbarians, strangers to all discipline." Despite these discouraging warnings the two Jesuits continued on their way; they sailed from a Flanders port, were twice put ashore on the English coast, where they had to conceal themselves for almost two weeks, and on the last day of 1541 arrived in Edinburgh and visited the king, then at Stirling Castle, presenting him with a letter from the pope. At the Scottish court the two Fathers were introduced by the French Ambassador and by some Scots who had known the Jesuits in Rome. James V promised to remain faithful to the Church; though his uncle Henry VIII had renounced his religion, Scotland's king would not follow him. On February 12, 1542, James gave the Jesuits a letter of recommendation to the "people of the islands and to all Scotland's allies and friends."[8] Their business with James V concluded, the papal emissaries were anxious to move on to Ireland. Salmeron writes to Ignatius:

It is harder to find out anything about Ireland here than in Rome.

And the information we gather is of dubious value, one telling us one thing, another the very opposite; and not one man can we find who can speak from personal experience. Nearly everyone—including the Archbishop of Glasgow—advises us not to go; the French Ambassador has kept urging their Majesties to prevent us, saying that we would be risking our lives in a useless cause. . . . Besides, three Irish priests on their way to Rome, whom we met here, told us that the two principal Irish chieftains, O'Neill and O'Donnell, have recently made submissions to the English King and O'Neill has surrendered his heir as hostage. These priests also told us that the few remaining Catholics still faithful to Rome have fled to the mountains where they perpetually fight among themselves. Master Paschal [Broet] went to Glasgow to see if he could meet any Irishmen there, for they frequently come to that town to trade and to study; in this way we thought we should have more news and from people with first-hand information. . . . But alas, Glasgow afforded no more information regarding Ireland than Edinburgh, and not a merchant or student from Ireland could he find there; he proceeded to Irvine, five leagues from Glasgow, to see if he could find out anything there . . . at this time he had changed his gown for an Irish kilt. . . . Now he has come back to Edinburgh; but though he heard of no sailing from either Glasgow or Irvine, he learned something from various merchants and some Irish; their reports lead us to believe that things are not quite so bad in Ireland as we were given to understand since coming here. . . . So we are off to explore Hibernia.[9]

They landed at the beginning of Lent, 1542, somewhere in the North; their arrival was not unknown to the Viceroy in Dublin, whose espionage system was both efficient and widely spread. A price was set upon their heads, any man or family harboring the pope's emissaries being liable to death and confiscation of all lands and goods. They had to sleep in a different place every night; for five weeks the papal envoys traversed the country. Salmeron describes their experiences:

God be praised for all things! Our stay in Ireland was not without our having to bear a share of the cross of Christ Our Lord; there we went hungry and thirsty, and often at night had no place to lay our heads, nor any space in which to say one *Pater Noster* in peace. It was Lent when we were there, a good time to do penance.[10]

They had arrived in disguise, still in kilts no doubt. They soon found out that there was no one to whom they might hand the pope's briefs, for Henry having by then taken the title of King of Ireland, almost all the chieftains, even O'Neill and O'Donnell, had acknowledged him as "Supreme Head, under Christ, of the Church of England and Ireland." "All their chiefs save one, who is on the point of overtaking his fellows, have made confederacy with the King of England, swearing to him allegiance as their spiritual as well as temporal sovereign and promising to put into the fire the papal bulls we bring, and to enchain and deliver to the Viceroy any person whom they may capture." Even Conn O'Neill, the strongest of the native chiefs, capitulated. In his biography of Conn O'Neill's son, Hugh, *The Great O'Neill*, Sean O'Faolain writes:

> For English contemporaries the entry into sixteenth-century Ireland was an entry into a world as strange as the Indies were to Columbus, nine-tenths of it an uncharted Thibet, and the O'Neills and O'Donnells and all its chief princes as remote and as unimaginable as the Great Khan. So that had some English traveller reported that there lived deep in Ireland tribes who wore their heads, like the anthropophagi, beneath their shoulders, London would have believed him; and in fact well after the Tudors, men were still picking up books from the counters of the booksellers under St. Paul's that made reports of things just as fantastic.[11]

For the travelers from Renaissance Europe, Fathers Salmeron and Broet, the Ireland of 1542 must have seemed the most outlandish place on earth. At the end of Lent the two Fathers received an order from the pope to return—for Paul III had heard of the order made against his nuncios. So they took ship for Scotland. The report they sent to Cardinal Cervini was, as might be expected, not a very encouraging one. Of the thirty Irish bishops, twenty-one had followed the example of Dr. Browne and sworn allegiance to Henry; the feuds between the Irish chieftains greatly perplexed the two Jesuits (one a native of Picardy, the other of Toledo); it was incomprehensible to them how men of one nation could waste time and energy and life and wealth in fighting one another on issues seemingly petty, while both the nation and the faith were being undermined and despoiled by an enemy who found excellent opportunity in the lack of unity among the Irish.

When the two missionaries got back to Scotland, all those who had

warned them against going to Ireland, received them "with much surprise, not having expected to see us ever again in this life."[12] King James
gave the papal nuncios a passage to Dieppe, and they made their way to
Paris. It must have been pleasant to arrive in Paris sometime in May,
after spending from New Year's Eve until well after Easter in the mists
and rain and snow and bitter winds of the northern islands. Leaving
Zapata in Paris to study, Broet and Salmeron set out for home later in the
year; they were a sorry-looking pair of ambassadors, so tattered and torn
that at Lyons they were arrested as possible spies. It took the united efforts of two cardinals to get them released and set on the road to Rome.
They arrived back to Ignatius in November. When Dr. Wauchope heard
their story, he said, "Now I see that unless the sheep hear the voice of the
shepherd, I shall do little good." The pope, however, wished him to go to
Germany just then; he did so, but eventually must have succeeded in
reaching Ireland, as Moore's *History of Ireland* mentions him as having
visited Culmer Fort on Loch Foyle some years later. MacGeoghegan mentions that he left Ireland and died at the Jesuit house in Paris in 1551.

Thus ended the mission to Hibernia. Of all those undertaken by the
first Jesuits, it was the only one which seemingly was a complete failure.
Yet within twenty years Pius IV was to send to Ireland a Limerick-born
member of the Society, Father David Wolfe, S.J., the first of the long line
of Jesuit priests, lay-brothers, and scholastics who dared king's edicts
and queen's writs to minister to a stricken people. Edmund Daniel, S.J.,
was hanged, drawn and quartered by Sir John Perrott in Cork; later the
Jesuit novice Maurice Eustace was hanged and quartered in Dublin and
Brother Dominic Collins, S.J., was executed in Youghal. Bishop Tanner,
Father Rochford, and Father Lea were among the most devoted workers
in Ireland's "underground" church. These were but the vanguard. After
them Father Archer, Father Lynch, Father Malony, Father Nicholas
Field, and others took up where the earlier generation left off; after them
the Jesuit teachers came, setting up little schools which migrated from
one provincial center to another as the persecution caught up with them;
the motto of these badgered academies might well have been "the
teacher makes the school." At first they kept moving about between
Limerick, Kilmallock, Clonmel, and Youghal. They were strong in
Waterford; later they began in Artane near Dublin. "The Jesuits," says
Mahaffy in his history of Trinity College, of which institution he was Provost, "by their vigorous and able action during the closing years of the
sixteenth century, saved Ireland for the papacy. It was they who trans-

lated the quarrel of race into one of creed." Ignatius, human enough to be disappointed by the results of the Broet-Salmeron mission to Ireland, did not live to see his sons return "to save Ireland for the papacy." But Irishmen of the Society of Jesus lived—and died—true to the orders of the man who wrote for the first two Jesuits he sent to Ireland, "If necessary for the glory of God and the common good, do not refuse to risk your lives."

The young nobleman, Zapata, whom Broet and Salmeron left in Paris to continue his studies, finished his university course and, returning to Rome, became a Jesuit novice. Despite qualities which indicated lack of suitability for the life—and one flagrant break with the already established traditions of obedience, which will be related in the next chapter—Ignatius, mindful of his former services, forgave Zapata and allowed him to remain in the order.[13] One day, when sent out on an errand, he beheld the Majorcan Father Jerome Nadal preaching near the Sant' Angelo Bridge. Nadal made a point of preaching at the bridge because there was a market and fairground nearby, frequented by jugglers, musicians, pedlars, and all the riffraff that gathered about such entertainers. While giving his sermons, Nadal used to mount a *banco* or rough bench. Zapata, passing by, thought the opportunity too good to resist; so he stopped to call *"monte banco"* [mountebank] at the preacher. Later that night the father whose duty it was to report to the General on all that had happened during the day related the incident. Though it was very late and the novices had retired hours before, Zapata was aroused and told he must leave by daybreak. The offense, not on the face of it very serious, might have been tolerated in a wilful young scamp like Ribadeneira. In Zapata, a mature man who had been a papal notary, who had escorted the pope's nuncios to a foreign land, who had completed his studies in Paris, who had, moreover, been pardoned for a graver offense, it confirmed whatever defect Ignatius had noted in his character years before when he kept putting him off each time he asked permission to enter the Society. Zapata went away in tears; but though not suited for the Jesuit order, he later joined the Franciscans and persevered as a friar of much learning and holiness, remaining on friendly terms with the Fathers of the Society until his death.[14]

The Father Nadal at whom Zapata had jeered with such serious repercussions to himself came from Palma, which is today a leading Mediterranean tourist center. He had met Ignatius in Paris and held out against him; after an exceptionally brilliant scholastic career, he mooned about in a state of melancholy from which nothing aroused him until chance brought a letter of Francis Xavier's his way. By this time Nadal had been ordained priest. He was amazed to read of the subsequent history of Ignatius and the Companions, of whom he had not heard for several years, they having left Paris about the time he had left for Avignon where he spent several years studying Hebrew. He decided to go at once to Rome to see for himself the new order founded by Ignatius. For a month Nadal, determined not to be lured into doing the Exercises, that net which had drawn so many of his old friends into the Society, lodged at some distance from the Jesuits. Yet he could not help calling now and again, and Ignatius occasionally coaxed him to stay for dinner. One evening when the others had left the table, Nadal said, "Father, these others have been stuffing me with talk of the Exercises; but I am well up to their game—they want me to join your Society. Now I just want you to sit here while I give you the reasons which will show you how unsuited I am for your Institute." Ignatius sat and listened while Nadal told him "everything but my sins." The other merely commented, "If Our Lord wants you in this Society, you won't lack for work." Nadal did the Exercises with a young Valencian Father, Domenech. During the first days "I was burning with the wish for something strange to happen to me—a vision, a sign, some sort of revelation." Later he steadied down, after making a general confession to Ignatius; but when midway through, he became perturbed and distracted "so that I could not keep either my mind or my body still." This depression overcome, he finished well, having determined to join the Society.

Nadal was nothing if not temperamental and, his long retreat over, he found himself vacillating, saying again and again that he would take the Jesuit vows but unable to take the initial step of entering. Finally he did enter and was allotted tasks in the kitchen and garden; in the kitchen he was given a broom which previous novices had worn almost to the handle; once he was put to dig the garden, "wearing a very long coat," while Ignatius and a visitor walked up and down. Nadal became suddenly ravenously hungry, but was too scrupulous or too shy to ask if he might go and get something to eat. All at once Ignatius stopped and called to him, "Jerome, my poor fellow; go and get yourself something to eat." When Lent came, Nadal was told not to fast. "But some of those in the house may be scandalized if they see me eating," he objected. "Show me who they are and I'll show them the door," replied Ignatius. Nadal had poor health, was moody and suspicious by nature, but was the soul of loyalty and probably the most brilliant of all the early Jesuits.[15]

In 1548 Ignatius sent Nadal to open a Jesuit College at Messina in Sicily, and a new phase in the history of the Society began. During the previous six years Jesuit Colleges had been opened in Italy, Portugal, the Netherlands, Spain, Germany, and an existing College in India had been reorganized by Francis Xavier; but all these were intended for young Jesuit students, the need for ten colleges in six years being a reliable indication of the rapid growth of the new order. The Sicilian foundation was significant in that it marked the admission of lay students. When founding the Society and during his first years as General, Ignatius—as is clear from Part Four of the *Constitutions*—had no intention of including teaching among the order's activities, his legislation regarding schools and studies being obviously planned for Jesuit seminarists. He yielded to combined Spanish and Sicilian pressure only when the pope added his request to the appeals already made. He soon saw that educational work did not run counter to his principle that his sons should go where souls were in the most need, where the most good could be done. Once the decision was made to engage in the education of lay students, Ignatius' zeal, vision, and tremendous capacity for organization sprang into action, the same motive that inspired all his undertakings—"the greater glory of God"—impelling him to give of his best for the furtherance of his new apostolate.

"St. Ignatius was a man," writes Ribadeneira, "who was constantly thinking about what means he could find to remedy the great evils which he saw springing up throughout Europe and particularly in Germany."[16] In the education of lay students he saw not only a means whereby the scholars might be aided to attain perfection in their studies, but a means through which they could be helped to save their own souls and also to become a powerful factor in the salvation of Europe. "He hoped," writes Father Ganss, S.J., "that they might vigorously and intelligently leaven their social environment with the doctrine and spirit of the Kingdom of Christ, which for him obviously meant the Catholic Church."[17] This entry of Ignatius and his order into the field of education was one of the most constructive steps towards reform taken within the Church, studding Europe with excellent secondary schools and universities, and—in the wise and practical rules framed and codified for the guidance of those to whom the administration of these educational institutes was entrusted—giving clear and sure directives for educators, both contemporary and modern.

It is difficult for Europeans of the present day to form any concept of Catholic, much less Jesuit, university education, for the administrative control of the universities of Europe has—with a very few exceptions—long since passed from the control of the Church. Since the restoration of the Society of Jesus in the eighteenth century, Jesuit educational activities in Europe have, for the most part, been confined to the secondary schools, with the result that English-speaking peoples of modern times, excepting those in the United States, are unfamiliar with the educational views of St. Ignatius. This is rather a pity, for most people are agreed that the need for changes in education to meet the problems peculiar to modern times is urgent, acute, and widespread; besides—apart from the spiritual sphere—in no other work did the genius of Ignatius display itself so fully as in the educational plan he devised to meet the needs of his time.

Through his own experiences in the universities of Europe, through the opinions—often conflicting—which he heard expressed concerning the merits and demerits of various colleges, the organization of studies, the methods of teaching in use, he discerned and appraised the good points and the shortcomings of the older medieval and the newer Renaissance education. When he came to plan and organize, he chose the golden mean between the old and the new, being always on the alert for what was good and useful in contemporary educational developments and enterprising enough to experiment and keep abreast of his age. "To adapt himself to the needs and interests of his times," says Father Ganss, "was one of the most prominent features in his outlook, in education no less than in his spirituality."

The singleness of purpose—God's greater glory—which motivated all his actions enabled him to see the potentialities of this new work. Through educated laymen the whole social structure of Europe might be permeated with the true Christian spirit and teaching. Such apostles needed a firm foundation, "a solid and strong intellectual formation," to secure which he appropriated the best features in the educational systems he knew, adapting some if necessary, the better to achieve his purpose. His idea of education is thus summarized by the author already quoted:

> The harmonious development of the whole man with all his faculties, natural and supernatural, that through his activity and thought he may have a well-reasoned Catholic outlook on life; that he may become a copy of Christ in his being and his actions; that, conse-

quently, he may be happy in this world as a citizen beneficial to society both ecclesiastical and civil, and eventually have a rich participation in the eternal joys of the beatific vision.[18]

He regarded order and organization as of the highest importance in the curricula of all the schools and colleges. Remembering his own unfortunate experience in Alcala, when his lack of proper grounding and his attempt to learn everything at once meant that most of the lectures were lost on him, he insisted that younger boys do a thorough course in Latin grammar before proceeding to the other "humanities"—poetry, rhetoric, and history. This course was done by boys between the ages of ten and thirteen, and it presupposed a knowledge of "how to read and write and converse in Latin." By the time he reached thirteen, the secondary schoolboy was expected to have mastered the art "of speaking, reading, and writing Latin, with elegance when possible." This preparatory period was considered as an essential before the student proceeded to three years of Arts studies—logic, physics, metaphysics, moral science, and mathematics—which led to the B.A. degree, that degree in turn being an essential qualification for all doing courses in law, theology, or medicine. Thus the students took their Arts degrees at sixteen (in theory if not always in actual practice!). The theology course lasted four years: six years if the student wished to do a doctorate.*

It will be noted that considerable emphasis was given to linguistic and literary study, Latin in particular having to be used in the debates through which the students recapitulated the subject matter of the various cultures. In Ignatius' time, Latin was not only among the attainments of every educated Catholic but, to a large extent, the language of international communications, of law, medicine, and world politics. In the theology courses, Ignatius stipulated that the *Summa* of St. Thomas Aquinas was to be the principal textbook used and he wished the students, Jesuit and non-Jesuit, to acquire—through a thorough study of the whole organic structure of Catholic theology—a critical, reasoning approach to religious knowledge and to be capable of holding their own in discussions on controversial points. It took no little courage to give St.

* *Note:* Part IV of the Jesuit *Constitutions*, with its more than two hundred paragraphs, is entirely devoted to the intellectual formation of Jesuit students and how the apostolate is to be exercised in schools and colleges. From these, and from the Saint's many letters on the subject of education, Father Ganss has summarized fourteen cardinal principles of Catholic higher education in his book *St. Ignatius' Idea of a University*.

Thomas pride of place, Peter Lombard's *Sentences* having been the work on which, for the previous four centuries, the teaching of theology was based.

It may be asked why Ignatius concentrated on secondary and university education only. For one thing the demands made on the Society—demands reinforced by the pope's authoritative request—were for higher education, and the supply of Jesuits was insufficient to staff even the colleges; for another, the first Jesuits were all men eminently fitted to educate at secondary and university level. It will be remembered that, before Ignatius acceded to the pressure brought to bear on him to open colleges, his own inclination and that of the early Companions was to devote all possible time to catechetical instruction of poor children and the uneducated everywhere. His letter to Archdeacon Cassador of Barcelona in 1536 had said that his aims were:

> . . . just to preach in a lesser capacity things that anyone can understand, things easy and elementary and lowly, hoping in God Our Lord that if I stick to the smallest and most humble He will send His grace so that in some way we may be able to contribute to the praise and service which are His due.[19]

In the *Constitutions* he wrote:

> To teach persons to read and write could also be a work of charity if the number of persons in the Society were sufficient for us to undertake all things, but on account of the lack of members we do not ordinarily teach them.[20]

Memories of his own struggles to overcome the handicap of not having begun his studies until the age of thirty-three were strong in him; the tremendous efforts of the long eleven years from the day he first sat with the small boys singing Latin verbs in Master Ardevoll's schoolroom in Barcelona until the great day when he "took the rock" in Paris gave him an esteem for learning not infrequently lacking in those whose learning costs less time and labor. "But he also esteemed . . . many temporal and eternal objectives beyond the school to which the mastery of learning can honorably be a means." He sought through education to aid others to the knowledge and love of God and to pour into society capable leaders whose opinions would be respected and sought as molders of policy. "Practical wisdom was his gift," writes Father Ganss, "both in reducing Catholic educational theory to practice and ordering education as a means to worthy temporal and eternal ends."[21]

*. . . . If nobody wishes to precede me in starting this work [the open-
ing of a home for Magdalens] let someone at least follow me. . . .*
(St. Ignatius to the members of the Company of Grace,
a Roman Confraternity.)

*. . . . The Ambassador [Ortiz], while making the Spiritual Exercises,
became depressed while considering the Four Last Things; when Ignatius
saw that he was feeling the strain, to cheer him up and rouse him from his
stupor he danced one of the Basque dances, reviving the retreatant's
drooping spirits greatly; the Ambassador was then able to resume his
meditations with renewed enthusiasm and continued until the end of the
thirty days . . . .* *(Lancisius.)*

I N the *Constitutions*, Ignatius wrote that special care should be taken
of souls who have no one to look after their spiritual welfare; hence, it
is not surprising to find him devoting much time and care to orphans, the
numbers of whom had greatly increased in Rome since the famine of the
preceding decade. He caused the Orphan Society of Rome to be founded
by Paul III and organized on an efficient basis, he himself starting two orphanages, one for boys and one for girls, with the donations he begged
from wealthy Romans for the purpose. At St. Catherine's of the Rope-
Makers he founded a refuge for young girls in need of protection. He also
established a house for converted Jews and made representations to in-
sure that they would not suffer for their conversion through having their
property confiscated by their fellow Jews of the Ghetto when they forsook the synagogue for the church.

One work which earned Ignatius Loyola much hatred in Rome was
the foundation of St. Martha's, a refuge for women of the streets. Administered by a confraternity known as the Company of Grace, this work
was so successful that within four years over three hundred souls were
admitted and, forsaking their previous haunts, began to live in peace and
sin no more. Excavations on the little square facing the Jesuit house pro-
videntially unearthed some marble slabs dating from the days of ancient
Rome; with the hundred gold crowns their sale realized, Ignatius began
to build St. Martha's , telling the rich and titled members of the Company

of Grace, "if nobody wishes to go before me in starting this work, let them at least follow me." The inevitable opposition from the ultra-good was encountered, many of whom poured cold water on the project by telling the saint that he was attempting the impossible; it was a waste of time, they said, even to try to draw the Magdalens from their ways, much less to induce them to follow the better life. To these he made the well-known reply: "I would consider no labor too much, if by my exertions I were able to prevent one soul from sinning for even one night for the sake of my Lord Jesus Christ, and even if I knew that immediately afterwards the sinner would return to the paths of sin." [1]

Marguerite of Austria, Eleanor Osorio de Vega, wife of the Spanish Ambassador, and other great ladies of Rome came to the assistance of Ignatius, not only raising money for the project but seeing to the domestic arrangements of the new institution. All the helpers seem to have been enkindled by the charity burning in the heart of the saint. Father Ferron, writing to Portugal, tells of how Vittoria Colonna, the Marquesa of Pescara, took in and sheltered in her own palace one who wished to give up her former ways but "who had been attacked and suffered much from the sons of the prince of darkness, so much so that Her Excellency feared for the girl's life if she once ventured outside." Hearing of this, Father Ignatius collected some gentlemen of the Ambassador's household early one morning and went to the house of the Marquesa and escorted the girl safely to St. Martha's, not paying any heed to the scandalous calumnies which followed on his action." [2] The Spanish Ambassador's wife not only kept the overflow from St. Martha's in her house, but went into the highways and byways seeking—and finding—many who only needed a kind word and a little help to start them on the road back to God. The spiritual care of the new foundation was given to Ignatius; and he appointed his own confessor, Father Diego de Eguia, who had by that time become a Jesuit, as chaplain to St. Martha's. It was typical of him to entrust to no other save a confessor of whose holiness and kindness he himself had practical, intimate knowledge the care of those souls whose conversion caused joy in heaven.

As might be expected, the vicious, deprived of sources of profit and pleasure, retaliated against St. Martha's and all it stood for. For months the piazza in front of the Magdalen home was packed each night with a mob yelling threats and obscenities; Ignatius and the Companions were vilely calumniated, in particular by one Cassiano, Master of the Pontifical Post, who went so far as to force his way into the chapel of St.

Martha's and drag Father de Eguia from the confessional, threatening to use his influence to destroy the house and its work of reform if a certain penitent did not return to him and her former life. The campaign of defamation was so fierce that Ignatius took a slander action against this official; the defendant did not appear in court and an injunction was issued threatening him with the loss of his goods and office if he repeated the falsehoods any more; the judge added a statement vindicating the Fathers of the Society—"men of uncorrupted doctrine, exemplary lives and good works." It is pleasant to record that a few years later Ignatius completely won over his calumniator, Cassiano, and the Master of the Pontifical Post became one of the saint's friends.[3]

Although Ignatius never lacked for enemies, he seems to have had a genius for making and keeping friends; they were legion and of every age and class. Not the least welcome was old Mateo from Viscaya, a Basque seaman who, each time his ship anchored in the mouth of the Tiber, made his way to the Jesuit house and made his confession to Ignatius. His sins disposed of, he probably settled himself down for a chat, telling the saint of where he had been since his last visit, of the ports to which his ship had called, the peoples he had seen, the news he had heard. Other penitents who were also personal friends of the saint were the Spanish Ambassador and his wife, and a young painter, Jacopino del Conte, not long arrived in Rome from Florence. But for Ignatius there was no friend like One—all human friendships, as everything else, were subordinated to the greater glory of the Friend above all friends.

Soon a friendship with one to whom Ignatius owed much had to be broken, for it hindered the spiritual aim towards which he steered so undeviating a course. Memories of the poor pilgrim were still so vivid in Barcelona, and affection for him so strong, that eventually Isabel Roser and a friend, Isabel Jose, sold their goods, left their home and native city, and sailed to Rome. Dona Roser had been for some years a widow and always had followed from afar the ups and downs of the Society. Ignatius had told all the first Fathers of her goodness and her frequent donations to him; she it was who had made possible his education, vying with Ines Pasqual in her efforts to support the poor student of Paris and Venice. The Fathers called her Dona Isabel and their "sister in God," recommending themselves to her prayers and sending their respects whenever Ignatius wrote to her. The other Isabel who accompanied her was—according to the Barcelona process for the canonization of St. Ignatius—a Latin scholar "who had studied the philosophy of Scotus

Erigena and who had been asked to preach publicly in Barcelona Cathedral." This lady's reputation for learning had preceded her to Rome and, shortly after her arrival, "she was invited to debate on abstruse theological questions before the assembled cardinals." Isabel Jose also had an extraordinary gift for converting Jews.[4]

The two Isabels were accompanied by Dona Roser's maid, Francesca Cruyellas; and a girl named Lucrezia Bradine joined them in Rome, though it is not clear whether the latter was a maid they employed or one of the group. Isabel Jose might be the intellectual one of the quartette, but Isabel Roser was the woman of action who initiated and carried through the venture. In the autumn of 1542, she wrote to Ignatius telling him that she and others in Barcelona planned to go to Rome to live under his spiritual direction and under obedience to him, and asked his advice on the matter. He replied, expressing the opinion that she and her companions would derive from a journey to Rome and a stay in the Eternal City much spiritual fruit; as though he had a presentiment of what was to happen, he said not one word to encourage the aspirations of the ladies to live as an offshoot of the Society.[5]

So, as Father Tacchi-Venturi relates in his magnificent history of the Company of Jesus in Rome, neither summoned nor invited, but solely on her own, or, as she herself later testified in a court of justice, "by the devotion she had for Master Ignatius," she set out for Rome, arriving there early in November, 1543. Ignatius received her with his usual innate courtesy and with the fine sense of gratitude he had towards all his benefactors. An old lay-brother, Stefan de Eguia (brother to Father Diego, confessor to St. Martha's) was deputed to escort the four ladies all over Rome. A nobleman of Alcala in his time, Brother Stefan was always called upon to attend on the nobility of Rome when they came to see the Fathers. For two years, 1544 and 1545, he attended on Isabel and her ladies, "being so humble that he swept out their rooms, and followed behind when she (Dona Roser) rode, carrying in readiness in his hand the overshoes which Spanish ladies used when in the saddle." Besides Brother Eguia, another lay-brother, Gian Paolo Borrell, was also lent to the ladies who had settled in St. Martha's, "the Fathers supporting him, not Dona Isabel whom he served." Ignatius was not happy about the whole position; but Isabel, as though sensing his unwillingness to take on the direction of a community of women "who wished to be affiliated and related to the Society as other religious orders of women are to the religious order founding them," betook herself to the pope and obtained a rescript permitting herself and her three companions to make solemn vows under obedience to the Company.[6]

The pope's merest wish was law to Ignatius, so at once he took over the care of the little community, giving to their spiritual direction all the care he was accustomed to give to enterprises entrusted to him by the pontiff. At first the ladies were very docile and obedient, relieving Ignatius of much worry in regard to St. Martha's, which institution they directed and ran. Isabel Roser, in particular, distinguished herself by her zeal for the reclamation work the Company of Grace engaged in, and was responsible for "turning many poor sinners from vice and attracting them towards good." But soon, not content with acting as the very efficient matron of St. Martha's, she wished to take a hand in the domestic management of the Jesuits; she visited their house and insisted on being allowed to attend the sick there—and no doubt found fault with the housekeeping. At the same time, two of her nephews arrived in Rome and set up in the city, living in some style; she also visited them a good deal.

Before many months the direction of this small band of women became an impossible burden, hampering Ignatius in his work for the Society. They made unreasonable demands upon his time, calling him in to advise about scruples, about doubts, and even to settle the disputes women can start about the most infinitesimal matters. "These four ladies and their souls give me more trouble than the whole Company," the harrassed General confided to a friend.[7] Finally, convinced that Isabel's general tone of behavior was "in strident discord with that of the life of perfection," he decided to disentangle himself from a care that obviously hindered and conflicted with his and the Society's sole aim—God's greater glory.

He wrote to Isabel, as gently and considerately as he could, telling her that he had applied to the pope to free him from the obligation of having hers or any other community of women affiliated to his order and thus directly under his care and in obedience to the Company:

Indeed I would willingly—for the greater glory of God—satisfy your good desires and retain you and the others in obedience, as I have done for some time past, being solicitous for your greater good and the salvation of your soul. However, not feeling disposed to continue and not being in the best of health because of my continual illnesses, moreover having already too much to occupy me in matters which are my principal obligation both to God and to His Holiness, our ruler in God's name; and also, as my conscience tells me that this Society cannot fittingly discharge the special care of matrons with vows of obedience (which I explained to His Holiness about half a year ago), it seems to me better, for God's greater glory, to resign this work and retire from it altogether. No longer do I hold you in obedience as my spiritual daughter, but as a good and pious mother, such as you have been to me over so many years for the greater glory of God Our Lord. And so, for the greater service, praise, and glory of His eternal goodness, as far as I can, but always subordinating myself to superior authority, I remit you all four to the eminently prudent judgment, decision, and wish of His Holiness, so that your soul may in all things be tranquil and consoled to the greater glory of God.[8]

Paul III granted the dispensation and Ignatius was free of all responsibility for Dona Roser and her three companions. Isabel failed to appreciate the argument that it was not fitting that the Society, vowed to strive for the greater good of the greater number—for God's glory—should occupy itself with the microscopic affairs of this community of four women. Being but human, it was natural that she should recall that but for her there might have been no Society—her advice, encouragement, and generous alms having helped to start Ignatius in 1524 and having sustained him until the foundation of his order. Being a woman, it was natural that she should feel deeply hurt and aggrieved. She left St. Martha's at once and took up residence in the house of a Spanish friend and protector; at first she remained indoors, giving out that she was ill; then "while still waiting for a sailing to Barcelona, she went about, filling all Rome with her laments." One of her nephews, Dr. Ferrara, who disliked Ignatius, instituted a law suit against the Jesuits for moneys which he claimed were owing to his aunt.

Before long the whole city was discussing the matter, and there were pro-Roser and pro-Jesuit factions. Among Ignatius' champions were the Spanish Ambassador and his wife; the lady ventured to interview "la Roser," as all Rome was calling Isabel, telling her that she ought to take herself home to Spain without further ado. But la Roser said that she had given Master Ignatius "A hundred scudi and a mule" and that St. Martha's owed her a lot of money. Ignatius said that, as he told Isabel at the time, he did not wish to accept gifts from her and had given the mule—probably the mount behind which poor humble Brother Eguia had run, carrying Isabel's overshoes—for the use of the church of Our Lady of Montserrat, where he sometimes preached. Ignatius at this stage suggested that Dona Roser's grievances, real or imaginary, should be pleaded by two referees, he to name one, she the other. If this two-judge tribunal failed to decide matters, the pope's vicar might be asked to arbitrate "so that further scandal may be avoided, as Rome is ringing with it and I expect Barcelona is too, some people favoring her, some us." But the lady's relatives would have no referees; the papal vicar being absent from Rome, they carried the case to his substitute. At first, this judge, influenced as he admitted afterwards by the tears of la Roser, was inclined to uphold the lady's claim but, on examining the case more closely, he found "that while she supplied the Fathers with ready money and goods to the value of 144 *scudi*, they on their part had expended 323 *scudi* on her account." Not the least interesting feature of the court case for the Roman ladies who flocked to see la Roser and to hear the judge's verdict was the long list produced by Isabel's Catalan notary listing all the items she said she had sent to the Fathers. Dozens and half dozens of towels; some second-hand clothes "in good condition"; "one altar pall of white satin embroidered with letters of gold and fringed with silk and gold. One thick white coverlet for Master Miona's bed, the which she herself carried to their house and which was worth two *escudos*. And fifty doubloons given to Master Pietro Codazzo for the work of St. Martha's."[9]

When the verdict went against her, la Roser prepared to leave; but before her departure she signed a legal attestation stating that the priests of the Company had neither robbed her nor appropriated her money or goods, and that the reports going the rounds in Rome which alleged that the Fathers had treated her with injustice were untrue. In May, 1547, she sailed home, accompanied by her maid, Francesca Cruyellas, who right through the lawsuit had opposed her mistress and given evidence in favor of Ignatius. Lucrezia Bradine had already become a nun in Rome. Later Isabel Roser became a Franciscan Sister of the Jerusalem convent in Barcelona. The learned Isabel Jose is mentioned in one document as a nun in the same convent. In December, 1547, and in April, 1554, Sister Isabel Roser wrote her last two letters to Ignatius Loyola; by then her anger had been stilled and resentment was dead, the generosity that had for a time been smothered by her sense of injury and the knowledge that her dear friend Ignatius had cast her adrift, awoke again within her. She acknowledged her bad conduct and expressed her regret for it in the humblest terms; and she begged the servant of God to pardon and bless her and frequently recommend her to

God. It may be taken for granted that, if anyone grieved more than Isabel over the whole sorry affair, it was Ignatius; for he was a warm-hearted man and always deeply conscious of the gratitude he owed to benefactors.[10]

The commotion and annoyance caused by the Roser affair only helped to unite the Companions more closely; just one discordant voice made itself heard within the walls of the Jesuit house. Francisco Zapata, the former escort of the papal legates on their journey to Ireland, was now a priest in the Society and sadly scandalized all the brethren by taking la Roser's part. When sent with Father Codazzo to interview the lady, he took the side of the weeping Isabel and told all and sundry that the Fathers of the Company had done a bad day's work when they bade adieu to their "sister in God" and declined to keep her in obedience. Worse still, one evening in the presence of several Fathers, when Ignatius asked him to reply to a certain question, Father Zapata snapped back, "I am a man, not a beardless boy, and I would rather obey fifty than you alone." And he "persevered in this attitude for several months, with scandal to all in the house and injuring and defaming the Company to externs."[11]

Although Ignatius was the one against whom Zapata had principally offended, the General did not himself penalize him, though his breaches of rule merited instant dismissal. Six Fathers considered the case and, mainly owing to Ignatius' influence, he was retained on condition that he did the penances his judges deemed most fitting for his offences and calculated to remedy his pride, his disrespect toward the superior, and lack of loyalty to the Company. Father Francisco humbly thanked the tribunal, professed himself to be overjoyed at having been allowed to remain in the Society, and undertook to perform the penances. One of the members of this tribunal was Nadal and the penance he prescribed as most beneficial "for such traitorous conduct" was that for a time in the refectory during meals Zapata was to have a slate bearing the title "Judas Iscariot" tied about his neck. It may have been a lingering desire to get even with Nadal that prompted Zapata to shout *"monte banco!"* [Mountebank!] when he saw Nadal preaching at the fairground, "which the said Father Nadal used to undertake out of humility, to earn himself some infamy."[12] For this offence Francisco Zapata was, as has already been related, drummed out of the Company that very night. Ignatius, who forebore to dismiss him for an offence against himself, could not tolerate that a subject lacking in loyalty, earnestness, and humility should sneer and jeer at a fellow Jesuit who was a shining example of those identical virtues.

Troubles seldom come alone. On the heels of the Roser law suit Ignatius had difficulties with Portugal, where the slack rule of Rodriguez was producing a generation of Jesuits with very hazy ideas about obedience and very extraordinary notions of spirituality. Reports reached Rome of students, young Jesuits of the great College of Coimbra, who during lectures contemplated the skulls they fetched into the halls of the university and placed on their desks; others were allowed to do the most extravagant penances on the public streets, moving the onlookers more to derision than to piety or the wish to serve God. Ignatius summoned Father Simon, one of the first nine Companions of the Paris days, to Rome to discuss matters—but Rodriguez, who had become King John's right arm, stayed where he was while the King wrote saying that he could not possibly allow him to leave Portugal as he was superintending the education of the heir to the throne.

So for all of twelve years Rodriguez continued between the court and Coimbra, admitting Portuguese youths into the Company in great numbers and with little regard to suitability. In 1547 Ignatius wrote to the Society in Portugal the famous letter on perfection,[13] checking certain impulses already showing in an ardent but not well directed body of young Jesuits; in this letter he outlined his idea of what a Jesuit should be. Finally, in 1551, Simon visited Rome; Ignatius was rather dismayed at finding how attached to his own opinion and the favor of his royal patron Rodriguez had become; his uneasiness regarding the Portuguese province increased. The following year he wrote his "Letter on Obedience" to the Jesuits in Coimbra.[14] He decided to appoint a new provincial and won the King of Portugal round to his point of view; to make things easier for Rodriguez he offered him a choice of two new provincialates: Aragon (for Spain now had two Jesuit provinces) or Brazil, an infant mission where Simon might hope in the far west to emulate Xavier (who had already traversed Japan) in the far east. But Rodriguez was not to be mollified, and he made things distinctly uncomfortable for the new provincial. Although summoned to Rome several times, he did not go until a threat of excommunication finally brought him there in 1553. Ignatius received him as though he were the beloved Francis Xavier, gone to heaven by way of Sancian, an island at the closed gates of China, just a year before. But Rodriguez remained in a huff and demanded a trial; he was given not only the trial but his choice as to the four judges. All four found him "guilty on all counts" and, as in Zapata's case, suitable penances—but watered down in consideration of his undoubted services to the Society—were given him. Ignatius at once remitted them all, except the command that Rodriguez should never return to Portugal.

The difficult, thorny man then expressed a wish to visit the Holy Land and was given a traveling companion and sufficient money for the pilgrimage. Rodriguez found fault with the priest who had been sent with him, with the Turks who prevented him from doing anything but hang about Venice for a whole year, with everything in life. In 1555, a year before Ignatius died, Rodriguez betook himself to the little hermitage where in 1537 he had spent forty days in retreat preparing himself for the priesthood. While there, mulling and musing on his misfortunes, he suddenly remembered how Ignatius had left his own retreat in that August of 1537 to hurry to nurse Rodriguez through a fever. Just as the memory of that kindness struck him, Father Nadal arrived, seemingly out of nowhere in particular; and poor, touchy intractable Simon Rodriguez experienced a re-conversion. He writes to Ignatius for a big blessing, big enough to reach from Rome to his hermitage. He lived for another twenty-four years, doing great good for the Church in Italy and Spain and, in his old age, going back to Portugal, in which country he stayed till his death.[15]

In 1546, that year of sorrows and the loss of so many friends, Peter Favre, worn out at forty, came home to Rome to die. For six years he had traversed Germany, Spain, and France, preserving, through much hardship and ceaseless labors for the Church and the Society, that equanimity and strength of spirit that had always signalized him. Having been named by Paul III as one of the leading papal theologians at the Council of Trent, he was summoned from Spain to Rome. When the order came, he was suffering from a fever and friends sought to dissuade him from making the journey. "It is necessary to obey, but not to live," he replied, and embarked on the next ship. After his arrival in Rome he rallied a little but, having a relapse, he died on the first day of August, with Ignatius by his side to speed his departing soul. His favorite petition, "Heavenly Father, give me the Good Spirit," was granted to Blessed Peter Favre in good measure; for he made friends and converts all over Europe and, though his labors in Germany showed little result during his lifetime and helped to bring him to an early grave, who knows how much Martin Luther and Philip Melanchthon and Bucer and Suleiman and Henry VIII and others owed and owe to the prayers of this gentle-souled and holy man who named them one by one in his prayers everyday of his life? It was Favre who wrote to Lainez, who was by no means so tolerant: "Anyone who desires to aid the heretics of our time should take care to be charitable and loving towards them, banishing from his mind anything that might lessen his esteem for them. The next step is to gain their goodwill so that they may love us and have us in their hearts.''[16]

Lainez did not always remember this good advice. When he and Salmeron were sent to the second session of the Council of Trent in 1551, they were lodged in "a small room that I can only call an oven, full of smoke and cluttered up with an old harp, a sword, a huge portmanteau, and boots ... not to mention the bed and a truckle bed which, when pulled out, leaves no room to walk a step." So inconducive to sleep was this apartment in the middle of a warm summer that Salmeron betook himself elsewhere, while Lainez and a lay-brother John "so that we all might not appear to be clearing out of the room allotted to us, resigned ourselves to the oven." When the papal legate's secretary put in his head to ask if they needed anything, Lainez could not refrain from replying, "Everything!" He added that, for the time being, a candle to save them from falling over the ancient harp and sword would be most acceptable, and a candlestick to hold it would also be appreciated. Finally, lack of sleep and the impossibility of either studying or receiving callers drove Father Lainez to the cardinal-nuncio to protest against their accommodation. The cardinal, probably feeling the sultry Trent summer a bit trying on himself, observed with some asperity that they who preached patience to others should practice it themselves; to which Lainez, now quite nettled, replied that he was simply pointing out that a delegate to the Council of Trent should not be without the means of preparing his addresses and doing study on the various questions before the Council; his oven was bad, but nothing to what he had suffered in his tent in North Africa when with the Emperor's troops the previous year. A good religious, he apologized to the cardinal and at once wrote to Ignatius, confessing his hastiness and asking a penance.

Before the Jesuits left for Trent, Ignatius had drawn up a most comprehensive list of instructions for them, one of which he probably underscored for Lainez and Salmeron:"Be slow to speak and then only in a friendly and thoughtful manner ... be careful to displease nobody." Another delegate to the Reform Council was Father Melchior Cano, a Spanish Dominican famed as a preacher and writer. For some years previously, Father Cano had roundly condemned the Society, claiming to have found heresy in the *Exercises* and denouncing Ignatius and the Companions as "forerunners of Antichrist, *Illuminati*, visionaries, worse than Lutherans." Fathers Lainez and Salmeron, finding themselves and the Dominican in one small city, had a brain wave; they would meet him and tell him all about Ignatius and the Society of Jesus; when his misapprehensions were dispelled, the good man could not but love them.[17]

As the oven was no fit place for a calm, dispassionate discussion—and decidedly no apartment in which to receive a man whom they hoped would shed his anti-Jesuit antipathies, if not all at once, at least by degrees during their conversation—they decided to call upon Father Cano. Alas for Ignatius' instructions! Three Spaniards, all rather quick-tempered, arguing on a controversial topic for a few hours, were bound to reach boiling point before long. The meeting ended in hard-hitting remarks on both sides, the insulted callers making their exit without much regard for leave-takings. Lainez boiled over altogether before he got out and turned on the threshold to throw a parting brick—in the shape of an unparliamentary expression—at the Dominican. When he reached the street "repenting of what he had done, he rushed back, went on his knees before Cano, and begged his forgiveness." But Father Melchior's opinion of the Society, at no time good, had now dropped to below zero, never to rise again. His anti-Jesuit phobia remained; and some times afterwards, as proof of the evils he claimed to find in these "worse than Lutherans," he used to refer to his own shocking encounter with the two Jesuits at Trent, never repeating the epithet used by Lainez, but leaving blanks for listeners or readers to fill in.[18]

Ignatius probably received another letter from Lainez confessing this fault. If he did, poor Father Lainez would have received a dressing down; for, as Ignatius was grooming two or three Fathers, one of whom he thought might succeed him as General, he treated them with exceptional severity, checking them for faults he would have passed over or excused in others. Lainez, Nadal, and Polanco were the three who most often felt the weight of the Founder's correction. Ribadeneira writes:

> Our blessed Father assured me that there was not one to whom our Society owed more than to Father Lainez. . . . Yet before his death, for a whole year he was so severe towards this Father as to make him completely miserable. Father Lainez himself told me that he used to pray to Our Lord, saying: "Lord, what have I done against the Society for this saint to treat me in such a way?" The reason was that our blessed Father wished to make a saint of Father Lainez and to make him used to hardship with a view to becoming General, so that by enduring he might learn how to govern.[19]

256

Meanwhile, throughout Europe the lights that shed so fierce a glare on the first half of the sixteenth century were being extinguished one by one. Luther died in February, 1546. On January 27, 1547, Henry VIII, having sent Lord Surrey to the block the week before and condemned Norfolk to be executed on the 28th, died. Two months after the death of Henry, Francis I called for his confessor, for he had many sins to deplore and much for which to beg mercy. He died on March 31. Toward the end of 1549, Paul III died. The Emperor Charles, with the victory of Muhlberg in 1547, had reached the zenith of his power. At forty-seven he was already aged and beginning to think of how happy he could be if he could rid himself of those *incubi*, wealth and power and worldly splendor.

And Father Ignatius, writing to his sons in the College of Padua who are suffering much because of their extreme poverty, consoles them and rejoices that they are getting an opportunity to practice a virtue so dear to Christ: "For poverty makes us the friends of the Eternal King; and the love of poverty makes us kings, not only in this world, but in heaven."[20]

. . . . On feastdays we would treat our Father to a few roasted chestnuts, that being a dish of his native place. . . . (Father da Camara.)

. . . . I shall do penance in your stead every time I have a stomach-ache. . . .   (St. Ignatius to a novice who had received a penance.)

. . . . The Father used to show great affection for young novices who were tempted, as with one Fleming, an unlettered youth with no head for learning; to cheer him up Ignatius used to throw his arms round him and hug him, but had to jump to do this, the fellow being so tall. . . .
                                                                (FN [I] : 554–556.)

ON the very day of Peter Favre's death in 1546, the last decade of life began for Ignatius Loyola. During these ten years he suffered much from poor health. Two doctors prescribed for him, advising His Paternity "to beware of catarrh, which arises from the following causes: too much food, too much wine, too much head covering, too much and too strenuous exercise, too much exposure of the head to the rays of the sun or the moon, too much activity after dinner, too much concentrated, continuous thinking, and lack of judicious exercise."[1] As the Fathers in Rome, like those of Padua, were in dire financial straits during Ignatius' latter years—mainly because the Romans believed that Francis Borgia brought the Order all his great wealth when he became a Jesuit—the warnings not to eat or drink too much were superfluous. As it happened, the real ailments from which the General was suffering, and which were revealed only after his death, made eating more of a trial than a pleasure; and, in any case, he seldom noticed what he ate, for many of his meals were taken standing up to avoid loss of time; he worked for twenty hours a day and slept four to extend his working time to the uttermost. The prescriptions warn against eggs, meat, and wine; fennel is ordered; aniseed and coriander seed are to be taken.[2]

Not the least marvelous feature of Ignatius' life, so full of spiritual and temporal activities, is the fact that the man who accomplished so much was physically handicapped. It is true that he got a good start: the robust constitution bequeathed him by hardy Basque forebears, and the ideal rural conditions of his infancy and childhood, laid the foundations for later health and strength. The only mention of illness during the first thirty years of his life is the nasal catarrh which afflicted and shamed him at Arevalo, and which yielded to saline douches. But his leg wound at Pamplona brought him to death's door, and his departure from Loyola before it was fully healed was a grave mistake. "It always gave him a good deal of pain, never drying up properly; even when he was General the suppuration—then chronic—from that wound was so bad that he began to suspect cancer. If he walked any distance it ulcerated afresh."

In Manresa and right through his life he suffered from gastric trouble, catarrhal conditions, and fevers, though only once—on the departure of the pilgrim ship from Venice in 1523—is there any mention of his having been overcome by nausea. By then his health had been already ruined by long fasts of several days' duration, by disciplinings to blood, by little and disturbed sleep, by wretched, inadequate food, by force marching his weary frame on long journeys, by the enduring of extremes of heat and cold, by brutal drubbings—such as those received from the Turks and Saracens in Palestine and from the negro hired to attack him after the reform of the Old Angels in Barcelona—by heroic, self-imposed severities as on that night in Paris when he waited, up to the chin in icy water, for the footstep of the passing sinner whom he hoped to win to repentance, by ten years of intense study, an occupation to which he was little inclined by nature and which his lack of early schooling made especially difficult for him, by long and fervent prayers, with the suspension of the organic functions that occurs in the mystical states. "What constitution," asks Father de Iriarte, "could stand all that?"

When the doctors and embalmers performed an autopsy on his dead body, the true nature of his maladies became apparent. He had suffered from gallstones and cirrhosis of the liver; "the condition of his internal organs was such," says Polanco, "that the doctors considered it a miracle that he should have lived to be so old, for his disease was long-standing."[3]

These details, in themselves of no great interest, show that apart from all Ignatius suffered from without, persecutions, oppositions, the cares of founding and governing an Order—two offices requiring different qualities and gifts, but which he discharged with supreme ability—he always had to bear the burden of ill-health, suffering pain and discomfort that would possibly have long before prostrated or killed a person of lesser will power, a man of lesser grace. Not much imagination is needed to realize what these ailments meant in the life of so active a man; yet he seldom complained and only consented to lie down when unable to stand on his feet.

From earlier descriptions it will be remembered that he was a small sized man, only barely five feet tall, and that his voice was "thin and delicate." Towards the end of his life he tended to grow stouter. The hair which in bygone days "fell to his shoulders, blonde and beautiful," had faded to "the color of ripe wheat." The Saint's high color and his habit of "blushing like a girl," referred to elsewhere, surprised and disedified at least one poor novice. "I was greatly scandalized and began to criticize him in my own mind, thinking that our Father had daubed and painted his face to make himself look well."*[4]

Father da Camara says that "the continual interior devotion of our Father showed itself in a great peace and composure of countenance. Neither for any news told him, nor for anything else that might happen, joyful or sad, spiritual or temporal, did any interior change show itself by facial expression or bodily gesture. When he went to meet someone to whom he wished to show kindness, his face used to light up with such joy that he really seemed to receive that person into his innermost soul. . . . He had bright eyes, with a penetrating glance that read one through and through, but his modesty seldom allowed him to raise them. They were sunken in the sockets, and in his later years his eyelids were so wrinkled from the tears he shed at Mass and when praying that when he went about with his eyes cast down one would think they were the eyes of a dead man." Father Manares said that "judging by human standards, our Father was not very good looking." Other Fathers claimed that he had "a distinguished appearance." Cardinal Quiroga, very well acquainted with Ignatius, said that his facial expression "was not altered, either by adversity or prosperity, success or failure . . . always he appeared to be imbued with a deep, unchanging peace . . . never have I seen a human face with an expression remotely resembling that of Father Ignatius."[5]

Smiles and laughter seemed to come to him as readily as tears, and "joy welled up in him at sight of the Fathers, so much so that he had trouble in preserving the serious demeanor he himself had laid down in the

---

* It was not unknown in the time of Ignatius for gentlemen, old and young, cleric and lay, to use cosmetics; not only the ladies attempted to adorn youth and beauty and conceal age.

Constitutions; sometimes a smile or laugh escaped his lips in spite of his self-control, and he took to disciplining himself for this excessive mirth—a lash for each laugh."[6] Even when he severely reprimanded the three, Lainez, Nadal, and Polanco, in whom he would tolerate no fault, laughter was never far away. One day the unhappy Nadal, who had reached such a state of nerves that he used to begin to quake every time he got a summons to the General's room, was called to account. "I stood there listening while Father Ignatius gave me a piece of his mind, making such scathing remarks that I felt as though the world had fallen in ruins around me. He walked towards me and began a second round, berating me for all he was worth for my fault. There was nothing I could do, only stand and shrug my shoulders, which I did. And then what do you think he did?—walked away laughing!"[7] The melancholy face of Nadal must have been a study as he watched his retreating General.

"He liked to see smiling faces in the house," records another Father; "and indeed he himself promoted the same by every honest means. He liked the superiors to make much of festival days, letting all contribute of their gifts and talents to the general entertainment. Sometimes Ignatius would ask Father Frusio to come and play him some melodies on the clavichord, "but never on a Friday or a Saturday, on which days he denied himself music for love of Our Lord and Our Lady." His love for music has been referred to in an earlier chapter; once he told a Father: "If I followed my own inclination, I would certainly have choir and sung office in the Company, but for our work, it seemed to me that it were better for us to forego the chant." When, after a particularly trying day, he thought that he might allow himself to relax a little "for the greater glory of God," he used to send for a holy and ingenuous lay-brother, whose one specialty in entertainment was a piece of mimicry in which he gave an imitation of the blind beggars of Rome. Ignatius, whose sense of humor evidently had always retained the salty Basque tang, would sit back and enjoy the performance hugely while the brother went through his little act, repeating the tall tales of the mendicants, some of them blind, some feigning blindness, their prayers, not always pious, the whining patter of the children who led them from one Roman church to another—"all of which the good brother used to mimic to perfection, with the very air and voice of the *lazarillos*."[8]

The novices who could sing well were sent to sing cheerful songs for any sick person who was inclined to melancholy and depression. But not if they were persons whom the sick man disliked. One of the rules drawn up for infirmarians reveals the understanding, practical Ignatius: "The infirmarian must ask the sick man which members of the community he likes and would prefer to see and talk to; these are the ones he is to admit to the sick room, and no others, so that the patient may be kept happy." His care for the sick was something he would delegate to no one, no matter how great the pressure of business or how ill he himself felt. The pewter tableware, the blankets off the beds, anything that could be sold or pawned had to go if times were bad and the doctor had ordered special food which the infirmarian was unable to buy for some sick Father or lay-brother.

When Francis Borgia, afterwards St. Francis Borgia, came to Rome in 1550, he gave Ignatius a large sum of money with which the saint founded the Roman College, which he intended as a model for Jesuit Colleges the world over; later, in recognition of the abundant alms of Gregory XIII, it was called the Gregorian University. "No other university still in existence," writes Father Brodrick, "can boast of having had two canonized Saints for its founders."[9] In 1552 Ignatius founded the German College for students from Luther's country, who he hoped would return to their own land and link it once again with the See of Peter. The scarlet cassocks and hats of the students of this college have ever since been a familiar sight in Rome.

While the Roman College was being built, the money ran short and the treasurer, Father Polanco, was at his wits' ends for funds. He had twenty-eight students housed in a building more like a shed than a college when Ignatius sent word that preparations were to be made at once for a hundred students, who would arrive in a day or two. Polanco had no money, only five gold crowns which he was holding on to for dear life to pay the workmen. He tried to beg some money while his helper, Father Manares, went around borrowing furniture and food from friends; next day the General came to see how things were going, and the two Fathers, thinking, that they had not done too badly in rounding up a sufficiency of beds and chairs, showed him into the long shed-like erection. "So this is where you are going to house our poor brothers for the winter, Master Polanco!" said Ignatius. "Is this how the poor fellows must live during rain and snow? Not a thing between them and heaven only a few tiles." Polanco apologized and explained; even the five gold crowns turned out to be underweight and were unacceptable as legal tender; they owed so much no one would lend them another penny. "Go ahead and add another storey, my dear Polanco," said the General; "we simply can't let the

students sleep in this shack. God will send His servants something."
Polanco set off to raise a loan—he was an obedient man—and "next day
the Hieronymite Fathers topped a loan of five hundred gold crowns given
him by a Spanish archdeacon with a much larger sum. And soon after,
sufficient alms was given us by devout persons to enable us to repay the
money, and thus the need of the moment was tided over."[10]

A young Jesuit, Benito Palmio, not yet ordained, was already permitted to preach, "which he had a great talent for and was well aware of
that same." One day, meeting a little old lady—very devout and very fond
of listening to sermons—in the street, the eloquent young preacher told
her when and where he would deliver his next pulpit discourse and invited her to come and hear him. The story reached Ignatius' ears and "he
was very tickled at this frank self-advertisement; and afterwards, when
giving Father Palmio any task to do, he would add, smilingly, 'Now,
Benito, if you do this well for me I promise to recruit all the devout little
old women I can to go and hear your sermons'." The same young preacher had an enormous appetite and was an outsize in Jesuits. Ignatius often
sat beside him in the refectory, delighted to see his giant thrive—for the
greater glory of God—and, no doubt, often helping the ever hungry
Benito to the food he himself was seldom able to eat.[11]

When there was a feast day, the community would treat Ignatius to
a few roasted chestnuts, "that being a dish of his native valley"[12]; five or
six decades before, the same dainty had been eaten in Errazti's forge and
the chestnuts had been picked in that faraway valley of the Iraurgi in the
trees around the *Casa-Torre*. If some Fathers were invited out to dinner,
he was delighted when they returned saying that they had got a good
meal; once a number of the Fathers returned from a dinner at which they
had been guests, rather doleful-looking when they found that the community meal was over. Ignatius, as usual, enquired how they had fared
and one Father wryly replied, "We got toothpicks wrapped in sage-
leaves; that would have been fine if we had anything we could use them
on; there was only one course—eggs." The uninvited laughed as heartily
as those who came home hungry, and the General laughed more than any.
But he did not laugh on another occasion when the Father Minister, having failed to provide a good dinner, arrived afterwards telling how he
had just been dining with a Cardinal who did things royally, giving his
guests lampreys. Ignatius at once chased him out to buy lampreys for all
in the house, the unfortunate man having to find the money by begging or
borrowing, "our Father acting in this manner not because he wanted us

to live on lampreys but because he wanted the Father Minister to have more charity and care for the brethren." And da Camara adds that the dinner provided for the Fathers of the house had "consisted of nothing but a few wretched sardines."[13]

By this time the Jesuits had lost their place as the youngest order in the Church. St. Philip Neri's Oratorians had been founded in 1548, and the genial Father Philip—*Pippo Buono* to half Rome—one of the most frequent callers to the Jesuit house, often discussed with Ignatius the great pilgrim hostel and the preparations for the Holy Year of 1550. Pippo's visits were followed by searches for needle and thread and quick repair work on the part of the Jesuits; "for he twirled the buttons off their soutanes while talking to them."[14] Philip and Ignatius shared a detestation of slovenliness. No Father would dream of appearing before the General untidily dressed; neatness and cleanliness were a fetish with him; for one blot or misspelt word a whole letter would have to be rewritten. Hundreds of incidents bearing on the day-to-day life of Ignatius and his religious family during that last decade of his life could be told; for many of the Fathers who lived with him left their recollections of the founder, and the records run to volumes.

All the time Ignatius continued to lead a life of intense, continuous prayer; sometimes his fervor, tears, and mystical experiences weakened him so much that he was obliged to curtail the time of prayer and to leave off saying Mass. As he toiled upstairs, or stepped out on to his little balcony, the Fathers would occasionally hear him sigh: "Alas for me! Poor sinner! Miserable wretch! Alas, my poor soul!" Hardly any miracles or visions or supernatural occurrences are mentioned in connection with St. Ignatius, especially during his years in Rome. When he heard stories told of persons who worked wonders or received extraordinary revelations, his attitude was of extreme reserve and prudence; when told of a stigmatist in Italy whose reputation for sanctity was widespread, he remarked that what impressed him most was the fact that the person in question was obedient. He sharply rebuked a Father who, on a journey from Lisbon to Rome, went out of his way to visit the famous Spanish *beata*, Magdalena de la Cruz, who afterwards proved to be an imposter.[15]

Although Francis Xavier died in December, 1552, word of his death did not reach Rome until the middle of 1554; and even then, the news having come through some merchants and no confirmatory reports arriving from the Fathers in India and the east, it was almost another year before the whole glorious story of Francis' immense labors and noble death was read by Ignatius and the brethren. Soon the great missionary's letters were being sent from Rome and Coimbra to Jesuit houses all over the continent, and in Paris and other European universities young men were listening to the ardent appeals of an apostle gone to his reward—and many were fired with the same eager desire that had moved Xavier to leave all things and follow souls to the ends of the earth. The Jesuits, numbering by 1556 almost a thousand, were dispersing in all directions. Some were going east in the footsteps of Xavier; Fathers were sailing to Brazil; three others were preparing themselves to enter Abyssinia; others were scattered throughout Germany, Scandinavia, and the various lands lost to the Church since the beginning of the century.

After 1550, when Ignatius almost died during one of his bouts of serious illness, Father Nadal kept pressing him to leave the Fathers some account of his life up to his conversion and the founding of the Society. After considerable coaxing, and after having Masses and prayers said to obtain light as to what was God's will in the matter, he agreed to do so and began to dictate to Father da Camara:

> In the year 1553, on the morning of Friday, August 4, the vigil of Our Lady of the Snows, our Father being in the orchard adjoining the house called "the Duke's house," he agreed to do that which Maestro Polanco and Maestro Nadal had asked, promising to tell me his recollections every Sunday. So in September one day he sent for me and began dictating the events of his life, including his youth with its sins. His mode of narration was clear and distinct; I never needed to ask him anything; his life seemed to pass before him there. I have added nothing, not one word, to what he told.[16]

There were three or four sessions that September, and the narration had gone as far as the days in Manresa. Then Ignatius stopped for a whole year when Nadal, returning from Spain to find that the project had been shelved, returned to the attack. Ignatius did nothing regarding the memoirs in early 1555, but on September 22 the Father General summoned da Camara "to the red tower" and resumed the interrupted dictation of his reminiscences, completing them in October with the words "and now Master Nadal can tell you the rest." This brief autobiography of Ignatius explains the *Exercises* and *Constitutions* and shows their sanctifying and apostolic power as exemplified in his own life.

No man in Rome received the news of Paul IV's election in 1555 with greater trepidation than Ignatius. The new Pope was none other than that Cardinal Carafa with whom he had clashed at Venice and who then and later made efforts to induce the Jesuits to amalgamate with St. Cajetan's Theatine Fathers, the founding of which Order had been largely Cardinal Carafa's doing. Ignatius was at dinner when news of the new pope's election was brought. "He shook and every bone in his body trembled and he paled"; rising, he went at once to the chapel; after a few minutes he returned, all smiles. "This pope will be good to us," he told the Fathers, who, not unnaturally, were concerned at the news that the cardinal most opposed to them was now pope.[17] The new pontiff, however, was friendly; but after a little time, when war broke out between Philip II of Spain and Paul IV, an order with a Spanish General and many Spanish members was under suspicion. One day the Governor of Rome combed the house from attic to basement searching for arquebuses and other hidden arms. Nothing was found, but it was the beginning of an uneasy period. The Society found things more difficult. For Ignatius, however, behind the maroon-robed figure of the pope there stood Christ; if His representative was less favorable than those who had preceded him in the pontifical office, that did not mean that those specially pledged to obey Christ's vicar should show less respect or lose any of their eagerness to serve.

In April, 1556, Polanco writes: "Our Father has failed much in health."[18] When the summer heat came, Ignatius, on the advice of the doctors, moved to a little villa on the Aventine which had been bought to house the ever-increasing number of Jesuit students. Although forty letters were sent out by Polanco—"the saint's hands and feet"—in his capacity as secretary to the General between July 20 and 31, of the dozen written on the 20th it is certain that Ignatius wrote at least one himself, for it dealt with a matter of conscience and was written in reply to a young Jesuit Father in Tivoli who had seemingly tied himself in a mental knot both regarding his temptations and his methods of fighting them. To no one, not even to the trusted Polanco, would the Founder delegate the duty of replying to this troubled son. *"Esteban carissimo,"* he begins, "Dearest Stephen," and proceeds to write three hundred words of counsel and encouragement to the young Father whose spirit, buffeted by inner storms, was weathering a time of turmoil and stress; it was an affectionate letter, saintly, wise, and fatherly, treasured by Esteban Casanovae to the end of his days and then handed on to the brethren to be preserved among the dead General's thousands of letters. Ignatius returned to the professed house on July 24.[19]

The next seven days were sultry. The unhealthy Roman summer had begun to exact its yearly toll in the city by the Tiber. Fevers swept in from the marshes, sparing neither high nor low, saint nor sinner. By Thursday, July 30, almost all the Fathers of the professed house were fever-stricken; in the evenings two doctors, one a Jesuit, visited the sick. Ignatius, hearing that they were doing the rounds of the house, asked to see them. They came, but did not think that there was any cause for alarm; the General had had indifferent health for many years past; he seemed much as usual—no better, no worse. Later that evening Polanco was called by Ignatius and asked to go to the Holy Father and get a last blessing.

Overworked, understandingly irritable, the secretary began to demur. The doctors had just said that all was well. And those important letters which he had been warned to get out before midnight had yet to be written and dispatched by fast messenger if they were to catch the ship sailing from Genoa.

"Your Reverence," he ventured, "the physicians see no grave danger in this illness; and I myself hope that God will preserve you yet some years for His service. Do you really feel so ill?"

"So ill," replied Ignatius, "that nothing remains for me but to give up my soul."

Still Polanco hesitated, mentioning the letters that could not wait and asking the Founder if the request for the papal blessing could not be put off till the morrow.

"I had rather," said the sick man, "that it were done today, and the sooner the better. But do what you think best in the matter. I leave myself entirely in your hands."

Having had decision thus thrust upon him, Polanco thought that he could very well defer the visit to the Vatican until the following day. By that time the wave of depression, the customary sequel to a bout of fever, would have passed away and Ignatius would be the first to recognize his request for what it was—unreasonable, a sick man's whim. Father Ignatius would be the last to expect Polanco or any of the few Fathers able to be up and about to rush off to the Vatican anoying the Holy Father for a man in no danger of death. But when later that night one of the doctors was again going around the house, Polanco, perhaps a trifle uneasy in mind because of his earlier remonstrance regarding the General's request, took the physician to Ignatius' room. They sat there while the patient had supper. For the two years before his death, Ignatius had had better health and could eat his food. "He ate his supper and conversed with us," Polanco wrote later, "so that I went to bed without suspecting any danger from his illness."

The summer night was short; the room, stifling. At dawn Brother Cannicaro, who had remained in the room with the sick man, went to fling open the casements, tight-hasped against the fever-laden breezes of the night. In the leaden light he suddenly noticed a great change in Ignatius, although during the night—except for his customary ejaculation, "Ah, Jesus!"—the General to all appearances rested fairly well; the Brother called Father Polanco and others. "We found Father Ignatius *in extremis;* so I went with all speed to St. Peter's and the pope, showing great sorrow at the news, sent him his loving benediction and all the other spiritual helps possible."Poor Polanco was evidently stricken with remorse for not having done as Ignatius asked the previous evening. Father Madrid, a doctor who had some time before become a Jesuit, sent the brother to the kitchen to beat up and cook "two fresh eggs." Father Frusio came, this time bringing neither clavichord nor lute. It is not quite clear who, if any, were present at the end, as the accounts are rather contradictory.[20] Ribadeneira records the saint as having said, when he heard them sending the brother for the egg cordial, "This is not the time for such things." Another account says that one of the Fathers present went for the saint's confessor, while another went to the kitchen to see what was delaying the brother, and that the doctor went to summon those of the community who were able to rise. But whether many or few, friends or enemies, surround a deathbed, each man has to die alone, to go forth unaccompanied on the journey from which there is no return. When Polanco rushed back from the Vatican, Ignatius was dead. The secretary states that Fathers Madrid and Frusio had been present. "Thus two hours after sunrise (at half-past five) in the presence of Father-Doctor Madrid and Master Andreas Frusio, the blessed Father gave up his soul to his Creator and Lord, dying without any difficulty."

The community, coming too late for a last word or even a last look from their beloved Father, assembled about his bed "all weeping, though we felt certain that he was in heaven." Meanwhile, the news of the Jesuit founder's death had spread throughout Rome. The events of the afternoon were duly recorded:

> We deferred his burial until Saturday after Vespers. The concourse of the pious and their devotion was great, though he remained in the room where he died. Some kissed his hands; others, his feet; they touched his body with their rosaries. . . . We did all we could to keep off those who wanted to take away bits of his biretta or clothes. . . . They took his shoelaces, his nightcap, and other belongings of his, though we gave nothing and, when we found what they were doing, did not allow the like to continue. Some artists made likenesses of him, which he had never permitted during his lifetime, though often asked.[21]

Despite their grief, the Fathers "endeavored to have something made, a memento which in his lifetime they did not obtain." An artisan who understood the technique of taking *mascarillas*, or deathmasks, was sent for and a plaster cast was taken from the dead man's features. Jacopino del Conte, the Florentine painter who had been a penitent of Ignatius, had come there earlier, set up his easel, and painted Ignatius—the living Ignatius he had known so well. From the plaster mould some wax models were cast—certain faults, such as where the plaster had compressed the nostrils and lips a little, being corrected. One of these reproductions was in the Jesuit professed house at Madrid up to the time of the Spanish civil war. When the communists burned that and several other religious houses in the Spanish capital, the library containing many priceless and irreplaceable manuscripts—and the *mascarilla* of St. Ignatius—went up in flames. Another of the early wax *mascarillas* is preserved in the ancestral home of St. Ignatius at Loyola, a favorite visiting place for summer visitors to nearby San Sebastian; fittingly, it is kept in that Chapel of the Conversion, the "Upper Room" of the house of Loyola, where it is enshrined just inside the sanctuary rails to the right of the main altar which bears the inscription, "Here Inigo de Loyola surrendered himself to God."

Yet a third *mascarilla* of the saint was in Rome until the time of the suppression of the Society of Jesus. It was sent for safe keeping to the Empress Maria Theresa of Austria and after her death came into the possession of the Benedictines—an Order which always claimed spiritual affinity with St. Ignatius, since it was at their monastery of

Montserrat he made his first great dedication of life and later he spent periods of time at Monte Cassino, where he wrote some of the Jesuit *Constitutions*. When the Society was restored, the Austrian Benedictines, as a gesture of friendship and congratulation, gave back to the Roman Jesuits the *mascarilla* of their founder.[22]

But even had no material likeness of Ignatius survived the centuries, there remains the direct image of his spirit as expressed in his writings. These have a special reality for a man like Ignatius, whose letters and scholarhsip were scanty and whose introspective activity was, on the other hand, extraordinarily intense. The *Spiritual Exercises*, the Jesuit *Constitutions*, the *Autobiography*, the few pages salvaged from his intimate *Spiritual Diary*, and almost seven tnousand letters—some running to great length—condense the essence of his privileged soul. And even had he left no written word, he left stamped upon his Order the unmistakable, indelible imprint of his indomitable will, of his boundless zeal and ambition to win the whole world "for God Our Lord."

In his personal life, as in his dealings with others, every effort of Ignatius was motivated by the conviction that "man was created to praise, reverence and serve God Our Lord, and by this means to save his soul." His decisions, while taking cognizance of changing circumstances, were based on that one unchanging principle; his ruling on which works the Society should undertake was "One must always discern, at any given time, the works that are most universal, most urgent, most likely to prove lasting in the service of God Our Lord."

He was not an intellectual; he did not hold with criticism—deserved or undeserved—of the Church, as may be seen in his "Rules for Thinking with the Church." He belonged to an older world: to the feudal, almost medieval Basque culture, to pre-Renaissance Spain. Many of the innovations of his time, many of the Roman customs, must have irked him in later years; yet he was no traditionalist, no upholder of tradition for tradition's sake. He was one of the first to dispense with the chanting of office in choir, with the wearing of a distinctive religious habit; he accepted the fact that change is inevitable and adapted his Society to a world in transition. The Pope who canonized him did not praise his organizing genius, his flair for leadership, his manifold apostolic achievements, but his immense and unceasing solicitude for the interests of God and the People of God. The Pontiff added, "Ignatius had a heart bigger than the world."

We leave him in 1556, when man stood—as he stands today—at a turning point in human evolution. Christ's teaching seemed to many then, as it does to many today, out-dated and incongruous. There was the same impatience with a Church that appeared to lag behind a world straining forward towards a future that promised fantastic benefits. There was the same material and intellectual wealth of the few, the same poverty of the many. It was a rather sick world, as ours is a rather sick world. Ignatius did not despair of his world, nor would he despair of ours. For the sickness of the world, in the twentieth as in the sixteenth century, is like that of Lazarus: *Not unto death, but for the glory of God* (John 11:4).

Appendix

Notes on Ignatian Biography and Sources

Until fairly recent times the writings of St. Ignatius Loyola, essential for the study of the saint, were little known outside Jesuit ranks. Biographers relied on excerpts and summaries which, due to a continuous process of quotation (always at second-hand) and in the course of translation through several languages, had come to lack the integrity and force of the originals. Today, thanks to the labors of Jesuit historians in Rome and Madrid over the past sixty years, the writings of St. Ignatius may be read in the original texts. These researchers have also amassed a vast amount of documented information concerning their founder, his associates, his times, and his work. The student of Ignatian and early Jesuit history is deeply indebted to the industry and scholarship which have put at his disposal so much relevant material—already assembled, sifted, and assessed; he is further indebted to the efficiency which has marshaled the mass of documents into admirable order, annotating, indexing, and editing them in a manner that renders the task of reference comparatively simple.

All this data is to be found in the massive *Monumenta Historica Societatis Jesu* (MHSJ), a collection totaling to date 117 large volumes, many of them running to more than a thousand pages. A sub-section of MHSJ, *Monumenta Ignatiana* (MI), comprises eighteen volumes the contents of which include almost seven thousand letters of the saint, his autobiography, the *Spiritual Exercises*, the *Constitutions of the Society of Jesus*, and the pages of his spiritual diary which escaped the destruction of that intimate journal; MI also contains the evidence of the 75 witnesses examined for the canonization processes and various memoirs, as well as impressions of the saint recorded by his contemporaries, Jesuit and non-Jesuit. The MI section, with the MHSJ volumes known as *Fontes Narrativi*, forms the basis of the present work. Other volumes in the MHSJ series have also been drawn upon, particularly those containing the recollections and letters of Ignatius' first Companions and their accounts of the beginnings of the Society. The general reader has been spared references which, if interpolated throughout the text, might prove tedious.

One biography of the saint ranks with the MHSJ volumes as a primary source; it is the well-known *Life* of Ribadeneira, completed in 1569, thir-

273

teen years after Ignatius' death, and published three years later. Pedro Ribadeneira, the Jesuit founder's Benjamin, had been jotting down incidents concerning the saint and recording the sayings of Ignatius long before the latter's death, with a view to eventually incorporating them in a *Life*. Another Jesuit, Maffei, published a *Life* in 1585. Both these writers had access to some of the saint's writings; the great bulk of the General's letters, however, which now fill twelve hefty tomes of MHSJ, were scattered not merely throughout Europe but had found their way to the most distant parts of Asia and to the Jesuit missions in Brazil and Africa. After the publication of these two lives, the superiors of the Order decided that Ignatius' writings should not be made available for later biographers; it was thought that the fragmentary nature of the documents and the founder's lack of literary style would, if made public, detract from his reputation and possibly cause disillusionment not only among the younger Jesuit brethren but among the faithful at large.

So, for a long period, the papers of Ignatius Loyola reposed undisturbed in the Roman archives of the Order he founded, while biographers had to be content to base their works on either Ribadeneira's or Maffei's. The majority plumped for Maffei, whose elegant Latin style conformed to the prevalent literary vogue; few noted the ring of authenticity in Ribadeneira's more ingenuous pages. Father Iparraguirre, a modern authority on Ignatian biography, commenting on the results of this "Maffeian" trend in the Lives of St. Ignatius published in the late sixteenth and early seventeenth centuries, writes:

> Maffei adorned the unfortunate years of the saint's youth—described by Ignatius' secretary, Polanco, as "dissolute and vain"—in a lamentable manner, evidently thinking that to disclose the true circumstances of the founder's early life was to diminish his stature and detract from his sanctity. With Maffei began those extraordinary divagations which have encrusted the saint's childhood with pious but unsubstantiated legends and completely misrepresented the character of the young Ignatius.

Maffei and those who followed him were responsible for an Ignatius who, while admirable as a founder and organizer, had all the essentials of sanctity except the human nature on which to base it. For the real Ignatius was substituted an aloof, dehumanized figure, a saint for admiration only, hard to imitate, impossible to love. The simple speech of

Ignatius who—Basque to the core to the end of his days—had always spoken briefly, to the point, and in homely, brusque manner, was touched up by Maffei, probably with the best of intentions but with rather grotesque results. For the amplification of the Saint's ordinary remarks into eloquent perorations presented the reader with a person who spoke out of character; the day-to-day life of Ignatius was almost completely ignored while the extraordinary was emphasized. For all Maffei's "fluid and terse style, so much in keeping with the taste of his time," his St. Ignatius was little more than a marionette whose strings his biographer pulled.

Those who chose to follow Maffei rather than Ribadeneira continued in the same strain, each adding his own measure of decoration, each stressing the extraordinary. Father Iparraguirre says:

> Thus the followers of Maffei helped to forge a grandiose image—almost cyclopean in proportions and weighted down with ornamentation—of a providential and unique founder of a never seen Order. . . . The human aspect of the saint was all but buried beneath a mountain of accumulated grandeurs. . . . In this sacerdotal figure, magnified to giant size, no psychological reactions could be discerned, no emotions seemed to register, no pulse-beat indicated that in Ignatius a warm heart throbbed.

After the canonization of the Saint in 1622, information of great value to biographers was made public, the most notable contribution being the testimony of the witnesses at the various Processes. Great must have been the confusion and mortification of those writers who had pinned their faith to Maffei rather than Ribadeneira, basing their lives of Ignatius on his! An anonymous *Life* published in Rouen in 1629, and Bartoli's *Life* published in Rome in 1650, heralded a new era in Ignatian biography, the canonization evidence available making for a more authentic *Life* as well as providing more detail. Nevertheless there was the same tendency to stress the unique and to overlook the commonplaces of life that make the warp and woof of sanctity. Ignatius the Founder, Ignatius the General, Ignatius the Paladin of the Counter-Reform, Ignatius the Saint—all got due attention while Ignatius the man again escaped notice. In vain one looks through these lives for the Father of the Company sitting in his little room in Rome or strolling in the garden as he chatted with his spiritual sons; who was happy when, in lean times, some kind friends invited the Fathers to dinner and on their return would inquire how they had fared; who wondered how those away on the missions were getting along and "whether they were bitten by many fleas or few"; who could stop in the middle of a harangue to laugh at the doleful face of the Father he was reprimanding; who could find excuses for the pranks and faults of a high-spirited, very young novice; who would ask one of the brethren to play him a few melodies on the clavichord and another to cheer him up by giving his imitation of the blind beggars of Rome. Those who lived with Ignatius, when asked for their memories and impressions of the beloved Father, recorded all these and many similar incidents; yet St. Ignatius as he appeared to the Roman Fathers might as well not have existed for all the notice his seventeenth century biographers took of him.

Not only the French, Italian, and German writers but even the Spaniard, Father Garcia—who had a decided advantage over all his predecessors and contemporaries in that he was able to draw on hitherto untapped sources, the Madrid archives—chose to write in the fashion of the age. To fact Garcia added pious legend; his Ignatius, like St. Francis of Assisi, is born in the stable of the paternal mansion, although from 1556 to the present day all visitors to the *Casa-Torre* of Loyola were shown the room which was the saint's birthplace. At his baptism in Azpeitia the infant (according to Garcia), on *hearing* his sponsors tell the priest that he is to be christened Beltran like his father, speaks up, saying: "No, I must get the name Ignatius"—to the consternation no doubt of the good Basque lady in whose arms he had been carried to the church. Father Garcia's *Life* was typical seventeenth century hagiography; the reading public liked its saints thus embellished, and authors should not be unduly blamed for acceding to popular demand.

In 1731 the Bollandist, Juan Pien, published a sound, historical account of Ignatius in the *Acta Sanctorum* (VII); included was the Autobiography or Acts of St. Ignatius, then published for the first time. Father Fluvia of Barcelona incorporated the fruits of Father Pien's studies in a *Life* published in 1735 but, as Father Iparraguirre remarks, "the adjectival refrain *extraordinary, prodigious,* and *heroic* made every chapter wearisome and gave the tone of the whole." Father Mariani of Bologna, also utilizing the material published by the Bollandists, published a five-volume *Life* in 1741 but his work was marred through having followed Maffei in his account of Ignatius' youth. Fluvia's and Mariani's lives, nevertheless, marked the initiation of the trend towards historical truth. In the following decade it was planned to establish in Madrid an academy for Jesuit historians with a view to publishing a critical edition of documents relevant to the Society's early history. Owing to the prevailing anti-Jesuit animus, the project fell through and, with the suppression of the Order in 1773, there seemed little likelihood that any further study of the Society or its Founder could continue. During the diaspora, however, a start was made on the task of collecting the Saint's letters by Father Menchaca in Spain and Father Genelli in Innsbruck; in an introduction to his collection Father Genelli makes a plea "to let St. Ignatius himself be heard giving the reasons for his actions." These collections formed the nucleus of the present imposing series, MHSJ.

Meanwhile Ribadeneira's *Life* had lain for more than a century practically unnoticed by the rhetoricians and apologists. Towards the end of the eighteenth century a French Jesuit, Pere Clair, led the return to Ribadeneira and the primary sources, while at Bruges Pere Michel published a life entitled *Histoire de St. Ignace d'apres les documents originaux*. Early in the nineteenth century—and not before its time!—St. Ignatius began to emerge from the artificial trappings under which he had so long remained hidden. Interest in the *man*, Ignatius Loyola, quickened; and the desire to know more about him spurred research. Father Cabre in Spain and Pere Cros in France were in the vanguard of the scientific investigators who, with all the verve and eagerness of their contemporaries then rushing across land and sea in quest of gold, began digging in the archives of Azpeitia, Madrid, Alcala, Rome, Venice, and other cities and towns, for the documental treasure that eventually saw publication with the first volume of MHSJ in 1894. Biographers no longer need rely on their predecessors of the sixteenth, seventeenth, and eighteenth centuries, for in 1978 the 117th volume was added to the MHSJ series which offers ample and original material not only for the biography of the Jesuit Founder but for many of his Companions.

In the bibliography appended to these notes, the principal lives of St. Ignatius written during the nineteenth and twentieth centuries have been given, as also several studies of important aspects of the Saint, his life, his work, and his spiritual teaching. It is significant that none of these studies appeared until the original documents were made available. Not all modern biographers of Ignatius Loyola have dealt kindly with him. Like all great men he has attracted some writers whose chief preoccupation and function seems to be that basely-named, graceless activity known as de-bunking. The spiritual viewpoint being out of focus,

Ignatius who is an astute politician and intriguer, a spiritual dictator, an unlikable, untrustworthy man, and that anomaly—an unholy saint.

Before concluding, it may be remarked that, except for the researches of Father Fita published in 1890–1893, little has been done to fill in the hiatus existing in regard to the Saint's youth in Castile; this field offers considerable scope for further research, and a careful scrutiny of all the documents concerning Juan Velasquez de Cuellar, Major-Domo of Castile (which are probably among the State Papers in Simancas), should throw some light on Inigo de Loyola's movements between 1507 and 1518, when he was a page and later a gentleman-of-the-household of Velasquez. Eleven years, especially the eleven years between a person's sixteenth and twenty-seventh years, are too long and important a period to leave unaccounted for in the record of a life.* Finally, it remains only to note that the latest entrants into the field of Ignatian biography have been the psychologists, and already many interesting character-studies have appeared, those of Father de Iriarte of Salamance University, a Jesuit theologian and psychologist, having won considerable notice and acclaim on the continent since their publication. Adopting the latest methods of character-study, and with the elements afforded by the existing knowledge of Ignatius—the three most authentic paintings, the death-masks, the descriptions recorded of his appearance and character, and the Saint's own writings—Father de Iriarte set out to see what manner of man all this data added up to or if a faithful likeness could be obtained. He modestly admits to having obtained "at least an interesting silhouette." But anyone who has read his articles must prefer to accept the psychological findings: "Ignatius was a fully integrated man; a person whose every action being directed toward one end achieved a noble balance, a glowing maturity, without losing any of his sensibility." Those who ignore this point miss the essential Ignatius, whose every effort went to the achieving of one aim—the greater glory of God.

* As the present work goes to press my attention has been drawn to the work of Father C. de Dalmases, S.J., *El Padre Maestro Ignacio* which devotes several pages to Ignatius' life with Juan Velasquez. An English translation of Father de Dalmases' book is in preparation.

Source List

Apart from MHSJ volumes, the *Life* by Ribadeneira, and the Life of the *Acta Sanctorum* (Julii; VII: pp. 420–645. Bollandists), the following books were used for reference.

A—LIVES OF ST. IGNATIUS

Arteche, Jose de: *San Ignacio de Loyola.* (Barcelona, 1941.)

Astrain, Antonio: Vol. I of *Historia de la Compania de Jesus en la Asistencia de Espana.* (Madrid, 1912 edition.)

Casanovas, Ignacio: *San Ignacio de Loyola, fundador de la Compania de Jesus.* (Barcelona, 1944 edition.)

Creixell, Juan: *San Ignacio en Barcelona.* (Barcelona, 1907.)
San Ignacio de Loyola. Vols. I and II (Barcelona, 1922.)
La espada de San Ignacio ofrendada a la Virgen de Montserrat. (Barcelona, 1931.) *San Ignacio: nacimiento, juventud, caballero, heroe.* (Barcelona, 1945.)

Dudon, Paul: *S. Ignace de Loyola.* (Paris, 1934.) (English translation by William J. Young, S.J. Bruce, Milwaukee, 1949.)

Garcia-Villoslada, Ricardo: *Ignacio de Loyola: un Espanol al Servicio del Pontificado.* (Sarragossa, 1956.)

Gonzalez Olmedo, Felix: *Introduccion a la Vida de San Ignacio de Loyola.* (Madrid, 1941.)

Leturia, Pedro de: *El Gentilhombre, Inigo Lopez de Loyola.* (Barcelona, 1949.)

B—VARIOUS WORKS ON IGNATIUS AND THE JESUIT ORDER

Bernoville, Gaetan: *Les Jesuites.* (Paris, 1934.)

Bouix, Marcel: *Lettres de S. Ignace.* (Paris, 1870.)

Brodrick, James: *The Origin of the Jesuits.* (London, 1940.) *The Progress of the Jesuits.* (London, 1947.)

Brou, Alexander: *S. Ignace, Maitre D'oraison.* (Paris, 1925.) *La spiritualite de S. Ignace.*(Paris, 1914.) (English translations by W. Young, S.J. Bruce, Milwaukee.)

Fita, Fidel: *San Ignacio de Loyola en la Corte de los Reyes Catolicos.* (Madrid. *Boletin de la Real Academia de la Historia.* XVII, pp. 492–520, 1890.)

Fitzpatrick, Edward A.: *St. Ignatius and the Ratio Studiorum.* (New York and London, 1933.)

Ganss, George E.: *St. Ignatius' Idea of a Jesuit University.* (Marquette, 1956.) *St. Ignatius the Educator; Guide amid Contemporary Problems.* (Rome, AHSI. *Commentarii Ignatiani:* Jan.–June, 1956, pp. 598–612.)

Goodier, Alban: *The Jesuits.* (London, 1929.) *St. Ignatius Loyola and Prayer.* (New York, 1940.)

Guibert, Joseph de: *La Spiritualite de la Compagnie.* (Rome, 1952.) (English translation by W. Young, S.J., Inst. Jesuit Sources, St. Louis, 1964.)

Iparraguirre y Dalmases: *Obras Completas de San Ignacio.* (Madrid, 1953. Edicion Manual. With Notes and Introductions.)

Iriarte, Mauricio de: *Figura y Caracter de Ignacio de Loyola.* (Madrid, *Razon y Fe:* Feb., March, June, July–Aug., 1944 and July–August, 1946.) *La personalidad de San Ignacio,* etc. (Madrid. *Razon y Fe:* Jan.–Feb., 1956.)

Iturrioz, J.: *Compania de Jesus; sentido historico y ascetico de este nombre.* (Manresa, Vol. 27, 1955.)

Larranaga, Victoriano: *La espiritualidad de San Ignacio y la de Santa Teresa de Jesus.* (Madrid, 1944.) *Obras Completas de San Ignacio.* Vol. I, with notes. (Madrid, 1947.)

Llanos y Torriglia, Felix de: *El capitan Inigo de Loyola y la dama.* . . . (Madrid: *Razon y Fe,* 124; 1941: pp. 33–70.)

Perez, Arregui, J. M.: *San Ignacio en Azpeitia.*

Rahner, Hugo: *The Spirituality of St. Ignatius.* (Newman, Maryland, 1955.)

Tacchi-Venturi, Pietro: *Le case abitate in Roma da S. Ignazio de Loyola.* (Rome, 1899.) *Storia della Compagnia di Gesu in Italia.* (Rome, 1951.) Vol. II, Parts I and II.

C—CONTEMPORARIES AND TIMES OF ST. IGNATIUS

Altamira y Crevea, Rafael: *A History of Spanish Civilisation.* (London, 1930.)

Belloc, Hilaire: *Paris.* (London, 1902.) *Towns of Destiny.* (New York, 1932.) *Characters of the Reformation.* (London, 1936.)

Bertrand and Petrie: *History of Spain.* (London, 1952.)

Boissonade, Prosper.: *Histoire de la Reunion de la Navarra a la Castille.* (Paris, 1893.)

Brodrick, James: *St. Francis Xavier.* (London, 1952.)

Cellini, Benvenuto: *Memoirs.* Symonds (1888) and Macdonell (1903) translations.

Cros, L. M.: *S. Francois Xavier: son pays, sa famille, sa vie.* (Toulouse, 1874.) *S. Francois Xavier: sa vie et ses lettres* 2 vols. (Toulouse, 1900.)

Gallop, Rodney: *A Book of the Basques.* (London, 1930.)

Garcia-Villoslada, Ricardo: *La Universidad de Paris durante los estudios de Francisco de Vitoria, O. P., 1507-1522.* (Rome, 1938.)

Gasquet, F. A.: *The Eve of the Reformation.* (London, 1900.)

Hayward, Fernand: *Histoire des Papes.* (Paris, 1929.)

Hughes, Philip: *The Reformation in England,* Vol. I. (London, 1950.)

Lamb, Harold: *Suleiman the Magnificent, Sultan of the East.* (London, 1952.)

Lojendio, Luis M. de: *Gonzalo de Cordoba, el Gran Capitan.* (Madrid, 1942.)

Martindale, C. C.: *In God's Army: Commanders in Chief.* (London, 1921.) *What are Saints? St. Francis Xavier,* pp. 69-75. (London, 1932.)

Newton and Others: *Travel and Travellers of the Middle Ages.* (London, 1926.)

Pastor, Ludwig Von: *History of the Popes.* Vols. X-XIII. (London, 1894-1933.)

Pidal, Ramon Menendez: *The Spaniards in Their History* (Trans. by Walter Starkie.) (London, 1950.)

Prescott, H. F. M.: *Mary Tudor.* (London, 1952 edition.)

Rait: *Life in Medieval Universities.* (Cambridge, 1912.)

Rashdall, H.: *Universities of Europe in the Middle Ages.* 3 vols. (Oxford, 1936.)

Sandoval, Prudencia: *Historia de la vida y hechos del Emperador Carlos V.* (Pamplona, 1614.)

Schurhammer, Georg: *Vida de San Francisco Javier.* (Bilbao, 1936.) *Vida de San Francisco Javier.* (Rome, 1955.) (English translation by M.J. Costelloe, Jesuit Hist. Inst., Chicago, 1973.)

Starkie, Walter: *Grand Inquisitor: Life and Times of Cardinal Ximenes de Cisneros.* (London, 1940.)

Suau, Pierre: *S. Francois de Borgia.* (Paris, 1910.)

Watson, Foster: *Luis Vives: el Gran Valenciano. Hispanic Notes and Monographs, No. IV.* (Oxford, 1922.)

Wyndham-Lewis, D. B.: *Francois Villon.* (London, 1928.)

Yeo, Margaret: *The Greatest of the Borgias.* (London, 1936.)

D—VARIA

Irish Jesuit Directory (1928), pp. 166 et seq. *The Society of Jesus in Ireland before the Suppression.* Article by Father MacErlean, S.J.

State Papers (Ireland) Reign of Henry VIII. (London, 1860.) Vols. III and IV.

Letters and Papers of the Reign of Henry VIII. (Foreign and Domestic) Vol. XVII.

La Universidad de Salamanca: Apunte Historico, by Cesar de la Riva. (Salamanca, 1953.)

Notes

For the convenience of those interested in the further study of St. Ignatius Loyola, it may be useful to indicate that in these notes secondary sources are referred to in full, while MHSJ references are listed under their appropriate section or title in that collection; e.g., MHSJ (*Nadal*) IV; MI⁴, II; MHSJ (*Chron. Pol.*) I; FN, I; MI¹(*Epp. et Ins. X*); etc.

PRINCIPLE ABBREVIATIONS

AA.SS.	Acta Sanctorum, vol. VII (Julii).
AHSJ	Archivium Historicum Societatis Jesu.
ASJR	Archivium Societatis Jesu Romanum.
Astr. Hist.	Astrain, *Historia de la Compania de Jesus en Espana*. 7 vols. Madrid, 1912.
Epp.	Letters of St. Ignatius in the MHSJ collection (12 vols.)
FN	*Fontes Narrativi* de S. Ignatio (2 vols. of the MHSJ collection). The letter A following a page number means that the extract is taken from the autobiography of the saint dictated to Father da Camara in 1553 and 1555.
Iriarte	de Iriarte, "Figura y Caracter de Ignacio de Loyola" (5 articles in the Jesuit review *Razon y Fe*, Madrid, 1944–1946).
Leturia	Leturia, *El Gentilhombre, Inigo Lopez de Loyola*. Barcelona, 1949.
MHSJ	*Monumenta Historica Societatis Jesu* (117 vols.; cf. App. III).
MI⁴	Documents relative to St. Ignatius (including evidence of witnesses at Canonization Processes) in MHSJ (2 vols.)
Rib (*Vida*).	Ribadeneira, *Vida de San Ignacio* (Books I, II, III, and IV).
TV (*Storia*).	Tacchi-Venturi, *Storia della Compagnia di Gesu in Italia*. 4 vols. Rome, 1922–1951.

CHAPTER I.

1. FN(I): Preface pp. 14–26; 153–4; 364–5 A.   ASJR: Folio 47 (V).
2. TV (*Storia*), Vol. II, Part I: 7.
3. Epp.(I): 329; (XII) 678.   FN(II): 393.   The Registers of Paris University for 1534, 1535, 1537 give "Ignatius de Loyola, Pampelonensis"; Loyola was in the diocese of Pamplona.
4. MI⁴(II): 190, 232.   MH(*Chron. Pol. VI*): 44
5. *ibid.*, (I): 516–17; MI⁴(II): 758.   Archives of Loyola and Azpeitia; a descendant of Martin Garcia, giving evidence at the canonization process of St. Ignatius, said that when Ignatius was born his oldest brother was 36 and "his mother so far beyond the age of child-bearing that it was considered a miracle. She [Dona Marina] hid herself, not believing that at her age she could be pregnant; even when assured that such was the case she replied

that it was possibly some illness but that she was far too old to bear a child."
The witness cited reliable persons including a near relative of Inigo's
mother.

6. MI⁴(II): 758.
7. FN(II): 513 n.7
8. (Footnote) *Un hermano de S. Ignacio*, article by de Olozago, S.J., in *Razon y Fe*
    (Madrid) January–February 1956: 275–284.
9. FN(I): 153 n.5.
10. Rib (*Vida*): Bk. I, Ch. 2.
11. FN(II): 513 n.7.   *St Ignatius of Loyola* by P. Dudon (Milwaukee 1949):18.
12. *Historia del Convento de Azpeitia* by Lizarralde (Santiago 1921): 64 ff.
13. FN(II): 513 n.7
14. *Introduccion a la Vida de S. Ignacio* by F. Olmedo (Madrid 1944): 60 ff.
15. TV(*Storia*), Vol. II, Part I: 9.   MI⁴(I): 587.
16. *El gentilhombre Inigo Lopez de Loyola* by P. de Leturia (Barcelona 1949): 37.
17. Wills in the Archives of Loyola and Azpeitia for 1431, 1461, 1496 and
    1549.   MH(*Chron. Pol.* I): 508–9.
18. *ibid.*, 531.
19. FN(I): 539; 641–42.   MI⁴(I): 194, 201, 423.   Iriarte in *Razon y Fe* (March
    1944): 262.
20. FN(II): 62.
21. Rib (*Vida*): Bk. IV, Ch. 18.   MI⁴(II) 471.
22. Lizarralde, *opus cit.*; (I) 75 ff.; 96 ff.; 184 ff.
23. Astr. Hist. (I): 86, n.5.
24. MI⁴(I): 394.
25. MI⁴(II): 868, article 2.
26. MI⁴(I): 595 ff.   MI⁴(II) 84–7.

CHAPTER II

1. *Historia de la vida y hechos del Emperador Carlos V* by P. Sandoval
    (Pamplona 1614): Vol. II, Ch. 21.
2. Leturia, *opus cit.*: 68.
3. *ibid.*: 68 ff.
4. MI⁴(I): 43.   *San Ignacio en la Corte* by F. Fita in *Boletin de la BAH* (Madrid
    1890) Vol XVII: 492–520.
5. *ibid.*
6. *Gonzalo de Cordoba, el Gran Capitan* by de Lojendio (Madrid 1942):
    300–01; 325; 360.
7. *Origenes de la Novela* by Menendez y Pelayo (Madrid 1925): 231–34.
8. MI⁴(I): 580–97.

9. *ibid.*: 340
10. *ibid.*: 584 ff.
11. *ibid.*: 596.
12. Lizarralde, *opus cit.*: 96–7.
13. MI⁴(I): 730.
14. de Lojendio, *opus cit.*: 375.
15. Fita, *opus cit.*: 504, 516.
16. MI⁴(II): 471.
17. TV(*Storia*), Vol. II, Part 1: 471.
18. MI⁴(II): 471.

CHAPTER III

1. MI⁴(I): 566.
2. Archivo de Simancas. Estado. leg. 345. (Spanish State Papers)
3. *Histoire de la Reunion de la Navarre a la Castile* by P. Boissonade (Paris 1893): 527–666.   Leturia, *opus cit*: 124–27.
4. *S. Francois de Xavier: sa vie etc.* by L.M. Cros, S.J. (Toulouse 1900): I, 84.
5. Boissonade, *opus cit.*: 527–666.
6. FN(II) (Nadal): 63.
7. Archivo de Simancas. Estado. leg. 345.
8. MH(*Chron. Pol.* I): 12.   FN(I): 155; 364 A.
9. MI⁴(I): 726.   FN(I): 155; 364 A.
10. MH(*Chron. Pol.* I): 12.
11. FN(I): 156; 366 A.   ASJR: folio 2, 9.
12. FN(I): 156; 364 A; 364 A; 370 A.   MH(*Nadal* II) 28.
13. *ibid.*
14. *Obras completas de S. Ignacio* by V. Larranga (Madrid 1947): 121–22 n.
15. Leturia, *opus cit.*: 140.
16. MH(*Chron. Pol.* I): 13.
17. Astr. Hist. (I): 18.   H. Bohmer in *Studien zur Geschichte der Gesellschaft Jesu* (Bonn 1914): Loyola, 17.
18. Azpeitia Archives.
19. Leturia, *opus cit.*: 142.
20. FN(I): 382 A.
21. MH(*Chron. Pol.* I): 507–8.
22. Leturia, *opus cit.*: 150–56.
23. FN(I): 370 A.   Lizarralde, *opus cit.*: 102–4.
24. *ibid.*
25. Leturia, *opus cit.*: 206.
26. FN(I): 376 A.

CHAPTER IV

1. FN(I): 372 A; 374 A.
2. *ibid*.: 376 A.
3. Lizarralde, *opus cit*.: 102–4.
4. FN(I): 376 A.
5. *ibid*.: 376 A; 378 A.
6. MI⁴(II): 193.   (Footnote) *ibid*.: 434–35.
7. *Spiritual Exercises of St Ignatius*: par. 74 (additional directions at the end of the Exercises for the First Week).
8. Leturia, *opus cit*.: 220 ff.
9. FN(I): 376 A.
10. *ibid*.: 107
11. *ibid*.: 376 A; 378 A.
12. *ibid*.: 380 A.
13. Lizarralde, *opus cit*.   (II): 8; 15–6.   Larranaga, *opus cit*.: 142 n.
14. FN(I): 380 A.   Rib (*Vida*): Bk. I, Ch. 3.
15. MI⁴(L): 379.
16. *ibid*.: 101.   FN(I) (*Epp. Lainii*): 76. n.9.
17. MI⁴(II): 821.
18. FN(I): 380 A.
19. MI⁴(II): 800–1; 821.
20. FN(I): 382 A; 384 A.
21. *ibid*.
22. *ibid*.: 386 A.

CHAPTER V

1. MI⁴(II): 387.
2. Larranaga, *opus cit*.: 152.
3. MI⁴(II): 441–45
4. *ibid*.: 83.
5. MH(*Nadal* IV): 826.
6. FN(I): 386 A.
7. *ibid*.: 386 A; 388 A.
8. *ibid*.: 389 A.
9. *ibid*.: 356 (Da Camara's Preface to the Autobiography)
10. *ibid*.: 388 A.   Rib (*Vida*): Bk. I, Ch. 4.
11. MI⁴(II): 82 ff.
12. *ibid*.: 83 ff.
13. *ibid*.: 378; 706.

14. MI⁴(I): *Epp. Lainii*: 78.
15. *ibid.*: 200.
16. FN(I): 584 A.
17. *ibid.*: 390 A.
18. *ibid.*: 390 A; 398 A; 400 A.
19. *ibid.*: 390 A.
20. *ibid.* (Polanco): 161.
21. *ibid.*: 394 A; 396 A.   Larranaga, *opus cit.*: 174.
22. FN(I): 396 A; 398 A.
23. *ibid.*
24. Larranaga, *opus cit.*: 174.
25. FN(I): 400 A; 402 A.
26. *ibid.*: 404 A.   MI⁴(I): 220.   MH(*Nadal* IV): 652.   Astr. Hist. (I): 106 n.l.
27. FN(I) (*Nadal*): 306–8.   AHSJ, No. 26 (1941) Leturia: *Genesis de los Ejercicios.*

CHAPTER VI

1. *Origin of the Jesuits* by J. Brodrick, S.J. (London 1940): 22.
2. MI⁴(I): 340; 353 ff.   MH(*Chron. Pol.* I): 23.   Rib (*Vida*): Bk. I, Ch. 17.
3. MI⁴(II): 707.   FN(I): 408 A.
4. FN(I): 412 A.
5. MI⁴(II): 85 ff.
6. *ibid.*: 88–9.
7. MI⁴(I): 733 ff.
8. *ibid.*
9. MI⁴(II): 680–81.
10. FN(I): 410 A; 412 A.
11. *ibid. Suleiman the Magnificent* by H. Lamb (London 1952) 55–64.
12. MI⁴(II): 709–10.
13. FN(I): 414 A.
14. MI⁴(II): 709–10.
15. FN(I): 414 A; 416 A.
16. *ibid.*: 418 A.
17. *ibid.*
18. Rib (*Vida*): Bk. I, Ch. 10.
19. FN(I): 420 A.
20. MI⁴(I): 243; 323.   Iriarte, *opus cit.*, *Razon y Fe* (July–August 1944): 92–6.
21. *Diary of Peter Fussli*, ed. H. Bohmer in *Studien zur Geschichte der Gesellschaft Jesu* (Bonn 1914).
22. *ibid.*

17. *ibid.*
18. Rib (*Vida*): Bk. I, Ch. 10.
19. FN(I): 420 A.
20. MI⁴(I): 243; 323.   Iriarte, *opus cit.*, *Razon y Fe* (July–August 1944): 92–6.
21. *Diary of Peter Fussli*, ed. H. Bohmer in *Studien zur Geschichte der Gesellschaft Jesu* (Bonn 1914).
22. *ibid.*
23. *ibid.*
24. FN(I): 420 A.
25. *Journal of Philip Hagen* ed. Conrady under title *Vier rheinische Palaestinapilgerschriften* (Wiesbaden 1882).

CHAPTER VII

This chapter is based on the diaries of Fussli and Hagen mentioned in Notes 21 and 25 of Chapter VI above; also on the following: FN(I) (*Itineris Palestinensis*): 1-3; (Lainez): 86-90; (Polanco): 167-69; and FN(I):420 A to 436 A.   FN(II) (*Nadal*): 67-8; (Polanco): 534-41.   Rib (*Vida*): Bk. I, Chs. 10, 11, 12.

CHAPTER VIII

1. MI⁴(II): 106, 273, 305, 319, 323   FN(I): 434 A; 436 A; 462 A.
2. Larranaga, *opus cit.*: 254.
3. Rib (*Vida*): Bk. I, Ch. 13.
4. Epp. (I): 102.
5. FN(I): 436 A.   Rib (*Vida*): Bk. I, Ch. 13.
6. FN(I): 436 A; 438 A.
7. MI⁴(II): 90 ff.
8. *ibid.*
9. *ibid.*
10. *ibid.*
11. *ibid.*
12. Rib (*Vida*): Bk. I, Ch. 13.
13. Epp. (I): 71–3.
14. FN(I): 438 A.   MI⁴(I): 607.
15. FN(I): 440 A; 442 A.
16. FN(I) (Polanco): 170; 472 A.

17. MI⁴(II): 194 ff.   FN(I): 440 A; 442 A.
18. FN(I): 444 A to 450 A.
19. FN(I) (Polanco): 174
20. MI⁴(I): 620; 621.
21. *ibid.*   FN(I): 450 A
22. FN(I): 450 A.   MI⁴(I): 598–627.
23. FN(I): 452 A; 454 A; 456 A.
24. *ibid.* and 460 A; 462 A.
25. *ibid.* and 464 A.
26. *ibid.*
27. MI⁴(II): 93–4.
28. Iriarte, *opus cit.*, *Razon y Fe* (June 1944): 614–15.

CHAPTER IX

1. *San Ignacio de Loyola, fundador* . . . . by I. Casanovas (Barcelona 1944): 193.
2. MI⁴(I) (*Lainez*): 110.
3. *Francois Villon* by D.B.Wyndham Lewis (London 1945): 199.
4. FN(I): 464 A; 466 A.
5. *ibid.*: 468 A.
6. Larranaga, *opus cit.*: 317 ff.
7. Epp. (I): 90–2.
8. MI⁴(I) (*Lainez*): 110
9. FN(I): 468 A.
10. Rib (*Vida*): Bk. II, Ch. 3.   MI⁴(I): 333–34.
11. FN(I): 476 A.
12. Iriarte, *opus cit.*, *Razon y Fe* (June 1944): 614–15.   FN(I): 470 A; 472 A.
13. MI⁴(I): 198.
14. Rib (*Vida*): Bk. V, Ch. 10.
15. FN(I): 474 A.   Larranaga, *opus cit.*: 349–50.
16. FN(I) (Polanco): 182.   MH(*Fabri Mon.*): 858.
17. Larranaga, *opus cit.*: 351 ff.
18. MI⁴(II): 182–252.
19. MH(*Fabri Mon.*): 493–95.
20. Wyndham Lewis, *opus cit.*: 19 ff.; 35 ff.
21. Dudon, *opus cit.*: 152.
22. Brodrick, *opus cit.*: 41.

23. MH(*Chron. Pol.* I), 49.   Astr. Hist. I: 73 ff.   Larranaga, *opus cit.*: 368 ff.
24. *ibid.*
25. MH(*Fabri Mon.*): 860.   MH(*Rod. Comment.*): 419 ff.   Dudon, *opus cit.*: 154 ff.

CHAPTER X

1. FN(I) (Polanco): 185.   FN(II): 568.   MH(*Rod. Comment.*): 461.   Rib (*Vida*): Bk. II, Ch. 5.
2. FN(I): 482 A.   MI⁴(I) (*Lainez*): 22.
3. MH(*Litt. quad.* I): 494.   FN(I) (Polanco): 181.   *ibid.*: 480 A; 482 A.   MI⁴(II): 3.
4. MI⁴(I) (*Lainez*): 102.   *ibid.*: 243; 340; 766.   MI⁴(II): 4 ff.; 83–7, 490.   Rib (*Vida*): Bk. IV, Ch. 18.
5. Epp. (I): 79–83.
6. *ibid.*
7. FN(I): 482 A.   MI⁴(II): 182–247.   *San Ignacio en Azpeitia* by P. Arregui (Madrid 1921):117 ff. (Fr. Arregui collected all local traditions in Azpeitia.)
8. *ibid.*
9. MI⁴(II): 182–247.
10. *ibid.*
11. *ibid.*
12. *ibid.*
13. *ibid.*
14. *ibid.*: 188
15. MH(*Chron. Pol.* I) : 501.   FN(II) (Polanco): 570.   MI⁴(I): 566–67.
16. MI⁴(I): 188.   MI⁴(I): 566–67.
17. MI⁴(II): 182–247.
18. MI⁴(I): 538.
19. MI⁴(II): 182 ff.; 209–52; 766.
20. MH(*Litt. quad.* I): 494.
21. FN(I): 486 A.
22. *ibid.*   MI⁴(I): 566.   Larranaga, *opus cit.*: 422–23.   MH(*Epist. Xav.* I): 9–12.   MH(*Fabri. Mon.*): 179. FN(I): 468 A.
23. Epp. (I): 319–20.   FN(I) (Polanco): 188.   MI⁴(I): 763–64.   MH(*Mon. Rib.* I): 152–54.   Larranaga, *opus cit.*: 428.
24. *Sulieman the Magnificent* by Harold Lamb (London 1952): 140–198.
25. *ibid.*
26. FN(I): 406 A; 488 A.

CHAPTER XI

1. FN(I): 488 A.
2. FN(II): 572
3. FN(I): 490 A; 492 A.
4. FN(II) (Polanco): 583
5. Epp. (I): 93–9.
6. Epp. (I): 99–107. *Spiritual Exercises*: rules in pars. 313, 316.
7. Epp. (I): 529.
8. Office for the feast of St Ignatius of Antioch, old Roman Breviary. *The Wisdom of Catholicism* ed. Anton C. Pegis (New York 1953): 4 –6
9. *The Spirituality of St Ignatius*, by Hugo Rahner, S.J. (Westminster, Maryland 1953): 59–60.
10. Epp. (I): 107–9.
11. Epp. (I): 509; (III): 502; (VI): 91. MI⁴(I): 520.
12. Epp. (III): 560.
13. *Spiritual Exercises*: annotation No. 2.
14. MI⁴(I): 343; 408. *St Teresa: Life* by A. Peers (London 1950): I, 145. *St Teresa: Book of the Foundations*: III, 12. Dudon, *opus cit.*: 225.
15. Epp. (II): 250.
16. MI⁴(I): 113. MH(*Rod. Comment.*): 460–86.
17. FN(I) (Polanco): 185. *ibid.*: 488 A. MH(*Rod. Comment.*): 474–77.
18. MH(*Rod. Comment.*): 474–75.
19. *ibid.*: 478–86. FN(I): 492 A.
20. *ibid.*
21. Epp. (I): 118–22.
22. Rib (*Vida*): Bk. II, Ch. 8.
23. FN(I)(Polanco): 194. *ibid.*: 494 A; 496 A. MI⁴(I): 116. MH(*Rod. Comment.*): 491. TV(*Storia*) II, 96. Rib (*Vida*): Bk. II, Ch. 9. Casanovas, *opus cit.*: 230.
24. *St Ignatius and the Ratio Studiorum* by E. Fitzpatrick (New York 1933): 10.
25. FN(II): 496–7.
26. FN(I) (Polanco): 193–4.
27. *S. Ignacio de Loyola etc.* by R. de Villoslada, S.J. (Sarragossa 1956): 133–4.
28. FN(II): 596
29. FN(I): 496 A; 498 A.
30. MI⁴(II) (*Lainez*): 74–5
31. FN(I): 498 A.
32. *ibid.*
33. *ibid.* Epp. (I): 161–5; 170–1; 274–6. Epp. (XII): 217–19.
34. FN(II): 578. MI⁴(I) (*Lainez*): 94.

CHAPTER XII

1. MI⁴(II): 830–1.   Larranaga, *opus cit.*: 514.   *Le case abitate in Roma da San Ignacio* by Tacchi-Venturi (Rome 1899).
2. MI⁴(I): 119.
3. Rib (*Vida*): Bk. II, Ch. 12.
4. Larranaga, *opus cit.*: 518-19
5. FN(I) (Polanco): 196.
6. *Lettres de S. Ignace de Loyola* etc. by M. Bouix, S.J. (Paris 1870).   *Note*: This collection of 145 letters contains some letters not in the MHSJ collection. This particular letter Bouix found in the Archives at Toledo, since destroyed during the Spanish Civil War.
7. FN(I) (Lainez): 124
8. *ibid.* (Lainez): 126
9. MH(*Epp. Broeti*): 491.
10. TV(*Storia*) II, Part 1. : 153–66.   MH(*Rod. Comment.*): 593.   FN(I) (Polanco): 201.   Epp. (I): 137–44.
11. *Epp. Mixtae* (I): 15–7.
12. Epp. (I): 136.
13. MH(*Rod Comment.*): 500 ff.   TV(*Storia*) II, Part 1,: 163.
14. MH(*Chron. Pol.*I): 65-6.   Rib (*Vida*): Bk. II, Ch. 13.   Larranaga, *opus cit.*, 554 ff.   Tacchi-Venturi (*Le Case*) 13-8.
15. *ibid.*
16. MH(*Chron. Pol.*I): 66–7; 81–2.   TV(*Storia*) II, Part 1: 178–85.
17. Epp. (I): 145–7.   MI⁴(II): 185; 217; 220; 242; 243.
18. MH(*Bob. Mon.*): 616.
19. *Epp. Mixtae* (I): 17.
20. MH(*Bob. Mon.*) : 602.
21. TV(*Storia*) II, (I) : 268 ff.   Brodrick, *opus cit.*: 78.
22. *Vida del P. Francisco Borgia* by Ribadeneira (Madrid 1945 ed.): 645 ff.   *The Greatest of the Borgias* by Margaret Yeo (London 1936): 68 ff.
23. *ibid.* (Yeo): 143.
24. MH(*Mon. Rib*): (I), 7.
25. *ibid.*: 12 ff.   TV(*Storia*) II, Part I: 316 ff.
26. *ibid.*
27. Epp. (I): 519–26.
28. Epp. (II): 264.
29. MH(*Chron. Pol.*I): 85.   TV(*Storia*) II, Part 1: 203
30. MH(*Fabri Mon.*): 50; 58.
31. MI⁴(II): 5–9
32. Epp. (IV): 669–81.

CHAPTER XIII

1. Epp. (I): 132–4.
2. MI⁴(I): 381 ff.
3. Brodrick, *opus cit.*: 104.
4. Epp. (I): 179–80.
5. *ibid.* Epp. (I): 727–30.
6. *ibid.*
7. Brodrick, *opus cit.*: 107.
8. MH(*Epp. Broet*): 197. Epp. (*Epp. Salmeronis*) I, 2–9.
9. *ibid.*
10. *ibid.*
11. *The Great O'Neill* by Sean O'Faolain (London 1947): 5.
12. MH(*Epp. Salmeronis*) I: 13.
13. FN(I) (Da Camara): 559. MI⁴(I): 629–45.
14. *ibid.*
15. MH(Epp. Nadab 1): 1–14. TV *Storia* II (Part 2) 38–41
16. Rib (*Vida*): Bk. IV, Ch.6.
17. *St Ignatius' Idea of a Jesuit University* by G. Ganss, S.J. (Milwaukee 1954): 18.
18. *ibid.*: 17; 45; 178 ff. *St Ignatius the Educator* by G. Ganss, S.J. in AHSJ (Rome 1956): 600; 602 ff.
19. Epp.(I): 95.
20. MH(*Const.*): Part IV, Ch. 12, par. 451.
21. Ganss, *St Ignatius . . . Educator,*(*opus cit.*): 612.

CHAPTER XIV

1. MI⁴(I): 356–7. TV(*Storia*) II, Part 1, 162–9.
2. Epp. (I): 372–**3**.
3. MI⁴(I): 270–375; 659–66. MH(*Chron. Pol.* I): 169.
4. MI⁴(II): 289; 290; 327. TV(*Storia*) II, Part I: 79 ff.
5. *Epp. Mixtae* (I): 311; 335.
6. MI⁴(I): 653. Epp. (I): 329; 372; 491. MH(*Chron. Pol.* I), 172 n.; 211. TV (*Storia*) II, Part I: 79 ff.
7. *ibid.* MI⁴(I): 656–9.
8. Epp. (I) 424; 439.
9. *ibid.*: 440; 441; 447; 493. MI⁴(I): 652 ff. TV(*Storia*) II, Part I: 81 ff.
10. *ibid.* Epp. (I): 488. *Epp. Mixtae* (I): 449; (II): 142; (IV): 148.
11. MI⁴(I): 641–5. FN(I): 559.

12. *ibid.*
13. Epp. (I): 495–510.
14. Epp. (IV): 669–81.
15. MI⁴(I): 673–707.   *Epp. Mixtae* (IV): 185.   Astr. Hist. I,: 619–21.
16. MH(*Fabri Mon.*): 485.
17. MH(*Lainii Mon.I*): 192 ff.
18. MH(*Epp. Nadal* II): 45.   Astr. Hist. I: 562.
19. MI⁴(I): 11; 202; 454; 468; 491.
20. Epp. (I): 572–77.

CHAPTER XV

1. Dudon, *opus cit.*: 426
2. MI⁴(I): 560–80.   Rib (*Vida*): Bk. I, Ch. 1; and Bk. IV, Ch. 18.   MH(*Pol. Hist.I*): 14.
3. MI⁴(II) (Polanco): 22.
4. *ibid.*: 490.
5. MI⁴(I): 243; (da Camara) 323.   MI⁴(II): 493; 762.
6. MI⁴(I): 490–1.   MH(*Epp. Nadal* I): 34–5
7. *ibid.*
8. MI⁴(I): 242; 449–53; 495; 726.
9. Brodrick (*Origin*): 199.
10. MI⁴(I): 521–2.
11. *ibid.*: 495–6.
12. FN(I) (da Camara): 641–2.
13. MI⁴(I): 248; 249; 497; 498. FN(I): 554–6.
14. *Memorie della Congreg. dell' Oratorio* by G. Marciano (Naples 1692) I, 88.
15. MI⁴(I): 251; 343; 403; 408
16. FN(I): 354 ff.
17. MI⁴(I): 198.   MH(*Chron. Pol.V*): 47.
18. Epp. (XI): 284.
19. Epp. (XII): 151–2.
20. MI⁴(I) (Polanco): 18 ff.   Rib (*Vida*): Bk. IV, Ch. 16.
21. MI⁴(II): 764–70.
22. MI⁴(I): 512 and footnote; 760; 761; 762.   MH(*Chron. Pol.* VI): 43.   TV(*Storia*) II: 367–8.